PHRBRAZIL

Portuguese

Essential For Effective Communication

ROUGH GUIDES

PHRASEBOOK FOR TRAVELLERS IN BRAZIL

Portuguese

Essential For Effective Communication

Compiled by
LEXUS

PUBLIFOLHA

Traduzido de "The Rough Guide Phrasebook Portuguese", edição de 2006, publicado por
Rough Guides Ltd, 80 Strand, Londres, WC2R 0RL, Inglaterra.
Título original: "The Rough Guide Phrasebook Portuguese"
Copyright © Rough Guides Ltd, 1996, 2006
Copyright do texto © Lexus Ltd 2006

Copyright © 2008 Publifolha – Divisão de Publicações da Empresa Folha da Manhã S.A.

ISBN 978-85-7402-934-4

PUBLIFOLHA

Divisão de Publicações do Grupo Folha
Al. Barão de Limeira, 401, 6° andar
CEP 01202-900, São Paulo, SP
Tel.: (11) 3224-2186/2187/2197
www.publifolha.com.br

COORDENAÇÃO DO PROJETO
PUBLIFOLHA
Assistência editorial: Rodrigo Villela
Produção gráfica: Soraia Pauli Scarpa
Assistência de produção gráfica: Mariana Metidieri

PRODUÇÃO EDITORIAL
EDITORA PÁGINA VIVA
Tradução: Anna Quirino
Revisão: Shirley Gomes
Consultoria técnica: Ibraíma Dafonte Tavares

Foto de capa: Juca Varella/Folha Imagem
Foto de 4ª capa: Jarbas Oliveira/Folha Imagem

ROUGH GUIDES
Compilação: Lexus com Norma de Oliveira Tait
Edição da Série Lexus: Sally Davies
Direção de Referência: Andrew Lockett
Edição da Série: Mark Ellingham

Dados Internacionais de Catalogação na Publicação (CIP)
(Câmara Brasileira do Livro, SP, Brasil)

Phrasebook for travellers in Brazil : portuguese / compilado por Lexus ; [tradução Anna
Quirino].– São Paulo : Publifolha, 2008. – (Coleção Guia de Conversação Para Viagens)

Título original: The Rough Guide Portuguese Phrasebook.
ISBN 978-85-7402-934-4

1. Inglês - Vocabulários e manuais de conversação - Português 2. Português -
Vocabulários e manuais de conversação - Inglês
I. Lexus. II. Série.

	CDD-428.2469
	-469.8242
08-08399	

Índices para catálogo sistemático:
1. Guia de conversação inglês-português : Lingüística 428.2469
2. Guia de conversação português-inglês : Lingüística 469.8242

CONTENTS

Introduction

*T*he *Rough Guide Phrasebook For Travellers in Brazil Portuguese*
is a highly practical introduction to the contemporary language. Laid out in clear A-Z style, it uses key-word referencing
to lead you straight to the words and phrases you want – so
if you need to book a room, just look up 'room'. The Rough
Guide gets straight to the point in every situation, in bars and
shops, on trains and buses, and in hotels and banks.

The main part of the book is a double dictionary: English-
Portuguese then Portuguese-English. Before that, there's a
section called **Basic Phrases**, and to get you involved in two-
way communication the Rough Guide includes, in this new
edition, a set of **Scenario** dialogues illustrating questions and
responses in key situations such as renting a car and asking
directions.

Forming the heart of the guide, the **English-Portuguese** section gives easy-to-use transliterations of the Portuguese words
wherever pronunciation might be a problem. Throughout this
section, cross-references enable you to pinpoint key facts and
phrases, while asterisked words indicate where further information can be found in a section at the end of the book called **How
the Language Works**. This section sets out the fundamental
rules of the language, with plenty of practical examples. You'll
also find here other essentials like numbers, dates, telling the
time and basic phrases. In the **Portuguese-English** dictionary,
we've given you not just the phrases you'll be likely to hear
(starting with a selection of slang and colloquialisms) but also
many of the signs, labels, instructions and other basic words you
may come across in print or in public places.

Near the back of the book you wil find an extensive **Menu
Reader**. Consisting of food and drink sections (each starting
with a list of essential terms), it's indispensable whether you're
eating out, stopping for a quick drink, or browsing through a
local food market.

boa viagem!
have a good trip!

Basic
Phrases

yes
sim
seeng

no
não
nowng

OK
está bem
eesta bayng

hello/hi
olá/oi

good morning
bom-dia
bohng dee-a

good evening/good night
boa-noite
boh-a noh-itee

see you!
até logo!
ateh logoo

goodbye
adeus
aday-oos

please
por favor
poor favohr

yes please
sim, por favor
seeng

thanks, thank you
(man/woman) obrigado(a)
ohbreegadoo, ohbreegada

no thanks, no thank you
não obrigado(a)
nowng

thank you very much
muito obrigado(a)
mweengtoo

don't mention it
não tem de quê
nowng tayng dee kay

not at all
de nada
dee

how do you do?
muito prazer
mweengtoo prazayr

how are you?
como está?
kohmoo eesta

fine, thanks
(man/woman) bem, obrigado(a)
bayng ohbreegadoo, bayng
    ohbreegada,

pleased to meet you
(man/woman) muito prazer em
    conhecê-lo(a)
mweengtoo prazayr ayng
    kohn-yaysayloo

excuse me
(to get past) com licença
kohng lees**ay**nsa
(to get attention) por favor
poor fav**oh**r
(to say sorry) desculpe
deesk**oo**lpee

(I'm) sorry
sinto muito
s**ee**ntoo m**wee**ngtoo

sorry?/pardon (me)?
(didn't understand) como?
k**oh**moo

what did you say?
o que disse?
oo kee d**ee**see

I see/I understand
entendo
aynt**ay**ndoo

I don't understand
não entendo
nowng

do you speak English?
fala inglês?
ingl**ays**

I don't speak Portuguese
não falo português
nowng f**a**loo pohrtoog**ays**

can you speak more slowly?
pode falar mais devagar?
p**o**dee fal**ar** mīs deevag**ar**

could you repeat that?
pode repetir?
p**o**dee Haypayt**eer**

can you write it down?
pode escrever isso?
p**o**dee eeskrayv**ayr ee**soo

I'd like...
queria...
keer**ee**-a

can I have...?
pode me dar...?
p**o**dee mee dar

do you have...?
tem...?
tayng

how much is it?
quanto é?
kwantw**eh**

cheers!
saúde!
sa-**oo**dee

it is...
é...; está...
eh; eest**a**

where is...?
onde é...?; onde está...?
ohndee eh; **oh**ndee eest**a**

is it far?
é longe?
eh l**oh**nJee

Scenarios

1. Accommodation

is there an inexpensive hotel you can recommend?
▶ pode me recomendar um hotel económico?
[**po**dee mee Hay**ko**hmayn**da**r oong oh**teh**l ayko**hnoh**meekoo?]

---

sinto muito, parece que estão todos lotados ◀
[**see**ntoo m**wee**ngtoo, par**eh**see kee ays**to**wng **toh**doos lo**hta**doos]
I'm sorry, they all seem to be fully booked

---

can you give me the name of a good middle-range hotel?
▶ pode me dar o nome de um bom hotel de preço médio?
[**po**dee mee da**ro**o **no**hmee dee oong bohng oh**teh**l dee pra**y**soo **meh**d-yoo?]

---

deixe-me ver; deseja ficar no centro? ◀
[**day**sheemee vayr; day**say**Ja fee**ka**r noo **say**ntroo?]
let me have a look; do you want to be in the centre?

---

if possible
▶ se possível
[see poh**see**vil]

---

importa-se que fique um pouco fora da cidade? ◀
[im**po**rtasee kee **fee**kee oong **po**hkoo **fo**ra da see**da**dee?]
do you mind being a little way out of town?

---

as long as it's not too far out
▶ desde que não seja muito longe
[**da**ysdee kee nowng **say**Ja m**wee**ngtoo **lo**hnJee]

---

where is it on the map?
▶ onde fica no mapa?
[**oh**ndee **fee**ka noo **ma**pa?]

---

can you write the name and address down?
▶ pode escrever o nome e o endereço?
[**po**dee ayskray**vay**r oo **no**hmee ee oo aynday**ray**soo?]

I'm looking for a room in a private house
▶ estou procurando um quarto numa casa de família
[ays**to**h prohkoo**ra**ndoo oong k**wa**rtoo **no**oma **ka**za dee fam**ee**l-ya]

15

2. Banks

bank account	conta bancária	[**koh**nta bankar-ya]
to change money	trocar dinheiro	[trohkar deen-**yay**roo]
cheque	cheque	[**sheh**kee]
to deposit	depositar	[daypohzee**tar**]
real	real	[Hay-**al**]
pin number	senha	[**sayn**-ya]
pound	libra	[**lee**bra]
to withdraw	retirar, sacar	[Hayteer**ar**]

can you change this into reais?
como quer o dinheiro? ◀
▶ poderia trocar isto por reais?
[**koh**moo kehr oo deen-**yay**roo?]
[pohdayree-a trohkar eestoo poor Hay-**ī**s?] how would you like the money?

small notes	big notes
▶ notas pequenas	▶ notas grandes
[**no**tas payk**ay**nas]	[**no**tas gr**an**dees]

do you have information in English about opening an account?
▶ há informações em inglês sobre como abrir uma conta?
[a infohrmas**oy**ngs ayng ingl**ays** **soh**bree **koh**moo abreer **oo**ma **koh**nta?]

sim, que tipo de conta quer? ◀
[seeng, kee **tee**poo dee **koh**nta kher?]
yes, what sort of account do you want?

I'd like a current account
▶ quero uma conta corrente
[**keh**roo **oo**ma **koh**nta koh-**Hayn**tee]

seu passaporte, por favor ◀
[**say**-oo pasap**or**tee, poor fav**ohr**]
your passport, please

can I use this card to draw some cash?
▶ posso usar este cartão para retirar dinheiro?
[**po**soo oo**zar** **ay**stee kart**ow**ng para Hayteer**ar** deen-**yay**roo?]

precisa ir ao caixa ◀
[pray**see**za eer ow k**ī**sha]
you have to go to the cashier's desk

I want to transfer this to my account at Banco do Brasil
▶ quero transferir isto para a minha conta no Banco do Brasil
[**keh**roo transfay**reer** **ee**stoo para m**een**-ya **koh**nta noo bankoo doo Braz**eel**]

tudo bem, mas teremos de cobrar a chamada telefônica ◀
[**too**doo bayng, mas tay**ray**moos dee k**ohbrar** a shamada taylay**fohn**eeka]
OK, but we'll have to charge you for the phonecall

3. Booking a room

shower	chuveiro	[shoov**ay**roo]
telephone in the room	telefone no quarto	[taylayf**oh**nee noo kw**ar**too]
payphone in the lobby	telefone público no hall	[taylayf**oh**nee p**oo**blikoo noo

do you have any rooms?
▶ há quartos vagos?
[a kw**ar**toos v**a**goos?]

para quantas pessoas? ◀
[p**a**ra kw**a**ntas pays**oh**-as?]
for how many people?

for one/for two
▶ para uma/para duas pessoas
[p**a**ra **oo**ma/para d**oo**-as pays**oh**-as]

sim, temos ◀
[seeng, **tay**moos]
yes, we have rooms free

▶ para quantas noites?
[p**a**ra kw**a**ntas n**oh**-itees?]
for how many nights?

just for one night
só por uma noite
[saw **oo**ma n**oh**-itee]

how much is it?
▶ quanto custa?
[kw**a**ntoo k**oo**sta?]

90 reais com banheiro e 70 reais sem banheiro ◀
[nohv**ay**nta Hay-**ī**s kohng ban-y**ay**roo ee sayt**ay**nta Hay-**ī**s sayng ban-y**ay**roo
90 reais with bathroom and 70 reais without bathroom

does that include breakfast?
▶ o café-da-manhã está incluído?
[oo kaf**eh** da man-y**a**ng eest**a** inklw**ee**doo?]

can I see a room with bathroom?
▶ posso ver um quarto com banheiro?
[p**o**soo vayr oong kw**ar**too kohng ban-y**ay**roo?]

ok, I'll take it
▶ tudo bem, fico com ele
[t**oo**doo bayng, f**ee**koo kong **ay**lee]

when do I have to check out?
▶ quando tenho de sair?
[kw**a**ndoo t**ay**n-yoo dee sa-**ee**r]

is there anywhere I can leave luggage?
▶ há algum lugar onde eu possa deixar a bagagem?
[a alg**oo**ng loogar **oh**ndee **ay**-oo p**o**sa daysh**a**r a baga**J**ayng?]

17

4. Car hire

automatic	automático	[owtomateekoo]
full tank	tanque cheio	[tankee shay-oo]
manual	manual	[manwal]
rented car	carro alugado	[kaHoo aloogadoo]

I'd like to rent a car
▶ eu gostaria de alugar um carro
[ay-oo gohstaree-a dee aloogar oong kaHoo]

por quanto tempo? ◀
[poor kwantoo taympoo?]
for how long?

two days
▶ dois dias
[doh-iJ dee-as]

I'll take the...
▶ fico com o...
[feekoo kohng oo...]

is that with unlimited mileage?
▶ a quilometragem é livre?
[a keelohmaytrajayng eh leevree?]

sim ◀
[seeng]
it is

posso ver sua habilitação, por favor? ◀
[posoo vayr soo-a abeeleetasowng, poor favohr?]
can I see your driving licence please?

e seu passaporte ◀
[ee say-oo pasaportee]
and your passport

is insurance included?
▶ o seguro está incluído?
[oo saygooroo eesta inklweedoo?]

sim, mas você tem de pagar os primeiros 100 reais ◀
[seeng mas vohsay tayng dee pagar oos preemayroos sayng Hay-īs]
yes, but you have to pay the first 100 reais

pode deixar um depósito de 100 reais? ◀
[podee dayshar oong daypozeetoo dee sayng Hay-īs?]
can you leave a deposit of 100 reais?

and if this office is closed, where do I leave the keys?
▶ e se a loja estiver fechada, onde posso deixar as chaves?
[ee s-ya loja eesteevehr fayshada, ohndee posoo dayshar as shavees?]

coloque-as nessa caixa ◀
[kohloky-as nehsa kīsha]
you drop them in that box

5. Communications

ADSL modem	modem ADSL	[modem a-day-**eh**see-**eh**lee]
at	arroba	[a**Ho**hba]
dial-up modem	conexão discada	[kohnay-ks**ow**ng dees**ka**da]
dot	ponto	[**poh**ntoo]
Internet	internet	[intayrn**eh**tee]
mobile (phone)	celular	[sayloo**lar**]
password	senha	[**sayn**-ya]
telephone socket adaptor	adaptador de tomada de telefone	[adaptad**ohr** dee tohm**a**da dee taylayf**oh**nee]

is there an Internet café around here?
▶ há algum cibercafé por aqui?
[a alg**oo**ng cybercafé poor ak**ee**?]

can I send email from here?
▶ posso mandar e-mail daqui?
[p**o**soo mand**a**r email dak**ee**?]

where's the at sign on the keyboard?
▶ onde é a arroba no teclado?
[**oh**ndee eh a a**Ho**hba noo taykl**a**doo?]

can you switch this to a UK keyboard?
▶ pode mudar para teclado britânico?
[p**o**dee mood**a**r para taykl**a**doo breet**a**neekoo?]

can you help me log on?
▶ pode ajudar a me conectar?
[p**o**dee a**J**ood**a**ramee kohn**a**ykt**a**r?]

can you put me through to...?
▶ pode me conectar com...?
[p**o**dee mee kohn**a**ykt**a**r kohng...?]

I'm not getting a connection, can you help?
▶ não consigo conexão, pode me ajudar?
[nowng kohns**ee**goo kohnay-ks**ow**ng, p**o**dee mee a**J**ood**a**r?]

where can I get a top-up card for my mobile?
▶ onde posso comprar recarga para o meu celular?
[**oh**ndee p**o**soo kohmprar Hayk**a**rga paroo m**a**y-oo sayloo**lar**?]

zero	five
zero	cinco
[**zeh**roo]	[**see**nkoo]
one	six
um	seis
[oong]	[says]
two	seven
dois	sete
[**doh**-is]	[**seh**tee]
three	eight
três	oito
[trays]	[**oh**-itoo]
four	nine
quatro	nove
[**kwa**troo]	[**no**vee]

19

6. Directions

hi, I'm looking for Avenida Brasil
▶ olá, estou procurando a Avenida Brasil
[ohla, eestoh prohkoorandwa avayneeda brazeel]

desculpe, nunca ouvi falar ◀
[deeskoolpee, noonka ohvee falar]
sorry, never heard of it

hi, can you tell me where Avenida Brasil is?
▶ olá, pode me dizer onde fica a Avenida Brasil?
[ohla, podee mee dizayr ohndee feeka avayneeda brazeel?]

também não sou daqui ◀
[tambayng nowng soh dakee]
I'm a stranger here to

hi, Avenida Brasil, do you know where it is?
olá, Avenida Brasil, sabe onde fica?
[ohla, avayneeda brazeel, sabee ohndee feeka?]

where?
onde?
[ohndee?]

which direction?
em que direção?
[ayng kee diraysowng?]

▶ virando a esquina
[feeka veerandoo aiskeena]
around the corner

▶ à esquerda, no segundo semáforo
[a eeskayrda, noo saygoondoo saymafohroo]
left at the second traffic lights

▶ depois, é a primeira rua à direita
[daypoh-is, eh a preemayra Hoo-a-deerayta]
then it's the first street on the right

à direita	em frente	mais adiante	saída
[a deerayta]	[ayng frayntee]	[mīj ad-yantee]	[sa-eeda]
on the right	opposite	further	turn off
à esquerda	em frente de	perto	sempre em frente
[a eeskayrda]	[ayng frayntee day]	[pehrtoo]	[saymprayng frayntee]
on the left	in front of	near	straight ahead
ali adiante		próximo	
[alee ad-yantee]		[prosimoo]	
over there	logo depois	next	para trás
	[logoo a saygeer]		[para tras]
depois do...	just after	rua	back
[daypoh-is doo...]		[Hoo-a]	
past the...		street	

7. Emergencies

accident	acidente	[asid**ay**ntee]
ambulance	ambulância	[amboolans-ya]
consul	cônsul	[**koh**nsool]
embassy	embaixada	[aymb**i**shada]
fire brigade	bombeiros	[bomb**ay**roos]
police	polícia	[pohl**ee**s-ya]

help!
▶ socorro!
[sohk**oh**Hoo!]

can you help me?
▶ pode me ajudar?
[**po**dee mee aJood**a**r?]

please come with me! it's really very urgent
▶ por favor, venha comigo! é realmente muito urgente
[poor fav**oh**r, **vay**n-ya kohm**ee**goo! eh Hay-alm**ay**ntee m**wee**ngtoo oorJ**ay**ntee]

I've lost (my keys)
▶ eu perdi (as minhas chaves)
[**ay**-oo payrd**ee** (as m**ee**n-yas sh**a**vees)]

(my car) is not working
▶ (meu carro) não funciona
[(m**ay**-oo ka**H**oo) nowng foons-y**oh**na]

(my purse) has been stolen
▶ (minha carteira) foi roubada
[(m**ee**n-ya kart**ay**ra) **foh**-i Hoh**ba**da]

I've been mugged
▶ fui assaltado
[fwee asalt**a**doo]

qual é seu nome? ◀
[kwal**eh** oo s**ay**-oo n**oh**mee?]
what's your name?

preciso ver seu passaporte ◀
I need to see your passport
[prays**ee**zoo vayr s**ay**-oo pasap**o**rtee]

I'm sorry, all my papers have been stolen
▶ sinto muito, roubaram todos os meus documentos
[s**ee**ntoo m**wee**ngtoo, Hohbar**ow**ng t**oh**dooz oos m**ay**-oos dohkoom**ay**ntoos]

21

8. Friends

hi, how're you doing?
▶ oi, tudo bem?
[oi **too**doo bayng?]

tudo bem, e você? ◀
[**too**doo bayng, ee vohs**ay**?]
OK, and you?

yeah, fine
▶ tudo bem
[**too**doo bayng]

not bad
▶ nada mal
[**na**da mal]

d'you know Mark?
▶ conhece o Mark?
[kohn-**yeh**s-yoo mark?]

and this is Ana
▶ e esta é a Ana
[ee **eh**sta eh a **a**na]

▶ sim, a gente se conhece
yeah, we know each other
[seeng, a **Jay**ntee see kohn-**yeh**see]

where do you know each other from?
▶ de onde vocês se conhecem?
[dee **ohn**dee vohs**ays** see kohn-**yeh**sayng?]

a gente se conheceu na casa do Daniel ◀
[a **Jay**ntee see kohn-yays**ay**-oo na **ka**za doo danee-**ehl**]
we met at Daniel's place

that was some party, eh?
▶ foi uma festa legal, não foi?
[**foh**-i **oo**ma **feh**sta lay**gal**, nowng **foh**-i?]

o máximo ◀
[oo **ma**seemoo]
the best

are you guys coming for a beer?
▶ querem tomar uma cerveja?
[**keh**rayng tohmar **oo**ma sayrvay**Ja**?]

▶ legal, vamos
[lay**gal**, **va**moos]
cool, let's go

não, vou me encontrar com a Maria
[nowng, **voh** mee aynkohntrar kohng a mar**ee**-a]
no, I'm meeting Maria

see you at Daniel's place tonight
▶ a gente se vê na casa do Daniel, hoje à noite
[a **Jay**ntee see vay na **ka**za doo danee-**ehl**, **ohJ**ee a-**noh**-itee]

até logo ◀
[ateh **lo**goo]
see you

9. Health

I'm not feeling very well
▶ não estou me sentindo muito bem
[nowng eest**oh** mee saynt**ee**ndoo m**wee**ngtoo bayng]

can you get a doctor?
▶ pode chamar um médico?
[p**o**dee sham**ar** oong m**eh**deekoo?]

▶ onde dói?	it hurts here
[**oh**ndee doy?]	▶ dói aqui
where does it hurt?	[doy ak**ee**]

▶ a dor é constante?	it's not a constant pain
[a dohr eh kohnst**a**ntee?	▶ não é uma dor constante
is the pain constant?	[nowng eh **oo**ma dohr kohnst**a**ntee]

can I make an appointment?
▶ posso marcar uma consulta?
[p**o**soo mark**ar** **oo**ma kohns**oo**lta?]

can you give me something for...?	yes, I have insurance
▶ pode me dar algo para...?	▶ sim, tenho seguro
[p**o**dee mee dar **a**lgoo para...?]	[seeng, **tay**n-yoo sayg**oo**roo]

antibiotics	antibióticos	[anteeb-y**o**teekoos]
antiseptic	pomada	[pohm**a**da
ointment	anti-séptica	antees**eh**pteeka]
cystitis	cistite	[seest**ee**tee]
dentist	dentista	[dent**ee**sta]
diarrhoea	diarréia	[d-yaH**eh**-ya]
doctor	médico	[m**eh**deeko]
hospital	hospital	[ohspit**a**l]
ill	doente	[dw**ay**ntee]
medicine	remédio	[Haym**eh**d-yoo]
painkillers	analgésicos	[analJ**eh**zeekoos]
pharmacy	farmácia	[farm**a**s-ya]
to prescribe	receitar	[Haysayt**ar**]
thrush	afta	[**a**fta]

10. Language difficulties

a few words	algumas palavras	[algoomas palavras]
interpreter	intérprete	[intehrpraytee]
to translate	traduzir	[tradoozeer]

seu cartão de crédito foi recusado ◀
[say-oo kartowng dee krehdeetoo foh-i Haykoozadoo]
your credit card has been refused

what, I don't understand; do you speak English?
▶ como? não entendo; fala inglês?
[kohmoo? nowng ayntayndoo fala inglays?]

ele não é válido ◀
[aylee nowng eh valeedoo]
this isn't valid

could you say that again?
▶ pode repetir?
[podee Haypayteer?]

slowly
▶ devagar
[dayvagar]

I understand very little Portuguese
▶ entendo muito pouco de português
[ayntayndoo mweengtoo pohkoo dee pohrtoogays]

I speak Portuguese very badly
▶ falo português muito mal
[faloo pohrtoogays mweengtoo mal]

não pode utilizar este cartão para pagar ◀
[nowng podee ooteeleezar aystee kartowng para pagar]
you can't use this card to pay

▶ entende?
[ayntayndee?]
do you understand?

sorry, no
▶ não, sinto muito
[nowng, seentoo mweengtoo]

is there someone who speaks English?
▶ há alguém que fale inglês?
[a algayng kee falee inglays?]

oh, now I understand
▶ ah, agora entendo
[ah, agora ayntayndoo]

is that ok now?
▶ está tudo bem agora?
[eesta toodoo bayng agora?]

11. Meeting people

hello
▶ olá
[oh**la**]

olá, meu nome é Joana ◀
[oh**la**, **may**-oo n**oh**mee eh Joo-**ana**]
hello, my name's Joana

Graham, from England, Thirsk
▶ eu sou Graham, de Thirsk, na Inglaterra
[**ay**-oo soh graham, dee thirsk, na inglat**eh**-Ha]

não conheço, onde fica? ◀
[nowng kohn-**yay**soo, **ohn**dee f**ee**ka?]
don't know that, where is it?

not far from York, in the North; and you?
▶ não muito longe de York, no norte; e você?
[nowng m**wee**ngtoo **loh**njee dee York, noo n**or**tee; ee vohs**ay**?]

sou de São Paulo; está aqui sozinho? ◀
[soh dee sowng **pow**loo; eesta ak**ee** soz**een**-yoo?]
I'm from São Paulo; are you here by yourself?

no, I'm with my wife and two kids
▶ não, estou com minha mulher e dois filhos
[nowng, eest**oh** kohng m**een**-ya mool-y**ehr** ee d**oh**-is f**ee**l-yoos]

what do you do?
▶ o que você faz?
[oo kee vohs**ay** fas?]

trabalho com computadores ◀
[trab**al**-yoo kong kohmpootad**oh**rees]
I'm in computers

me too
▶ eu também
[**ay**-oo tamb**ayng**]

here's my wife now
▶ aqui está a minha mulher
[ak**ee** eesta a m**een**-ya mool-y**ehr**]

prazer em conhecê-la ◀
[praz**ayr** ayng kohn-yay**say**loo]
nice to meet you

12. Post offices

airmail	correio aéreo	[koh-**Hay**-oo a-**ehr**-yoo]
post card	cartão-postal	[kar**tow**ng pohstal]
post office	correio	[koh-**Hay**-oo]
stamp	selo	[**say**loo]

what time does the post office close?
▶ a que horas fecha o correio?
[a k-y**o**ras f**eh**sha oo koh-**Hay**-oo?]

▶ às 17h horas durante a semana
[as dayzays**eh**tee **o**ras door**a**ntee a saym**a**na]
five o'clock weekdays

is the post office open on Saturdays?   até o meio-dia ◀
▶ o correio abre aos sábados?   [at**eh** oo m**ay**-oo d**ee**-a]
[oo koh-**Hay**-oo a**bree** ows s**a**badoos?]   **until midday**

I'd like to send this registered to England
▶ gostaria de mandar esta carta registrada para a Inglaterra
[gohstar**ee**-a dee mand**ar eh**sta k**a**rta para a inglat**eh**-Ha]

                                            pois não, são 10 reais ◀
                                    [**poh**-is nowng, sowng dehz Hay-**īs**]
                                        certainly, that will cost 10 reais

and also two stamps for England, please
▶ e também dois selos para a Inglaterra, por favor
[ee tamb**ayng** d**oh**-is **say**loos p**a**ra a inglat**eh**-Ha, poor fav**ohr**]

do you have some airmail stickers?
▶ tem adesivos de correio aéreo?
[tayng adayz**ee**voos dee koh-**Hay**-oo a-**ehr**-yoo?]

do you have any mail for me?
▶ tem correspondência para mim?
[tem koh-Hayspohnd**ayn**s-ya p**a**ra meeng?]

cartas	letters
pacotes/encomendas	parcels

13. Restaurants

bill	conta	[**koh**nta]
menu	cardápio	[kard**ap**-yo]
table	mesa	[**may**za]

can we have a non-smoking table?
▶ pode nos arrumar uma mesa para não-fumantes?
[**po**dee noos a**Hoo**mar **oo**ma **may**za para nowng foo**man**tees?]

there are two of us
▶ é para duas pessoas
[eh para **doo**-as payso**oh**-as]

there are four of us
▶ é para quatro pessoas
eh para kwatroo payso**oh**-as]

what's this?
▶ o que é isto?
[oo k-yeh **ee**stoo?]

é um tipo de peixe ◀
[eh oong **tee**poo dee **pay**shee]
it's a type of fish

é uma especialidade local ◀
[eh **oo**ma eespays-yalid**a**dee loh**kal**]
it's a local speciality

entre e eu lhe mostro ◀
[**ayn**tree ee **ay**-oo l-yi **mo**stroo)
come inside and I'll show you

we would like two of these, one of these, and one of those
▶ queremos dois destes, um desses e um daqueles
[kay**ray**moos **doh**-is **day**stees, oong **day**sees ee oong da**kay**lees]

▶ e para beber?
[ee para bay**bayr**?]
and to drink?

red wine
▶ vinho tinto
[**veen**-yoo **teen**too]

white wine
▶ vinho branco
[**veen**-yoo **bran**koo]

a beer and two orange juices
▶ uma cerveja e dois sucos de laranja
[**oo**ma sayrv**vay**Ja ee **doh**-is **soo**koos dee laran**Ja**]

some more bread please
▶ mais pão, por favor
[mīs powng, poor fav**ohr**]

▶ como estava a comida?
[**koh**moo eest**a**va a kom**ee**da?]
how was your meal?

excellent, very nice!
▶ excelente, muito boa!
[aysay**layn**tee, mw**een**gtoo b**oh**-a!]

▶ mais alguma coisa?
[mīz alg**oo**ma k**oh**-iza?]
anything else?

just the bill, thanks
▶ apenas a conta, obrigado
[a**pay**naz a **koh**nta, ohbreeg**a**doo]

14. Shopping

posso ajudá-lo? ◀
[**po**soo aJoodaloo?]
can I help you?

can I just have a look around?
▶ posso dar só uma olhada?
[**po**soo dar saw **oo**ma ol-**ya**da?]

yes, I'm looking for...
sim, estou procurando...
[seeng, eest**oh** prohkoo**ra**ndoo...]

how much is this?
▶ quanto custa isto?
[**kwa**ntoo **koo**sta **ee**stoo?]

32 reais ◀
[treen**ti**-d**oh**-is Hay-**ī**s]
thirty-two reais

OK, I think I'll have to leave it; it's a little too expensive for me
▶ tudo bem, acho que vou ter de desistir; é muito caro para mim
[**too**doo bayng, **a**shoo kee voh tayr dee dayzist**eer**; eh m**wee**ngtoo **ka**roo para meeng]

e que tal este? ◀
[ee kee tal **ay**stee]
how about this?

can I pay by credit card?
▶ posso pagar com cartão de crédito?
[**po**soo pa**ga**r kohng kart**ow**ng dee kr**eh**deetoo?]

it's too big
▶ é muito grande
[eh m**wee**ngtoo **gra**ndee]

it's too small
▶ é muito pequeno
[eh m**wee**ngtoo payk**ay**noo]

it's for my son – he's about this high
▶ é para o meu filho – ele é mais ou menos desta altura
[eh pa**ro**o m**ay**-oo **fee**l-yoo – **ay**lee eh m**ī**z oh m**ay**noos d**eh**sta alt**oo**ra]

▶ mais alguma coisa?
[m**ī**z alg**oo**ma k**oh**-iza?]
will there be anything else?

that's all thanks
▶ isso é tudo, obrigada
[**ee**soo eh **too**doo, ohbreeg**a**da]

make it 20 reais and I'll take it
▶ se fizer por 20 reais eu levo
[see feez**ehr** poor v**ee**ntee Hay-**ī**s **ay**-oo **leh**voo]

fine, I'll take it
▶ está bem, vou levar
[eest**a** bayng, voh layv**ar**]

aberto	open	liquidação	sale
caixa	cash desk	trocar	to exchange
fechado	closed		

15. Sightseeing

art gallery	galeria de arte	[galayree-a dee artee]
bus tour	excursão de ônibus	[ayskoorsowng dee ohneeboos]
city centre	centro da cidade	[sayntroo da seedadee]
closed	fechado	[fayshadoo]
guide	guia	[gee-a]
museum	museu	[moozay-oo]
open	aberto	[abehrtoo]

I'm interested in seeing the old town
▶ estou interessado em conhecer a cidade velha
[eestoh intayraysadoo ayng kohn-yaysayr a seedadee vehl-ya]

are there guided tours?
▶ há visitas guiadas?
[a veezeetas gee-adas?]

▶ sinto muito, estão lotadas
[seentoo mweengtoo, eestowng lohtadas]
I'm sorry, it's fully booked

how much would you charge to drive us around for four hours?
▶ quanto cobraria para nos levar para passear por quatro horas?
[kwantoo kohbraree-a para noos layvar para pas-yar poor kwatroo oras?]

can we book tickets for the concert here?
▶ podemos reservar aqui os ingressos para o concerto?
[pohdaymoos Hayzayrvar akee oos eengrehsoos paroo kohnsayrtoo?]

▶ sim, em nome de quem?
[seeng, ayng nohmee dee kayng?]
yes, in what name?

▶ qual é o cartão de crédito?
[kwaleh oo kartowng dee krehdeetoo?]
which credit card?

where do we get the tickets?
▶ onde pegamos os ingressos?
[ohndee paygamooz oos ingrehsoos?]

podem pegá-los na entrada ◀
[podayng paygaloos na ayntrada]
just pick them up at the entrance

is it open on Sundays?
▶ abre aos domingos?
[abree ows dohmeengoos?]

how much is it to get in?
▶ quanto é a entrada?
[kwantweh a ayntrada?]

are there reductions for groups of 6?
▶ tem desconto para grupos de seis pessoas?
[tayng deeskohntoo para groopoos dee says paysoh-as?]

that was really impressive!
▶ foi impressionante!
[foh-i imprays-yonantee!]

16. Underground/Bus/Train

to change trains	mudar de trem	[moodar dee trayng]
platform	plataforma	[plataforma]
return	bilhete de ida e volta	[beel-yaytee deedī volta]
single	bilhete de ida	[beel-yaytee dee eeda]
station	estação	[aystasowng]
stop	parada	[parada]
ticket	bilhete	[beel-yaytee]

how much is...?
▶ quanto é...?
[kwantweh...?]

a single, second class to
▶ um bilhete de ida, de segunda classe para...
[oong beel-yaytee dee eeda, dee saygoonda klassee para...]

two returns to...
▶ dois bilhetes de ida e volta para...
[doh-is beel-yaytees deedī volta para...]

for today	for tomorrow	for next Tuesday
▶ para hoje	▶ para amanhã	▶ para a próxima terça-feira
[para ohJee]	[paraman-yang]	[para prosima tayrsa fayra]

---

há um extra para a integração ◀
[a oong aystra para a intaygrasowng]
there's a supplement for the integration

deseja reservar o seu assento? ◀
[daysayJa Hayzayrvar oo say-oo asayntoo?]
do you want to make a seat reservation?

tem de mudar de trem na Sé ◀
[tayng dee moodar dee trayng na seh?]
you have to change at Sé

---

is this seat free?
▶ este lugar está livre?
[aystee loogar eesta leevree?]

excuse me, which station are we at?
▶ em que estação estamos?
[ayng kee eestasowng eestamoos?]

is this where I change for Vila Madalena?
▶ é aqui que mudo de trem para a Vila Madalena?
[eh akee kee moodoo dee trayng para a veela madalayna?]

English

→

Portuguese

A

a, an* um, uma [oong, **oo**ma]

about: about 20 mais ou menos vinte; cerca de vinte [mîs oh **may**noos **veen**tee]

it's about 5 o'clock são cerca de cinco horas [sowng **say**rka dee **seen**koo]

a film about Brazil um filme sobre o Brasil [oong **feel**mee **soh**bree oo braz**eel**]

above acima [a**see**ma]

abroad no exterior [noo eestayr-**yohr**]

absolutely! (I agree) com certeza! [kohng sayrt**ay**za]

absorbent cotton o algodão hidrófilo [algohd**owng** eedr**oh**feeloo]

accelerator o acelerador [asaylayrad**ohr**]

accept aceitar [asayt**ar**]

accident o acidente [aseed**ayn**tee]

there's been an accident houve um acidente [**oh**vee oong aseed**ayn**tee]

accommodation a hospedagem [ohspayda**J**ayng]

accurate exato [ayz**a**too]

ache a dor [dohr]

my back aches estou com dor nas costas [eest**oh** kohng dor nas **kos**tas]

across: across the road do outro lado da rua [doo **oh**troo ladoo da **Hoo**-a]

adapter o adaptador [adaptad**ohr**]

address o endereço [ayndayr**ay**soo]

what's your address? qual é seu endereço? [kwal**eh** oo **say**-oo]

address book a agenda de endereços [a a**J**aynda dee]

admission charge entrada; ingresso [ayntr**a**da; ingr**eh**soo]

adult (man/woman) o adulto [ad**oo**ltoo], a adulta

advance: in advance adiantado [ad-yantad**oo**]

aeroplane avião [av-y**ow**ng]

Africa a África

African (adj) africano [afreek**a**noo]

after depois [dayp**oh**-is]

after you você primeiro [vohs**ay** preemayr**oo**]

after lunch depois do almoço [dayp**oh**-is dwalm**oh**soo]

afternoon a tarde [**tar**dee]

in the afternoon à tarde

this afternoon esta tarde [**eh**sta]

aftershave a loção pós-barba [lohs**owng**]

aftersun cream a loção pós-sol

afterwards em seguida [ayng sayg**ee**da]

again outra vez [**oh**tra vays]

against contra [k**ohn**tra]

age a idade [eed**a**dee]

ago: a week ago há uma semana [a **oo**ma saym**a**na]

an hour ago há uma hora [**o**ra]

agree: I agree concordo [kohnk**or**doo]

airmail: by airmail por via aérea [poor **vee**-a-**ehr**-yl]

airmail envelope o envelope por via aérea [aynvaylopee]

airport o aeroporto [a-ehrohpohrtoo]

to the airport, please para o aeroporto, por favor [paroo – poor favohr]

airport bus o ônibus para o aeroporto [**ohn**eeboos]

aisle seat o assento no corredor [asayntoo noo koh-Haydohr]

alarm clock o despertador [deespayrtadohr]

alcohol o álcool [alkohl]

alcoholic alcoólico [alkoh-**o**likoo]

all: all the boys todos os meninos [**toh**dooz oos mayneenoos]

all the girls todas as meninas [**toh**daz as mayneenas]

all of them todos [**toh**doos]

that's all, thanks (said by man/woman) é tudo, obrigado(a) [eh **too**doo ohbreegadoo]

allergic: I'm allergic to... (said by man/woman) sou alérgico/alérgica a... [soh ale**hr**Jeekoo]

allowed: is it allowed? é permitido? [eh payrmeeteedoo]

all right está bem [eesta bayng]

I'm all right estou bem [eestoh]

are you all right? você está bem? o senhor está bem?

almond a amêndoa [a**may**ndwa]

almost quase [kwazee]

alone só [saw]

alphabet o alfabeto [alfab**eh**too]

a	a	j	Jota	s	**eh**see
b	bay	k	ka	t	tay
c	say	l	**eh**lee	u	oo
d	day	m	**ay**mee	v	vay
e	ay	n	**ay**nee	w	dabl-yoo
f	**eh**fee	o	o	x	shees
g	Jay	p	pay	y	**ee**pseelohn
h	ag**a**	q	kay	z	zay
i	ee	r	**eh**-Hee		

already já [Ja]

also também [tamb**ay**ng]

although embora [aymb**o**ra]

altogether totalmente [tohtalm**ay**ntee]

always sempre [**say**mpree]

am*: I am sou [soh]; estou [eest**oh**]

a.m.: at seven a.m. às sete horas da manhã [as – man-yang]

amazing (surprising) espantoso [eespant**oh**zoo]

(very good) maravilhoso [maraveel-y**oh**zoo]

ambulance a ambulância [amboolans-ya]

call an ambulance! chame uma ambulância! [shamee **oo**ma]

America a América

American (adj) americano [amayreek**a**noo]

I'm American (man/woman) sou americano/americana

among entre [**ayn**tree]

amount a quantia [**kwantee**-a]

amp: a 13-amp fuse um
fusível de treze ampères
[oong foo**zee**vil dee t**ray**zee
amp**ehr**ees]

and e [ee]

angry zangado [zang**a**doo]

animal o animal

ankle o tornozelo
[tohrnohz**ay**loo]

anniversary (wedding) o
aniversário de casamento
[aneevayrs**a**r-yoo (dee
kaza**mayn**too)]

annoy: this man's annoying
me este homem está me
importunando [**ay**stee
omayng ees**ta** mee
impohrtoon**a**ndoo]

annoying importuno
[import**oo**noo]

another outro [**oh**troo]
can we have another room?
pode nos dar outro quarto?
[**po**dee noos dar – k**war**too]
another beer, please ou**tra**
cerveja, por favor [sayr**vay**Ja
poor fav**ohr**]

antibiotics os antibióticos
[anteeb-yo**teek**oos]

antihistamines os anti-
histamínicos [eestam**ee**neekoos]

antique: is it an antique? é
uma antiguidade? [eh **oo**ma
anteegeed**a**dee]

antique shop o antiquário
[anteek**war**-yoo]

antiseptic o anti-séptico

any: have you got any bread/
tomatoes? tem pão/tomates?
[tayng powng]

do you have any? tem?

sorry, I don't have any
desculpe, não tenho
[deesk**ool**pee nowng **tayn**-yoo]

anybody* alguém [al**gayng**]
does anybody speak
English? alguém fala inglês?
[ing**lays**]

there wasn't anybody there
não tinha ninguém lá [nowng
teen-ya neeng**gayng** la]

anything* qualquer coisa
[kwalk**ehr** **koh**-iza]

dialogues

anything else? mais
alguma coisa? [mīs alg**oo**ma
koh-iza]
nothing else, thanks (said
by man/woman) mais nada,
obrigado(a) [ohbreeg**a**doo]

would you like anything to
drink? gostaria de beber
alguma coisa? [gohstar**ee**-a
dee bayb**ayr**]
I don't want anything,
thanks (said by man/
woman) não quero nada,
obrigado(a) [nowng k**ehr**oo]

apart from além de [al**ayng** dee]

apartment o apartamento
[apartam**ayn**too]

apartment block o prédio de apartamentos [**prehd**-yoo dee]

aperitif o aperitivo [apayreet**ee**voo]

apology as desculpas [deesk**ool**pas]

appendicitis a apendicite [apayndees**ee**tee]

appetizer a entrada [aynt**ra**da]

apple a maçã [ma**sang**]

appointment a hora marcada [**ora**]

dialogue

good morning, how can I help you? bom dia, posso ajudá-la? [bohng d**ee**-a, p**o**soo aJood**a**la?]

I'd like to make an appointment gostaria de marcar hora [gohst**a**ree-a]

what time would you like? que hora prefere? [k-y**o**ra prayf**eh**ree?]

three o'clock três horas [trayz **o**ras]

I'm afraid that's not possible, is four o'clock all right? infelizmente não é possível, quatro horas está bem? [infayleezm**a**yntee nowng eh poh**see**vil, kw**a**troo **o**ras eesta bayng?]

yes, that will be fine sim, está bem [seeng]

the name was...? seu nome é...? [**say**-oo n**oh**mee eh]

apricot o damasco [dam**a**skoo]

April abril [ab**ree**l]

Arab (adj) árabe [**a**rabee]

are*: we are somos [s**oh**moos]; estamos [eest**a**moos]

you are é [eh]; está [eest**a**]

they are são [sowng]; estão [eest**ow**ng]

area área [**ar**-ya]; região [HayJ-y**ow**ng]

area code o código de área

arm o braço [br**a**soo]

arrange: will you arrange it for us? pode arrumar isto para nós? [**po**dee aHoomar **ee**stoo – nos?]

arrival a chegada [shayg**a**da]

arrive chegar

when do we arrive? quando chegamos? [kw**a**ndoo shayg**a**moos?]

has my fax arrived yet? meu fax já chegou? [**may**-oo – Ja shayg**oh**?]

we arrived today chegamos hoje [shayg**a**moos **oh**Jee]

art a arte [**a**rtee]

art gallery a galeria de arte [galayr**ee**-a dee]

artist (man/woman) o/a artista [art**ee**sta]

as: as big as tão grande quanto [towng gr**a**ndee kw**a**ntoo]

as soon as possible logo que possível [**lo**goo kee poh**see**vil]

ashtray o cinzeiro [seenz**ay**roo]

ask perguntar [payrgoont**a**r]; pedir [payd**ee**r]

I didn't ask for this não pedi isto [nowng payd**ee ee**stoo]

could you ask him to...?
poderia pedir a ele que...?
[pohdayree-a paydeer a aylee kee...?]

asleep: she's asleep ela está dormindo [ehla eesta dohrmeendoo]

aspirin a aspirina [aspeereena]

asthma a asma

astonishing incrível [inkreevil]

at: at the hotel no hotel [noo]
at the station na estação [na eestasowng]
at six o'clock às seis horas [as sayz oras]
at Américo's na casa do Américo [dwamehreekoo]

athletics o atletismo [atlayteesmoo]

Atlantic Ocean o Oceano Atlântico [ohs-yanoo atlanteekoo]

attractive atraente [atra-ayntee]

aubergine a berinjela [bayreenJehla]

August agosto [agohstoo]

aunt a tia [tee-a]

Australia a Austrália [owstral-ya]

Australian (adj) australiano [owstral-yanoo]
I'm Australian (man/woman) sou australiano/australiana [soh]

automatic automático [owtohmateekoo]

automatic teller o caixa eletrônico [kisha aylaytrohneekoo]

autumn o outono [ohtohnoo]
in the autumn no outono [noo]

avenue a avenida [avayneeda]

average (not good) médio/regular [mehd-yoo/Haygoolar]
on average em média [ayng mehd-ya]

awake: is he awake? ele está acordado? [aylee eesta akohrdadoo?]

away: go away! saia! [sa-ya]
is it far away? fica longe? [feeka lohnJee]

awful horrível [oh-Heevil]

axle o eixo [ayshoo]

B

baby o bebê [baybay]

baby food a comida de bebê [kohmeeda dee]

baby's bottle a mamadeira [mamadayra]

baby-sitter a babá

back (of body) as costas [kostas]
(back part) a parte posterior [partee pohstayr-yohr]
at the back atrás [atras]
can I have my money back? pode devolver o meu dinheiro? [podee dayvohlvayr oo may-oo deen-yayroo?]
to come/go back voltar

backache a dor nas costas [dohr nas kostas]

bacon o bacon

bad mau [mow], (f) má

a bad headache uma dor de cabeça forte [**oo**ma dohr dee kabay**sa** fortee]

badly mal

bag o saco [**sa**koo]
(handbag) a sacola [sa**ko**la]
(suitcase) a mala

baggage a bagagem [baga**Ja**yng]

baggage check o controle de bagagem [kohntr**oh**lee]

baggage claim a retirada de bagagens [**Ha**yteerada]

bakery a padaria [pada**ree**-a]

balcony o balcão [bal**ko**wng]
a room with a balcony um quarto com balcão [oong **kwa**rtoo kohng]

bald careca [ka**reh**ka]

ball a bola
(small) a bolinha [bol**ee**n-ya]

ballet o balé

ballpoint pen a esferográfica [eesfayroh-gra**fee**ka]

banana a banana

band (musical) a banda

bandage a bandagem [banda**Ja**yng], a faixa [**fa**isha]

Bandaid® o curativo adesivo [koorat**ee**voo aday**zee**voo]

bank (money) o banco [**ba**nkoo]

bank account a conta bancária [ban**ka**r-ya]

bar o bar
a bar of chocolate uma barra de chocolate [**ba**Ha dee shohkoh**la**tee]

38

barber's o barbeiro [bar**ba**yroo]

basket o cesto [**sa**ystoo]
(in shop) o cesto de compras [dee koh**mpra**s]

bath o banho [**ba**n-yoo]
can I have a bath? posso tomar banho? [**po**soo tohmar]

bathroom o banheiro [**ba**n-**ya**yroo]
with a private bathroom com banheiro privativo [kohng – preevat**ee**voo]

bath towel a toalha de banho [**twa**l-ya]

bathtub a banheira [ban-**ya**yra]

battery a pilha [**pee**l-ya]
(for car) a bateria [batay**ree**-a]

bay a baía [ba-**ee**-a]

be* ser [sayr]; estar [ees**ta**r]

beach a praia [**pr**ī-a]
on the beach na praia

beach mat a esteira de praia [ees**ta**yra dee prī-a]

beach umbrella o guarda-sol [**gwa**rda sol]

beans os feijões [fay**Jo**yngs]
French beans as vagens [**va**Jayngs]
broad beans as favas [**fa**vas]

beard a barba

beautiful bonito [boh**nee**too]

because porque [poor**ka**y]
because of... por causa de... [poor **ko**wza dee]

bed a cama
I'm going to bed now vou para a cama agora [voh]

bedroom o quarto [**kwa**rtoo]

beef a carne de vaca
[karnee dee]

beer a cerveja [sayrvayJa]
two beers, please duas
cervejas, por favor [doo-as
sayrvayJas poor favohr]

before antes [antees]

begin começar [kohmaysar]
when does it begin? quando
começa? [kwandoo kohmehsa]

beginner (man/woman) o/a
principiante [preenseep-yantee]

beginning: at the beginning no
início [noo eenees-yoo]

behind atrás [atras]
behind me atrás de mim
[dee meeng]

beige bege

Belgian (adj) belga

Belgium a Bélgica [behlJeeka]

believe acreditar

below abaixo [abīshoo]

belt o cinto [seentoo]

bend (in road) a curva [koorva]

berth (on ship) a cabine
[kabeenee]

beside: beside the... junto
de... [Joontoo]

best o melhor [mayl-yor]

better melhor
are you feeling better? está se
sentindo melhor? [eesta see
saynteendoo]

between entre [ayntree]

beyond além [alayng]

bicycle a bicicleta [beeseeklehta]

big grande [grandee]
too big muito grande
[mweengtoo]

it's not big enough não é
grande o bastante [nowng eh
bastantee]

bikini o biquíni

bill a conta
(US) a cédula [sehdoola]
could I have the bill, please? a
conta, por favor? [poor favohr]

bin a lata de lixo [dee leeshoo]

bin liner o saco de lixo
[sakoo]

bird o pássaro [pasaroo]

birthday o aniversário
[aneevayrsar-yoo]
happy birthday! feliz
aniversário! [faylees]

biscuit o biscoito [beeskoitoo];
a bolacha [bohlasha]

bit: a little bit um pouco
[oong pohkoo]
a big bit um pedaço grande
[paydasoo grandee]
a bit of... um pedaço de...
a bit expensive um pouco
caro [pohkoo karoo]

bite (by insect) a picada
[peekada]
(by dog) a mordida
[mohrdeeda]

bitter (taste etc) amargo
[amargoo]

black preto [praytoo]

blanket o cobertor [kohbayrtohr]

bleach (for toilet) o alvejante
[alvayJantee]

bless you! saúde! [sa-oodee]

blind cego [sehgoo]

blinds as persianas [payrs-yanas]

blister a bolha [bol-ya]

blocked (road) interditada [intayrdeetada], bloqueada [blohk-yada]
(pipe, sink) entupido [ayntoopeedoo]
blond (adj) loiro [loh-iroo]
blood o sangue [sangee]
  high blood pressure a pressão alta [praysowng]
blouse a blusa [blooza]
blow-dry fazer escova [fazayr eeskohva]
  I'd like a cut and blow-dry queria cortar e fazer escova [keeree-a]
blue azul [azool]
  blue eyes os olhos azuis [ol-yoos azoo-is]
blusher o pincel de blush [peensehl dee]
boarding house a pensão [paynsowng]
boarding pass o cartão de embarque [kartowng d-yaymbarkee]
boat o barco [barkoo]
  (for passengers) o ferryboat
body o corpo [kohrpoo]
boiled egg o ovo cozido [ohvoo kohzeedoo]
boiler a caldeira [kaldayra]
bone o osso [ohsoo]
  (in fish) a espinha [eespeen-ya]
bonnet (of car) o capô [kapoh]
book o livro [leevroo]
  (verb) reservar [Hayzayrvar]
  can I book a seat? posso reservar um lugar? [posso – oong loogar]

dialogue

I'd like to book a table for two quero reservar uma mesa para dois [kehroo – ooma mayza para doh-is]
what time would you like it booked for? para que horas? [kyoras]
half past seven sete e meia [sehtee may-a]
that's fine está bem [eesta bayng]
and your name? e o seu nome? [yoo say-oo nohmee]

bookshop a livraria [leevraree-a]
bookstore a livraria [leevraree-a]
boot (footwear) a bota
  (of car) o porta-malas [porta]
border (of country) a fronteira [frohntayra]
bored: I'm bored (said by man/woman) estou chateado/chateada [eestoh shat-yadoo]
boring chato [shatoo]
born: I was born in Manchester nasci em Manchester [nasee ayng]
  I was born in 1960 nasci em mil novecentos e sessenta
borrow pedir emprestado [paydeer aympraystadoo]
  may I borrow...? posso pedir... emprestado? [posso]
both ambos [amboos]
bother: sorry to bother you desculpe incomodá-lo [deeskoolpee inkohmohdaloo]

bottle a garrafa [gaHafa]
 a bottle of house red uma garrafa de vinho da casa [**oo**ma – dee **vee**n-yoo da **ka**za]
bottle-opener o abridor de garrafa [abree**dohr** dee]
bottom (of person) o bumbum [boomb**oom**]
 at the bottom of... (hill) no sopé da... [noo soh**peh** da]
box a caixa [k**ī**sha]
box office a bilheteria [beel-yaytay**ree**-a]
boy o menino [mayn**ee**noo]
boyfriend o namorado [namoh-**ra**doo]
bra o sutiã [soot-yang]
bracelet a pulseira [pools**ay**ra]
brake o freio [fr**ay**-oo]
brandy o conhaque [kohn-**ya**kee]
Brasília Brasília [braz**eel**-ya]
Brazil Brasil [braz**eel**]
Brazilian (adj) brasileiro [brazeela**y**roo]
 I'm Brazilian (man/woman) sou brasileiro/brasileira [soh]
bread o pão [p**ow**ng]
 white bread o pão branco [**bran**koo]
 brown bread o pão preto [pr**ay**too]
 wholemeal bread o pão integral [intaygr**al**]
break quebrar [kaybr**ar**]
 I've broken the... quebrei... [kaybr**ay** oo]
 I think I've broken my wrist acho que quebrei o pulso [**a**shoo kee – oo p**oo**lsoo]

break down quebrar
 May car has broken down meu carro quebrou [**may**-oo k**a**Hoo kaybr**oh**]
breakdown (mechanical) a pane [p**a**nee]
breakdown service o serviço de guincho [sayrv**ee**soo drr g**ee**nshoo]
breakfast o café-da-manhã [kaf**eh** da man-y**ang**]
break-in: I've had a break-in minha casa foi roubada [**meen**-ya k**a**za f**oh**-i H**oh**bada]
breast o seio [**say**-oo]
breathe respirar [Hayspeer**ar**]
breeze a brisa [br**ee**za]
bridge (over river) a ponte [**poh**ntee]
brief breve [br**eh**vee]
briefcase a pasta [**pas**ta]; a maleta [mal**ay**ta]
bright (light etc) brilhante [breel-**yan**tee]
 bright red vermelho vivo [vayrma**y**l-yoo **vee**voo]
brilliant (idea, person) brilhante
bring trazer [traz**ayr**]
 I'll bring it back later trago isto de volta mais tarde [**tra**goo **ee**stoo dee – mis **tar**dee]
Britain a Grã-Bretanha [grang brayt**an**-ya]
British britânico [breet**a**neekoo]
brochure o folheto [fohl-**yay**too]
broken quebrado [kaybr**a**doo]
bronchitis bronquite [brohnk**ee**tee]
brooch o broche [br**o**shee]

broom a vassoura [vas**oh**-ra]
brother o irmão [eerm**owng**]
brother-in-law o cunhado [koon-yadoo]
brown marrom [ma**Hohng**], castanho [kastan-yoo]
brush (for hair, cleaning) a escova [ees**kova**]
(artist's) o pincel [peens**ehl**]
bucket o balde [**bal**dee]
buffet car o vagão-restaurante [vag**owng** Haystowr**an**tee]
buggy (for child) o carrinho de bebê [kaH**een**-yo dee bayb**ay**]
building o edifício [aydeef**ees**-yoo], o prédio [**preh**d-yoo]
bulb (light bulb) a lâmpada
bullfight a tourada [toh-**ra**da]
bullfighter o toureiro [toh-**ray**roo]
bullring a praça de touros [**pra**sa dee **toh**-roos]
bull-running a corrida de touros [koH**ee**da]
bunk o beliche [bayl**ee**shee]
bureau de change a casa de câmbio [**ka**za dee kamb-yoo]
burglary o roubo [**Hoh**boo]
burn a queimadura [kaymad**oo**ra]
(verb) queimar [kaym**ar**]
burnt: this is burnt isto está queimado [**ees**too eesta kaymad**oo**]
burst: a burst pipe um cano estourado [oong k**an**oo eestoh-r**a**doo]
bus o ônibus [**oh**neeboos]
what number bus is it to...? qual é o número do ônibus

para...? [kwal**eh** oo n**oo**mayroo doo]
when is the next bus to...? quando sai o próximo ônibus para...? [**kwan**doo sï oo pr**os**imoo]
what time is the last bus? quando sai o último ônibus? [**oo**ltimoo]

dialogue

> **does this bus go to...?** este ônibus vai para...? [**ays**tee]
> **no, you need a number...** não, tem de pegar o número... [nowng, tayng dee pag**ar** oo n**oo**mayroo]

business o negócio [nayg**os**-yoo]
bus station o terminal de ônibus [tayrmeen**al** dee **oh**neeboos]
bus stop o ponto de ônibus [**pohn**too]
bust o busto [**boos**too]
busy (restaurant etc) movimentado [mohveemaynt**a**doo]
I'm busy tomorrow (said by man/woman) estarei ocupado/ ocupada amanhã [eestar**ay** okoop**a**doo aman-y**ang**]
but mas [mas]
butcher's o açougue [as**oh**gee]
butter a manteiga [mant**ay**ga]
button o botão [boht**owng**]
buy comprar
where can I buy...? onde posso comprar...? [**ohn**dee **pos**oo]

by*: **by bus** de ônibus
[**ohn**eeboos]
by car de carro [dee ka**Hoo**]
written by... escrito por...
[eeskree**too** poor]
by the window à janela [a
Ja**neh**la]
by the sea à beira-mar
by Thursday na quinta-feira
[na **keen**ta **fay**ra]
bye! tchau!

C

cabbage o repolho [Hay**pohl**-
yoo]
cabin (on ship) o camarote
[kama**ro**tee]
cable car o teleférico
[taylay**feh**reekoo]; o bondinho
[bohn**deen**-yoo]
café o café [ka**feh**]
cake o bolo [**boh**loo]
cake shop a confeitaria
[kohnfaytar**ee**-a]
call chamar [sha**mar**]
(to phone) telefonar, ligar
[taylayfoh**nar**, lee**gar**]
what's it called? como se
chama isto? [**koh**moo see
shama **ees**too]
he/she is called... ele/ela
se chama... [**ay**lee/**eh**la see
shama]
please call the doctor por
favor, chame o médico
[poor favo**hr** sham-yoo
mehdeekoo]

please give me a call at...
a.m. tomorrow por favor,
ligue para mim amanhã às...
horas [**lee**gee para meeng
aman-yang as... **o**ras]
please ask him to call me
por favor, peça a ele que me
telefone [**peh**sa-a **ay**lee kee mee
taylay**foh**nee]
call back: I'll call back later
volto a telefonar mais
tarde [**vol**twa taylayfoh**nar**
mīs **tard**ee]
call round: I'll call round
tomorrow passo amanhã
[**pa**soo aman-**yang**]
camcorder a filmadora
[feelmad**oh**-ra]
camera a máquina
fotográfica [ma**keena**
fohtoh**gra**feeka]
camera shop a loja de
artigos fotográficos [**lo**Ja dee
ar**tee**goos fohtoh**gra**feekoos]
camp acampar
can we camp here?
podemos acampar aqui?
[poh**day**moos – a**kee**]
campsite o camping
can a lata
a can of beer uma lata de
cerveja [dee sayr**vay**Ja]
can*: can you...? você
pode...? [voh**say po**dee]
can I have...? pode me
servir um...? [mee sayr**veer**
oong]
I can't... não posso... [nowng]
Canada o Canadá

Canadian canadense
[kanadaynsee]
I'm Canadian (man/woman)
sou canadense [soh]
canal o canal
cancel cancelar [kansaylar]
candies as balas
canoe a canoa [kanoh-a]
canoeing a canoagem
[kanoh-a-Jayng]
can-opener o abridor de latas
[abreedohr dee latas]
cap (hat) o boné [bohneh]
(of bottle) a tampa
car o carro [kaHoo]
by car de carro
caravan o trailer
caravan site camping de
trailer
carburettor o carburador
[karbooradohr]
card (birthday etc) o cartão
[kartowng]
here's my business card
aqui está o meu cartão de
visitas [akee eesta oo may-oo
kartowng dee veezeetas]
cardigan o cardigã
cardphone o telefone de
cartão [taylayfohnee dee
kartowng]
careful cuidadoso
[kwidadohzoo]
be careful! cuidado!
[kwidadoo]
caretaker (man/woman)
o zelador [zayladohr], a
zeladora
car ferry o ferryboat

car hire o aluguel de carros
[aloogehl dee kaHoos]
carnival o carnaval
car park o estacionamento
[eestas-yonamayntoo]
carpet o carpete [karpehtee]
carriage (of train) o vagão
[vagowng]
carrier bag a sacola de plástico
[sakola dee plasteekoo]
carrot a cenoura [saynohra]
carry levar [layvar]
carry-cot o moisés
[moh-izehs]
carton a caixa de papelão
[kisha dee papaylowng]
carwash o lava-rápido
[lava Hapeedoo]
case (suitcase) a maleta
cash o dinheiro
[deen-yayroo]
(verb) descontar [deeskohntar]
will you cash this for me?
pode descontar isto para
mim? [podee – eestoo para
meeng]
cash desk a caixa [kisha]
cash dispenser o caixa
eletrônico [aylaytrohneekoo]
cassette a fita cassete
cassette recorder o gravador
de fita [gravadohr dee feeta]
castle o castelo [kastehloo]
casualty department o
serviço de emergência
[sayrveesoo dee aymayrJayns-ya]
cat o gato [gatoo]
catch pegar
where do we catch the bus

to...? onde pegamos o ônibus para...? [**oh**ndee payg**a**mooz oo **oh**neeboos]
cathedral a catedral [katayd**ral**]
Catholic (adj) católico [kat**o**likoo]
cauliflower a couve-flor [**koh**vee flohr]
cave a caverna
ceiling o teto [**teh**too]
celery o aipo [**ī**poo]
cellar (for wine) a adega [ad**eh**ga]
cellular phone o celular [sayloo**lar**]
cemetery o cemitério [saymeet**ehr**-yoo]
centigrade* centígrado [saynt**ee**gradoo]
centimetre* o centímetro [saynt**ee**maytroo]
central central [sayn-**tral**]
central heating o aquecimento central [akayseem**ayn**too]
centre o centro [**sayn**troo]
  how do we get to the city centre? como chegamos ao centro da cidade? [**koh**moo shayg**a**moos ow s**ayn**troo da seed**a**dee]
  how do we get to the sports center? como chegamos ao centro esportivo? [s**ayn**troo eesport**ee**voo]
cereal os cereais [saray-**ī**s]
certainly é claro [eh kl**a**roo], certamente [sehrtam**ayn**tee], certainly not é claro que não [kee nowng]

chair a cadeira [kad**ay**ra]
champagne o champanhe [shampan-**yī**]
change (money) o troco [tr**oh**koo] (verb: money) trocar [troh**kar**]
  can I change this for...? posso trocar isto por...? [**po**soo – **ee**stoo]
  I don't have any change não tenho troco [nowng t**ayn**-yoo]
  can you give me change for a 20 euro note? pode me trocar uma nota de vinte euros? [**po**dee mee troh**kar oo**ma – dee v**een**tee **ay**-ooroos]

dialogue

  do we have to change (trains)? temos de trocar de trem? [**tay**moos dee troh**kar** dee trayng?]
  yes, change at Sé/no, it's a direct train sim, troquem na Sé/não, a linha é direta [seeng tr**o**kayng na seh/nowng a l**ee**n-ya eh dir**eh**ta]

changed: to get changed trocar-se
chapel a capela [kap**eh**la]
charge o preço [pr**ay**soo] (verb) custar [koos**tar**]
charge card o cartão de débito [kart**owng** dee d**eh**beetoo]
cheap barato [bar**a**too]
  do you have anything cheaper? tem algo mais barato? [tayng **al**goo mīs]

check (US) o cheque [shehkee]
(US: bill) a conta
see bill
check verificar
could you check the...,
please? pode verificar o...,
por favor? [podee – oo... poor
favohr?]
checkbook o talão de
cheques [talowng dee shehkees]
check-in o check-in
check in fazer o check-in
[fazayr oo]
where do we have to check
in? onde temos de fazer o
check-in? [ohndee taymoos]
cheek (on face) a face [fasee]
cheerio! até logo! [ateh
lohgoo]
cheers! (toast) saúde!
[sa-oodee]
cheese o queijo [kayJoo]
chemist's a farmácia
[farmas-ya]
cheque o cheque [shehkee]
do you take cheques?
aceitam cheques? [asaytowng
shehkees]
cheque book o talão de
cheques [talowng dee shehkees]
cherry a cereja [sayrayJa]
chess o xadrez [shadrays]
chest o peito [paytoo]
chewing gum a goma de
mascar [gohma dee maskar]
chicken o frango [frangoo]
chickenpox a catapora
[katapora]; a varicela
[vareesehla]

child a criança [kry-ansa]
children as crianças
[kry-ansas]
child minder a babá
children's pool a piscina
infantil [peeseena infanteel]
children's portion a porção
para crianças [pohrsowng]
chin o queixo [kayshoo]
china a porcelana
[pohrsaylana]
Chinese (adj) chinês [sheenays]
chips as batatas fritas [batatas
freetas]
chocolate o chocolate
[shohkohlatee]
milk chocolate o chocolate
ao leite [ow laytee]
plain chocolate o chocolate
puro [pooroo]
a hot chocolate um
chocolate quente [oong
– kayntee]
choose escolher [eeskohl-yayr]
Christian name o nome
de batismo [nohmee dee
bateesmoo]; o primeiro nome
[preemayroo]
Christmas o Natal
Christmas Eve a noite de
Natal [noh-itee dee]
merry Christmas! feliz Natal!
[faylees]
church a igreja [eegrayJa]
cider a cidra [seedra]
cigar o charuto [sharootoo]
cigarette o cigarro [seegaHoo]
cigarette lighter o isqueiro
[eeskayroo]

cinema o cinema [seen**ay**ma]
circle o círculo [**seer**kooloo]
 (in theatre) a platéia [plat**eh**-ya]
city a cidade [seed**a**dee]
city centre o centro da cidade
 [**sayn**troo]
clean (adj) limpo [**leem**poo]
 can you clean this for me?
 você pode limpar isto para
 mim? [voh**say** p**o**dee leempar
 eestoo – meeng]
cleaning solution (for contact
 lenses) a solução de limpeza
 [sohloos**ow**ng dee leemp**ay**za]
cleansing lotion a loção de
 limpeza [lohs**ow**ng dee]
clear claro [klaroo]
clever inteligente
 [intaylee**Jayn**tee]
cliff o rochedo [Rohsh**ay**doo]
climb escalar [eeskalar]
cling film o filme de PVC
 [**feel**mee dee pay-vay-say]
clinic a clínica [kleen**ee**ka]
cloakroom a chapelaria
 [shapaylar**ee**-a]
clock o relógio [Haylo**J**-yoo]
close (verb) fechar [faysh**ar**]
closed fechado [faysh**a**doo]

dialogue

what time do you close?
a que horas fecham? [a k-
yoras fays**h**owng]
we close at 8 p.m. on
weekdays and 6 p.m. on
Saturdays fechamos às 20

horas durante a semana
e às 18 horas aos sábados
[faysha-mooz as v**ee**ntee **o**ras
doorant-ya saymana yas dayz**oh**-
ito **o**ras ows sabadoos]
do you close for lunch?
fecham para almoço?
[alm**oh**soo]
yes, between 1 and 2 p.m.
sim, entre as 13 e as 14
horas [seeng **ay**ntr-yas trayz-
yas kat**oh**rzee **o**ras]

cloth (fabric) o tecido [tays**ee**doo]
 (for cleaning etc) o pano de
 limpeza [panoo dee leemp**ay**za]
clothes a roupa [Hohpa]
clothes line o varal [varal]
clothes peg o prendedor de
 roupa [dee Hohpa]
cloud a nuvem [**noo**vayng]
cloudy nublado [noobladoo]
clutch a embreagem [aymbray-
 a**J**ayng]
coach (bus) o ônibus [**oh**neeboos]
 (on train) o vagão [vag**ow**ng]
coach station o terminal
 de ônibus [tayrmeenal dee
 ohneeboos]
coach trip a excursão de
 ônibus [ayskoors**ow**ng]
coast o litoral [leetohral]
 on the coast no litoral
coat (long coat) o sobretudo
 [sohbrayt**oo**doo]; o casacão
 [kazak**ow**ng]
 (jacket) o paletó [paleet**o**]; a
 jaqueta [Jak**ay**ta]

coathanger o cabide [kabeedee]

cockroach a barata

cocoa o cacau [kakow]

coconut o coco [kohkoo]

cod o bacalhau fresco [bakal-yow frayskoo]

dried cod o bacalhau seco [saykoo]

code (for phoning) o código de área (DDD) [kodeegoo dee ar-ya]
    what's the (dialling) code for Rio? qual é o código de área do Rio? [kwaleh oo – doo Hee-oo]

coffee o café [kafeh]
    two coffees, please dois cafés, por favor [doh-is kafehs poor favohr]

coin a moeda [moh-ehda]

Coke® a Coca-Cola

cold frio [free-oo]
    I'm cold estou com frio [eestoh kohng]
    I have a cold estou resfriado [eestoh Haysfree-adoo]

collapse: he's collapsed ele desmaiou [aylee deesmi-oh]

collar o colarinho [kohlareen-yoo]; a gola

collect buscar [booskar]
    I've come to collect... vim buscar... [veeng]

collect call a chamada a cobrar [shamada kobrar]

college a faculdade [fakooldadee]

colour a cor [kohr]
    do you have this in other colours? tem isto em outras cores? [tayng eestooo ayng ohtras kohrees]

colour film o filme colorido [feelmee kohlohreedoo]

comb o pente [payntee]

come* vir [veer]

dialogue

where do you come from?
de onde você é? [dee ohndee vohsay eh]
I come from Edinburgh
sou de Edimburgo [soh dee yadeenboorgoo]

come back voltar
    I'll come back tomorrow volto amanhã [voltoo aman-yang]

come in entrar [ayntrar]

comfortable confortável [kohnfohrtavil]

compact disc o CD [say-day]

company (business) a companhia [kohmpan-yee-a]

compartment (on train) o compartimento [kohmparteemayntoo]

compass a bússola [boosoola]

complain reclamar [Hayklamar]

complaint a reclamação [Hayklamasowng]
    I have a complaint tenho uma reclamação [tayn-yoo ooma]

completely completamente [kohmplehtamayntee]

computer o computador [kohmpootadohr]

concert o concerto [kohnsayrtoo]

concussion a concussão [kohnkoosowng]

conditioner (for hair) o condicionador de cabelo [kohndees-yohnadohr dee kabayloo]

condom o preservativo [prayzayrvateevoo]

conference a conferência [kohnfayrayns-ya]

confirm confirmar [kohnfeermar]

congratulations! parabéns! [parabayngs]

connecting flight o vôo de conexão [voh-oo dee kohnayk-sowng]

connection a conexão

conscious consciente [kons-yayntee]

constipation a prisão de ventre [preezowng dee vayntree]

consulate o consulado [konsooladoo]

contact contatar

contact lenses as lentes de contato [layntees dee kohntatoo]

contraceptive o anticoncepcional, [antee-kohnsayps-yonal]

convenient conveniente [kohnvayn-yayntee]

that's not convenient não é conveniente [nowng eh]

cook cozinhar [kohzeen-yar]

not cooked malpassado [mow pasadoo]

cooker o fogão [fohgowng]

cookie a bolacha [bohlasha]; o biscoito [beeskoh-itoo]

cooking utensils os utensílios de cozinha [ootaynseel-yoos dee kohzeen-ya]

cool fresco [frayskoo]

cork a rolha [Hohl-ya] (material) a cortiça [kohrteesa]

corkscrew o saca-rolhas [saka-Hohl-yas]

corner o canto [kantoo] in the corner no canto [noo]

cornflakes os flocos de milho [flokoos]

correct (right) certo [sehrtoo]

corridor o corredor [koh-Haydohr]

cosmetics os cosméticos [kohsmehteekoos]

cost custar [koostar] how much does it cost? quanto custa? [kwantoo koosta]

cot o berço [bayrsoo]

cotton o algodão [algoodowng]

cotton wool o algodão hidrófilo [eedrofeeloo]

couch (sofa) o sofá [sohfa]

couchette o beliche [bayleeshee]

cough a tosse [tosee]

cough medicine o xarope para tosse [sharopee]

could: could you...? poderia...? [pohdayree-a]
could I have...? gostaria de...? [gohstaree-a]
I couldn't... (wasn't able to) não consegui... [nowng kohnsaygee]

country (nation) o país [pa-ees]

(countryside) o campo [**kam**poo]

countryside o campo

couple (two people) o casal
[ka**zal**]; o par [par]

a couple of... um par de...

courgette a abobrinha
[abo**bree**n-ya]

courier (man/woman) o/a
guia de turismo [**gee**-a dee
too**rees**moo]

course (main course etc) o prato
[oo **pra**too]

of course é claro [eh **kla**roo];
certamente [serta**mayn**tee]

of course not é claro que não
[kee **now**ng]

cousin (man/woman) o(a)
primo(a) [**pree**moo]

cow a vaca [**va**ca]

crab o caranguejo
[karang**ay**Joo]

cracker a bolacha de água
e sal [bo**lasha** d-**ya**gwa ee]

craft shop a loja de artesanato
[**lo**Ja d-yartayza**na**too]

crash a colisão [kohlee**zow**ng]

I've had a crash tive uma
colisão [**tee**vee **oo**ma]

crazy doido [**doh**-idoo]

cream o creme de leite
[**kray**mee dee **lay**tee]
(lotion) o creme
(colour) creme

creche a creche

credit card o cartão de crédito
[kar**tow**ng dee **kreh**deetoo]

do you take credit cards?
vocês aceitam cartão de
crédito? [vohs**ayz** a**say**towng]

dialogue

can I pay by credit card?
posso pagar com cartão de
crédito? [**po**soo – kohng]

which card do you want
to use? que cartão deseja
utilizar? [kee kar**tow**ng
day**say**Ja ootelee**zar**]

yes, sir sim, senhor [**seen**g
sayn-**yor**]

what's the number? qual
é o número? [**kwal**eh oo
noomayroo]

and the expiry date? e a
data de validade? [ya **da**ta
dee valee**da**dee]

crisps as batatas fritas [ba**ta**tas
freetas]

crockery a louça [**loh**sa]

crossing (by sea) a travessia
[travay**see**-a]

crossroads o cruzamento
[krooza**mayn**too]

crowd a multidão
[moolteed**ow**ng]

crowded apinhado [apeen-
yadoo], cheio [**shay**-oo], lotado
[lo**ta**doo]

crown (on tooth) a coroa
[koh-**ro**-a]

cruise o cruzeiro [kroo**zay**roo]

crutches as muletas [moo**lay**tas]

cry chorar [sho**rar**]

cucumber o pepino [pay**pee**noo]

cup a xícara [**shee**kara]

a cup of..., please uma xícara
de..., por favor [poor fa**vohr**]

cupboard o armário [armar-yoo]
cure curar [koorar]
curly crespo [krayspoo];
  encaracolado [aynkarakohladoo]
current a corrente [koh-Hayntee]
curtains as cortinas [kohrteenas]
cushion a almofada [almohfada]
custom o costume
  [kohstoomee], o hábito [abeetoo]
customs a alfândega
  [alfandayga]
cut o corte [kortee]
  (verb) cortar
  I've cut myself eu me cortei
  [ay-oo mee kohrtay]
cutlery os talheres [tal-yehrees]
cycling o ciclismo [seekleesmoo]
cyclist (man/woman) o/a
  ciclista [seekleesta]

D

dad o papai
daily diariamente [d-yar-
  yamayntee]
  (adj) diário [d-yar-yo]
damage estragar [eestragar]
  damaged estragado
  [eestragado]
  I'm sorry, I've damaged
  this desculpe, estraguei isto
  [deeskoolpee eestragay eestoo]
damn! maldição! [maldeesowng]
damp (adj) úmido [oomeedoo]
dance a dança [dansa]
  (verb) dançar
  would you like to dance?
  quer dançar? [kehr]

dangerous perigoso
  [payreegohzoo]
Danish (adj, language)
  dinamarquês [deenamarkays]
dark (adj) escuro [eeskooroo]
  it's getting dark está
  escurecendo [eesta
  eeskooraysayndoo]
date*: what's the date today?
  que dia é hoje? [kee dee-a eh
  ohjee]
  let's make a date for next
  Monday vamos marcar para
  a próxima segunda-feira
  [vamoos – proseema saygoonda
  fayra]
dates (fruit) as tâmaras [tamaras]
daughter a filha [feel-ya]
daughter-in-law a nora
dawn o amanhecer [aman-
  yaysayr]
  at dawn ao amanhecer
day o dia [dee-a]
  the day after o dia seguinte
  [saygeentee]
  the day after tomorrow
  depois de amanhã [daypoh-is
  dee aman-yang]
  the day before o dia anterior
  [antayr-yohr]
  the day before yesterday
  anteontem [antee-ohntayng]
  every day todos os dias
  [tohdooz-oos dee-as]
  all day o dia todo [tohdoo]
  in two days' time dentro de
  dois dias [dayntroo dee doh-is]
  have a nice day bom-dia
  [bohng]

day trip a excursão de um dia [ayskoorsowng dee oong dee-a]

dead morto [mohrtoo]

deaf surdo [soordoo]

deal (business) o negócio [naygos-yoo]

it's a deal é negócio fechado [fayshadoo]

death a morte [mortee]

decaffeinated coffee o café descafeinado [kafeh deeskafay-eenadoo]

December dezembro [dezaymbroo]

decide decidir [dayseedeer]

we haven't decided yet ainda não decidimos [a-eenda nowng dayseedee-moos]

decision a decisão [dayseezowng]

deck (on ship) o convés [konvehs]

deckchair a espreguiçadeira [eespraygeesadayra]

deep fundo [foondoo]

definitely definitivamente [dayfeeneeteevamayntee]

definitely not é claro que não [eh klaroo kee nowng]

degree (qualification) o diploma [deeploma]

delay o atraso [atrazoo]

delicious delicioso [daylees-yohzo]

deliver entregar [ayntraygar]

delivery (of mail) a entrega [ayntrega]

Denmark a Dinamarca [deenamarka]

dental floss o fio dental [fee-oo dental]

dentist (man/woman) o (a) dentista [daynteesta]

dialogue

it's this one here é este aqui [eh aystee akee]
this one? este?
no, that one não, aquele [nowng akaylee]
here? aqui?
yes sim [seeng]

deodorant o desodorante [dayzohdohrantee]

department store a loja de departamentos [loja dee daypartamayntoos]

departure a saída [sa-eeda]

departure lounge a sala de embarque [d-yaymbarkee]

depend: it depends depende [daypayndee]

it depends on... depende de... [dee]

deposit (payment) o depósito [daypozeetoo]

dessert a sobremesa [sohbraymayza]

destination o destino [daysteenoo]

develop (film) revelar [Hayvaylar]

dialogue

could you develop these films? pode revelar estes filmes? [podee Hayvaylar aystees feelmees]
yes, certainly sim, é claro [seeng eh klaroo]

when will they be ready?
quando ficam prontos?
[**kwandoo feekowng prohntos**]
tomorrow afternoon
amanhã, à tarde [aman-**yang**
a **tardee**]
**how much is the four-hour
service?** quanto custa o
serviço de quatro horas?
[**kwantoo koosta oo sayrveesoo
dee kwatroo oras**]

diabetic (man/woman) diabético
[d-yab**eh**teekoo], diabética
diabetic foods os alimentos
para diabéticos [al**eemay**ntoos]
dial discar; digitar [dee**jeetar**]
dialling code código de área
(DDD) [**ko**deegoo d-**yar**-ya]
diamond o diamante
[d-ya**man**tee]
diaper a fralda
diarrhoea a diarréia [d-ya**Heh**-ia]
**do you have something for
diarrhoea?** tem algo para
diarréia? [tayng **al**goo **para**]
diary (for business) a agenda
[a**Jay**nda]
(for personal experiences) o diário
[d-yar-yoo]
dictionary o dicionário
[dis-yohn**ar**-yoo]
didn't* see not
die morrer [moh-**Hayr**]
diesel o diesel
diet a dieta [d-**yeh**ta]
I'm on a diet estou de dieta
[eest**oh** dee]
I have to follow a special diet

tenho de seguir uma dieta
especial [**tay**n-yoo dee sayg**eer
oo**ma – eespays-**yal**]
difference a diferença
[deefayr**ayn**sa]
what's the difference? qual é
a diferença? [kwal**eh**]
different diferente
[deefayr**ayn**tee]
this one is different este é
diferente [**ays**tee eh]
a different table outra mesa
[**oh**tra may**za**]
difficult difícil [dee**fee**seel]
difficulty a dificuldade
[deefeekool**da**dee]
dinghy o escaler [eeskal**ehr**]
dining room a sala de jantar
[dee **Jan**tar]
dinner (evening meal) o jantar
to have dinner jantar
direct (adj) direto [deer**eh**too]
is there a direct line? há uma
linha direta? [a **oo**ma **leen**-ya]
direction a direção
[deeray**sowng**]
which direction is it? em que
direção fica? [ayng kee – **fee**ka]
is it in this direction? fica
nesta direção? [**neh**sta]
directory enquiries a seção de
informações [say**sowng** dee
infohrmas**oyngs**]
dirt a sujeira [sooJ**ay**ra]
dirty sujo [**soo**Joo]
disabled deficiente físico
[dayfees-**yayn**tee]
**is there access for the
disabled?** há acesso para

deficientes físicos? [a as**eh**soo – f**ee**zeekoos]

disappear desaparecer [dayzaparays**ayr**]

it's disappeared desapareceu [dayzaparays**ay**-oo]

disappointed decepcionado [daysayps-yohn**a**doo]

disappointing decepcionante [daysayps-yon**a**ntee]

disaster o desastre [dayz**a**stree]

disco o disco [d**ee**skoo]

discount o desconto [deesk**oh**ntoo]

is there a discount? tem desconto? [tayng]

disease a doença [dw**ay**nsa]

disgusting nojento [nohJ**ay**ntoo]

dish (meal) o prato [pr**a**too]
(bowl) a tigela [teeJ**eh**la]

dishcloth o pano de prato [p**a**noo dee pr**a**too]

disinfectant o desinfetante [dayzeenfayt**a**ntee]

disk (for computer) o disquete [deesk**eh**tee]

disposable diapers/nappies as fraldas descartáveis [fr**a**ldas deeskart**a**vays]

distance a distância [deest**a**ns-ya]

in the distance ao longe [ow l**oh**nJee]

distilled water a água destilada [**a**gwa daysteel**a**da]

district o bairro [b**i**Hoo]

disturb perturbar [payrtoorb**a**r]

diversion (detour) o desvio [daysv**ee**-oo]

diving board o trampolim [trampohl**ee**m]

divorced divorciado [deevohrs-y**a**doo]

dizzy: I feel dizzy estou tonto [eest**oh** t**oh**ntoo]

do* fazer [faz**ayr**]

what shall we do? o que vamos fazer? [kee v**a**moos]

how do you do it? como se faz isso? [k**oh**moo see faz **ee**soo]

will you do it for me? você faria isso para mim? [vohs**ay** far**ee**-a– meeng]

dialogues

how do you do? como vai? [k**oh**moo v**i**]

nice to meet you bem, obrigado(a) [bayng ohbreeg**a**doo]

what do you do? (work) o que você faz? [kee vohs**ay**]

I'm a teacher, and you? (said by man/woman) sou professor(a), e você? [soh – ee vohs**ay**]

I'm a student sou estudante

what are you doing this evening? o que fará esta noite? [kee far**a** **eh**sta noh-**ee**tee]

we're going out for a drink, do you want to join us? vamos beber alguma coisa, quer vir conosco? [v**a**moos bayb**ay**r alg**oo**ma k**oh**-iza kehr veer kon**oh**skoo]

do you want cream? quer chantili? [kehr shanteelee]
I do, but she doesn't quero, mas ela não [kehroo maz ehla nowng]

doctor (man/woman) o médico [mehdeekoo], a médica
we need a doctor precisamos de um médico [prayseezamoos dee oong]
please call a doctor por favor, chame um médico [poor favohr shamee]

dialogue

where does it hurt? onde dói? [ohndee doy]
right here bem aqui [bayng akee]
does that hurt now? dói agora?
yes sim [seeng]
take this to the pharmacy leve isto à farmácia [lehvee eestwa farmas-ya]

document o documento [dohkoomayntoo]
dog o cachorro [kashoh-Hoo]
doll a boneca [bohnehka]
domestic flight vôo doméstico [voh-oo dohmehsteekoo]
donkey o burro [booHoo]
don't!* não! [nowng]
don't do that! não faça isto! [fasa eestoo]
door a porta

doorman o porteiro [pohrtayroo]
double duplo [dooploo]
double bed a cama de casal [dee kazal]
double room o quarto de casal [kwartoo]
doughnut a rosquinha [Hohskeen-ya]
down embaixo [aymbīshoo]
down here aqui embaixo [akee]
put it down over there ponha ali [pohn-ya alee]
it's down there on the right é ali, à direita [eh – a deerayta]
it's further down the road é nesta rua mais abaixo [nehsta Hoo-a mīs abīshoo]
downmarket (restaurant etc) econômico [aykohnohmeekoo]; barato [baratoo]
downstairs embaixo [aymbīshoo]
dozen a dúzia [dooz-ya]
half a dozen a meia dúzia [may-a]
drain (in sink, in road) o cano de esgoto [kanoo dee aysgohtoo]
draught beer chope [shohpee]
draughty: it's draughty tem uma corrente de ar [tayng ooma koh-Hayntee d-yar]
drawer a gaveta [gavayta]
drawing o desenho [dayzayn-yoo]
dreadful horrível [oh-Heevil]
dream o sonho [sohn-yoo]
dress o vestido [vaysteedoo]

dressed: to get dressed vestir-se [vaysteersee]

dressing (for cut) a atadura [atadoora]

salad dressing o tempero de salada [taympayroo]

dressing gown o roupão [Hohpowng]

drink a bebida [baybeeda] (verb) beber [baybayr]

a cold drink uma bebida gelada [ooma – Jaylada]

fancy a quick drink? quer beber algo? [kher baybayr algoo]

can I get you a drink? posso lhe oferecer uma bebida? [posoo l-yoh-fayraysayr ooma baybeeda]

what would you like (to drink)? o que gostaria de beber? [kee gohstaree-a dee]

I don't drink não bebo [nowng bayboo]

I'll just have a drink of water só um copo de água [saw oong kopoo dagwa]

drinking water a água potável [agwa pohtavil]

is this drinking water? esta água é potável? [ehsta – eh]

drive dirigir [deereeJeer]

we drove here viemos de carro [v-yaymoos dee kaHoo]

I'll drive you home levo você de carro para casa [lehvoo vohsay dee kaHoo para kaza]

driver (of car, of bus: man/woman) o/a motorista [mohtohreesta]

driving licence a carteira de motorista [kartayra dee]

drop: just a drop, please (of drink) só um pouco, por favor [saw oong pohkoo poor favohr]

drug o medicamento [maydeekamayntoo]

drugs (narcotics) a droga [droga]

drunk (adj) bêbado [baybadoo]

drunken driving dirigir embriagado [deereeJeer aymbr-yagadoo]

dry (adj) seco [saykoo]

dry-cleaner a tinturaria [teentooraree-a]

duck o pato [patoo]

due: he was due to arrive yesterday ele devia ter chegado ontem [aylee dayvee-a tayr shaygadoo ohntayng]

when is the bus due? quando o ônibus deve chegar? [kwandoo oo ohneeboos]

dull (pain) dor intensa [dohr intaynsa]

dummy (baby's) a chupeta [shoopayta]

during durante [doorantee]

dust o pó [paw]

dustbin a lata de lixo [lata dee leeshoo]

dusty empoeirado [aympo-ayradoo]

Dutch holandês [ohlandays]

duty-free (goods) duty-free

duvet o edredom [aydraydohn]

E

each (every) cada
  how much are they each?
  quanto é cada um? [kwantweh – oong]
ear a orelha [oh-rayl-ya]
earache: I have earache estou
  com dor de ouvido [eestoh kohng dohr d-yohveedoo]
early cedo [saydoo]
  early in the morning de
  manhã cedo [dee man-yang]
  I called by earlier passei aqui
  mais cedo [pasay akee mīs]
earrings os brincos [breenkoos]
east o leste [lehstee]
  in the east no leste
Easter Páscoa [paskwa]
easy fácil [fasil]
eat comer [kohmayr]
  we've already eaten,
  thanks (said by man/woman) já
  comemos, obrigado(a) [Ja kohmaymoos ohbreegadoo]
eau de toilette a água-de-
  colônia [agwa dee kohlohn-ya]
economy class classe
  econômica [klasee aykohnohmeeka]
Edinburgh Edimburgo
  [aydeenboorgoo]
eel a enguia [ayngee-a]
egg o ovo [ohvoo]
eggplant a berinjela
  [bayreenJehla]
either: either... or... ou... ou...
  [oh]

either of them qualquer um
  deles [kwalkehroom daylees]
elastic o elástico [aylasteekoo]
elastic band o elástico de
  escritório [dee ayskreetor-yoo]
elbow o cotovelo
  [kohtohvayloo]
electric elétrico [aylehtreekoo]
electrical appliances os
  eletrodomésticos [aylehtroh-
  dohmehsteekoos]
electric fire o aquecedor
  elétrico [akaysaydohr
  aylehtreekoo]
electrician o eletricista
  [aylaytreeseesta]
electricity a eletricidade
  [aylaytreeseedadee]
elevator (in building) o elevador
  [aylayvadohr]
else: something else outra
  coisa [ohtra koh-iza]
  somewhere else em outro
  lugar [ayng ohtroo loogar]

dialogue

would you like anything
else? deseja mais alguma
coisa? [daysayJa mīs algooma
koh-iza]
no, nothing else, thanks
(said by man/woman) não,
mais nada, obrigado(a)
[nowng mīs – ohbreegadoo]

e-mail o e-mail
embassy a embaixada
  [aymbīshada]

Em

57

emergency a emergência
[aymayrJ**a**yns-ya]

this is an emergency! isto é
uma emergência! [**ee**stoo eh
ooma]

emergency exit a saída de
emergência [sa-**ee**da dee
aymayrJ**a**yns-ya]

empty vazio [vazee-oo]

end o fim [feeng]

at the end of the street no
fim da rua [noo feeng da H**oo**-a]

when does it end? quando
acaba? [kw**a**ndoo]

engaged (toilet, telephone)
ocupado [ohkoop**a**doo]
(to be married) noivo [n**oh**-ivoo]

engine (car) o motor
[moht**oh**r]

England a Inglaterra
[inglat**eh**-Ha]

English (adj, language) inglês
[ingl**a**ys]

I'm English (man/woman) sou
inglês(esa) [soh]

do you speak English? fala
inglês?

enjoy: to enjoy oneself
divertir-se [deevayrt**ee**rsee]

dialogue

how did you like the film?
gostou do filme? [gohst**oh**
doo f**ee**lmee]
I enjoyed it very much; did
you enjoy it? gostei muito;
e você? [gohst**ay** mw**ee**ngtoo
ee voh**say**]

enjoyable divertido
[deevayrt**ee**doo]

enlargement (of photo) a
ampliação [ampl-yas**ow**ng]

enormous enorme [**a**ynormee]

enough suficiente
[soofees-y**a**yntee]

there's not enough... não há
suficiente... [nowng a]

it's not big enough não é
suficientemente grande
[eh soofees-yaynteem**a**yntee
gr**a**ndee]

that's enough, thanks
(said by man/woman) isso
basta, obrigado(a) [**ee**soo
– ohbreeg**a**doo]

entrance a entrada [aynt**ra**da]

envelope o envelope
[aynvayl**o**pee]

epileptic (man/woman) epiléptico
[aypeel**eh**pteekoo], epiléptica

equipment o equipamento
[aykeepam**a**yntoo]

error un erro [**a**yHoo]

especially especialmente
[eespays-yalm**a**yntee]

essential essencial [aysayns-ya**l**]

it is essential that... é
essencial que... [eh – kee]

EU UE [oo ay]

Euro o euro [**a**y-ooroo]

Europe a Europa [ay-oor**o**pa]

European (adj) europeu [ay-
oorohp**ay**-oo], (f) européia [ay-
oorohp**eh**-ia]

even: even the British até
os britânicos [at**eh**-oos
breet**a**neekoos]

even men até mesmo os homens [ateh maysmo ooz omayngs]
even if... mesmo se... [see]
evening a noite [noh-itee]
this evening esta noite [ehsta noh-itee]
in the evening à noite
evening meal o jantar [oo Jantar]
eventually no fim [noo feeng]
ever já [Ja]

dialogue

have you ever been to Curitiba? já esteve alguma vez em Curitiba? [Ja eestayvee algooma vays ayng kooreeteeba]
yes, I was there two years ago sim, estive lá há dois anos [seeng eesteevee la a doh-iz anoos]

every cada
every day todos os dias [tohdooz-ooz dee-as]
everyone todo mundo [tohdoo moondoo]
everything tudo [toodoo]
everywhere em toda parte [ayng tohda partee]
exactly! exatamente! [ayzatamayntee]
exam o exame [ayzamee]
example o exemplo [ayzaymploo]
for example por exemplo [poor]

excellent excelente [aysaylayntee]
excellent! excelente!
except exceto [aysehtoo]
excess baggage o excesso de bagagem [aysehsoo dee bagaJayng]
exchange rate a cotação cambial [kohtasowng kamb-yal]
exciting emocionante [emohs-yohnantee]
excuse me (to get past) com licença [kohng leesaynsa]
(to get attention) por favor [poor favohr]
(to say sorry) desculpe [deeskoolpee]
exhaust (pipe) o cano de escapamento [kanoo dee ayskapamayntoo]
exhausted (tired) exausto [ayzowstoo]
exhibition a exposição [ayspohzeesowng]
exit a saída [sa-eeda]
where's the nearest exit? onde é a saída mais próxima? [ohndee eh – mīs proseema]
expect esperar [eespayrar]
expensive caro [karoo]
experienced experiente [ayspayr-yayntee]
explain explicar [ayspleekar]
can you explain that? pode me explicar isso? [podee m-yayspleekar eesoo]

express (mail) urgente [oorjayntee]
(train) o expresso [aysprehsoo]
extension (telephone) o ramal [Hamal]

extension 221, please ramal duzentos e vinte e um, por favor [doozayntooz ee veent-yoong poor favohr]

extension lead a extensão [eestaynsowng]

extra: can we have an extra one? pode nos servir mais um/uma? [podee noos sayrveer mīs oong/ooma]

do you charge extra for that? isso é cobrado a mais? [eesoo eh kohbradoo a mīs]

extraordinary extraordinário [aystra-ohrdeenar-yoo]

extremely extremamente [aystraymamayntee]

eye o olho [ohl-yoo]

will you keep an eye on my suitcase for me? pode ficar de olho na minha mala? [podee feekar dee – na meen-ya mala]

eyebrow pencil o lápis de sobrancelha [lapees dee sobransayl-ya]

eye drops o colírio [kohleer-yo]

eyeglasses (US) os óculos [okooloos]

eyeliner o lápis de olhos [lapees dee ol-yoos]

eye make-up remover o demaquilante para os olhos [daymakeelantee]

eye shadow a sombra de olhos

F

face o rosto [Hohstoo]
factory a fábrica [fabreeka]
Fahrenheit* Fahrenheit
faint (verb) desmaiar [deesmī-ar]

she's fainted ela desmaiou [ehla deesmī-oh]

I feel faint sinto que vou desmaiar [seentoo kee voh]

fair (funfair, tradefair) a feira [fayra]
(adj) justo [Joostoo]

fairly bastante [bastantee]
fake falso [falsoo]
fall cair [ka-eer]

she's had a fall ela caiu [ehla kaee-oo]

fall (US) o outono [ohtohnoo]

in the fall no outono [noo]

false falso [falsoo]
family a família [fameel-ya]
famous famoso [famohzoo]
fan (electrical) o ventilador [vaynteeladohr]

(handheld) o leque [lehkee]

(sports: man/woman) o torcedor [tohrsaydohr], a torcedora

fan belt a correia do ventilador [koh-Hay-a doo vaynteeladohr]

fantastic fantástico
far longe [lohnJee]

dialogue

is it far from here? é longe daqui? [eh – dak**ee**]

no, not very far não, não é muito longe [nowng – m**wee**ngtoo]

well how far? bem, qual é a distância? [bayng kwal**eh** a dee**stans**-ya]

it's about 20 kilometres são mais ou menos vinte quilômetros [sowng mís oh m**ay**noos v**ee**ntee keel**oh**maytroos]

fare o preço do bilhete [pr**ay**soo doo beel-**yay**tee]
farm a fazenda [faz**ay**nda]
fashionable da moda
fast rápido [**Ha**peedoo]
fat (person) gordo [**goh**rdoo]
(on meat) a gordura [gohrd**oo**ra]
father o pai [pí]
father-in-law o sogro [**soh**groo]
faucet a torneira [tohrn**ay**ra]
fault a culpa [**kool**pa]; o defeito [day**fay**too]

sorry, it was my fault desculpe, foi culpa minha [deesk**oo**lpee f**oh**-i k**oo**lpa m**een**-ya]

it's not my fault a culpa não é minha [nowng eh m**een**-ya]

faulty com defeito [kohng day**fay**too]
favourite favorito [favoh-r**ee**too]
fax o fax
to send a fax mandar um fax

February fevereiro [fayvayr**ay**roo]
feel sentir [sayn**teer**]
I feel hot estou com calor [eest**oh** kohng kal**ohr**]
I feel unwell não me sinto bem [nowng mee s**een**too bayng]
I feel like going for a walk estou com vontade de caminhar [eest**oh** kohng vont**ad**ee dee kameen-y**ar**]
how are you feeling? como se sente? [**koh**moo see sayn**tee**]
I'm feeling better eu me sinto melhor [**ay**-oo mee s**een**too mayl-y**or**]

felt-tip (pen) a caneta hidrográfica [kan**ay**ta eedrohgr**a**feeka]
fence a cerca [**say**rka]
fender o pára-choques [para-sh**o**kees]
ferry o ferryboat
festival o festival [faysteev**al**]
fetch buscar [b**oo**skar]
I'll fetch him vou buscá-lo [voh boosk**a**-loo]
will you come and fetch me later? pode vir me buscar mais tarde? [**po**dee veer mee b**oo**skar mís t**ar**dee]

feverish febril [feb**reel**]
few: a few alguns [alg**oo**ns]
I'll give you a few dou-lhe alguns [d**oh**l-yalg**oo**ns]
a few days alguns dias [d**ee**-as]
fiancé o noivo [**noh**-ivoo]
fiancée a noiva

field o campo [kampoo]
fight a briga [breega]
figs os figos [feegoos]
fill in preencher [pray-aynshayr]
  do I have to fill this in? tenho de preencher isto? [tayn-yoo dee – eestoo]
fill up encher [aynshayr]
  fill it up, please encha o tanque, por favor [aynsha oo tankee poor favohr]
filling (in cake, sandwich) recheio [Hayshay-oo]
  (in tooth) a obturação [ohbtoorasowng]
film o filme [feelmee]

dialogue

do you have this kind of film? você tem este tipo de filme? [vohsay tayng aystee teepoo]
yes, how many exposures? sim, de quantas poses? [seeng dee kwantas pohzees]
36 trinta e seis [treenti-says]

film processing a revelação de filmes [Hayvaylasowng dee feelmees]
filter coffee o café de filtro [kafeh dee feeltroo]
filter papers os filtros de café [feeltroos]
filthy imundo [eemoondoo]
find encontrar [aynkohntrar]
  I can't find it não consigo encontrar [nowng kohnseegoo

I've found it encontrei-o [aynkohntray-oo]
find out descobrir [dayskohbreer]
  could you find out for me? pode descobrir para mim? [podee – meeng]
fine (weather) bom [bohng]
  (punishment) a multa [moolta]

dialogues

how are you? como vai? [kohmoo vī]
I'm fine, thanks (said by man/woman) bem, obrigado(a) [bayng ohbreegadoo]

is that OK? assim está bem? [aseeng eesta bayng]
that's fine, thanks está bem, obrigado(a)

finger o dedo [daydoo]
finish terminar, acabar
  I haven't finished yet ainda não terminei [a-eenda nowng tayrmeenay]
  when does it finish? quando é que termina? [kwandoo eh kee tayrmeena]
fire o fogo [fohgoo]
  (blaze) o incêndio [insaynd-yoo]
  fire! fogo!
  can we light a fire here? podemos fazer uma fogueira aqui? [pohdaymoos fazayr ooma fohgayra akee]
  it's on fire está pegando fogo

[eesta paygando **foh**goo]

fire alarm o alarme de incêndio [a**lar**mee dins**aynd**yoo]

fire brigade os bombeiros [bohmb**ay**roos]

fire escape a saída de incêndio [sa-**ee**da deens**aynd**-yoo]

fire extinguisher o extintor de incêndio [aysteent**ohr**]

first primeiro [pree**may**roo]

I was first (said by man/woman) eu fui o/a primeiro/primeira [**ay**-oo fwee]

at first no início [noo een**ees**-yoo]

the first time a primeira vez [vays]

first on the left primeira à esquerda [a ees**kayr**da]

first aid os primeiros socorros [pree**may**roos soh**ko**Hoos]

first aid kit o kit de primeiros socorros [dee]

first class (travel etc) primeira classe [k**la**see]

first floor o primeiro andar (US) o térreo [**teh**-Hy-oo]

first name o nome de batismo [**noh**mee dee bat**ees**moo]; o primeiro nome [pree**may**roo]

fish o peixe [**pay**shee] (verb) pescar [pays**kar**]

fishing village a aldeia de pescadores [al**day**-a dee payskad**oh**rees]

fishmonger's a peixaria [paysharee-a]

fit (attack) ataque [a**ta**kee],

acesso [a**seh**soo]

fit: it doesn't fit me não me serve [nowng mee **seh**rvee]

fitting room o provador [prohvad**ohr**]

fix (repair) consertar [kohnsayr**tar**]

can you fix this? (repair) pode consertar isto? [**po**dee – **ees**too]

fizzy gasoso [gaz**oh**zoo], com gás [kohng gas]

flag a bandeira [band**ay**ra]

flannel a flanela de limpeza [flan**eh**la dee leemp**ay**za]

flash (for camera) o flash

flat (apartment) o apartamento [apartam**ayn**too] (adj) plano [**pla**noo]

I've got a flat tyre estou com um pneu furado [eest**oh** kohng oong pn**ay**-oo foor**a**doo]

flavour o sabor [sab**ohr**]

flea a pulga [**pool**ga]

flight o vôo [**voh**-oo]

flight number o número do vôo [**noo**mayroo doo]

flippers as barbatanas [barbat**a**nas]

flood a inundação [eenoondas**owng**]

floor (of room) o chão [showng] (storey) o andar

on the floor no chão

florist a floricultura [flohreekoolt**oo**ra]

flour a farinha [far**een**-ya]

flower a flor [flohr]

flu a gripe [**gree**pee]

fluent: he speaks fluent Portuguese ele fala português

FI

63

fluentemente [**ay**lee
– pohrtoo**gays** flwenteemay**ntee**]
fly a mosca [**moh**ska]
(verb: person) ir de avião [eer d-
yav-**yowng**]; voar [voh-**ar**]
fog a neblina [nay**blee**na]
foggy: it's foggy tem neblina
[**tayng**]
folk dancing a dança folclórica
[**dan**sa fohl**klo**rika]
folk music a música folclórica
[**moo**zeeka]
follow seguir [say**geer**]
follow me siga-me [**see**gamee]
food a comida [koh**mee**da]
food poisoning a intoxicação
alimentar [intohkseekas**owng**]
food shop/store a mercearia
[mayrs-yar**ee**-a]
foot* (of person, measurement) o
pé [peh]
on foot a pé
football (game) o futebol
[foo**tay**bol]
(ball) a bola de futebol
football match a partida de
futebol [par**tee**da dee]
for: do you have something
for...? (headache/diarrhoea etc)
tem alguma coisa para...?
[tayng al**goo**ma k**oh**-iza]

dialogues

who's the feijoada for?
para quem é a feijoada?
[kayng eh a fayJ**wa**da]
that's for me é para mim
[eh – meeng]

and this one? e este?
[ee **ays**tee]
that's for her é para ela
[**eh**la]

where do I get the bus
for Copacabana? onde
posso pegar o ônibus para
Copacabana? [**ohn**dee p**os**oo
pay**gar** oo **oh**neeboos para
kopakab**a**na]
the bus for Copacabana
leaves from Praça XV o
ônibus para Copacabana
sai da Praça Quinze [sī da
pr**as**a k**een**zee]

how long have you been
here for? há quanto tempo
está aqui? [a k**wan**too t**ay**mpoo
eesta ak**ee**]
I've been here for two
days, how about you?
estou aqui há dois dias, e
você? [eest**oh** ak**ee** a d**oh**-is
dee-as ee voh**say**]
I've been here for a week
estou aqui há uma semana
[say**ma**na]

forehead a testa [**teh**sta]
foreign estrangeiro
[eestranJ**ay**roo]
foreigner (man/woman) o
estrangeiro/a estrangeira
forest a floresta [floh-**reh**sta]
forget esquecer [eeskay**sayr**]
I forget, I've forgotten eu me
esqueci [eeskay**see**]

fork o garfo [garfoo]
(in road) a bifurcação [beefoorkasowng]
form (document) o formulário [fohrmoolar-yoo]
formal (dress) roupa formal [fohrmal]
fortnight a quinzena [keenzayna]
fortunately felizmente [fayleesmayntee]
forward: could you forward my mail? poderia despachar minha correspondência? [podayree-a deespashar meen-ya koh-Hayspohndayns-ya]
forwarding address o novo endereço [nohvoo ayndayraysoo]
foundation cream a base [bazee]
fountain a fonte [fohntee]
foyer (of hotel, theatre) o foyer [fwi-ay]
fracture a fratura [fratoora]
France a França [fransa]
free livre [leevree]
(no charge) gratuito [gratweetoo]
is it free (of charge)? é gratuito? [eh]
freeway a rodovia [Hohdohvee-a]
freezer o freezer
French (adj, language) francês [fransays]
French fries as batatas fritas [batatas freetas]
frequent frequente [fraykwayntee]

how frequent is the bus to SWão Paulo? com que frequência há ônibus para São Paulo? [kohng kee fraykwaynsya a ohneeboos – sowng powloo]
fresh fresco [frayskoo]
fresh orange o suco de laranja natural [sookoo dee laranJa natooral]
Friday sexta-feira [saysta fayra]
fridge a geladeira [Jayladayra]
fried frito [freetoo]
fried egg o ovo frito [ohvoo]
friend (man/woman) o amigo [ameegoo], a amiga
friendly simpático [seempateekoo]
from de [dee]
when does the next bus from Porto Alegre arrive? quando chega o próximo ônibus de Porto Alegre? [kwandoo shaygoo prosimoo ohneeboos]
from Monday to Friday de segunda a sexta-feira [dee saygoonda saysta fayra]
from next Thursday a partir da próxima quinta-feira [a parteer da prosima keenta fayra]

dialogue

where are you from? de onde você é? [dee ohndee]
I'm from Slough sou de Slough [soh dee]

front a frente [frayntee]

in front em frente [ayng]
in front of the hotel em frente do hotel [doo]
at the front na frente [na]
frost a geada [Jay-ada]
frozen congelado [kohnJayladoo]
frozen food a comida congelada [kohmeeda]
fruit a fruta [froota]
fruit juice o suco de fruta [sookoo dee froota]
fry fritar [freetar]
frying pan a frigideira [freeJeedayra]
full cheio [shay-oo]
it's full of... está cheio de... [eesta – dee]
I'm full (said by man/woman) estou satisfeito/satisfeita [eestoh sateesfaytoo]
full board a pensão completa [paynsowng kohnplehta]
fun: it was fun foi divertido [foh-i deevayrteedoo]
funeral o funeral [foonayral]
funny (strange) estranho [eestran-yoo]
(amusing) engraçado [ayngrasadoo]
furniture a mobília [mohbeel-ya]
further mais adiante [mīs ad-yantee]
it's further down the road é mais adiante na rua [na Hoo-a]

dialogue

how much further is it to Santos? quantos quilômetros faltam para Santos? [kwantoos keelohmaytroos faltowng – santoos]
about 5 kilometres cerca de cinco quilômetros [sayrka dee seenkoo]

fuse o fusível [foozeevil]
fuse box a caixa de fusíveis/disjuntores [kīsha dee foozeevays/deesJoontoh-rees]
fuse wire o fio do fusível [fee-oo doo foozeevil]
future o futuro [footooroo]
in future no futuro [noo]

G

gallon* o galão [galowng]
game (cards, match etc) o jogo [Johgoo]
(meat) a carne de caça [karnee dee kasa]
garage (for fuel) o posto de combustível [pohstoo dee kohmboosteevil]
(for repairs, parking) a oficina [ohfeeseena]
garden o jardim [Jardeeng]
garlic o alho [al-yoo]
gas o gás [gas]
gas cylinder (camping gas) o botijão de gás [booteeJowng]

gasoline (US) a gasolina [gazooleena]

gas permeable lenses as lentes de contato semi-rígidas [layntees saymee-HeeJeedas]

gas station o posto de combustível [pohstoo dee kohmboosteevil]

gate o portão [pohrtowng] (at airport) o portão de embarque [d-yaymbarkee]

gay o homossexual [ohmoh-saykswal]

gay bar o bar gay

gearbox a caixa de câmbio [kīsha dee kamb-yoo]

gear lever a avalanca do câmbio

gears as marchas [marsha]

general (adj) geral [Jeral]

gents (toilet) banheiro masculino [ban-yayro maskooleenoo]

genuine (antique etc) autêntico [owtaynteekoo]

German (adj, language) alemão [alaymowng]

German measles a rubéola [Hoobeh-ola]

Germany a Alemanha [alayman-ya]

get (fetch) trazer [trazayr]
will you get me another one, please? pode me trazer outro, por favor? [podee mee trazayr ohtroo poor favohr]
how do I get to...? como vou até...? [kohmoo voh]
do you know where I can

get this? sabe onde posso comprar isto? [sabee ohndee posoo – eestoo]

dialogue

> **can I get you a drink?**
> posso lhe oferecer uma bebida? [posoo l-yo-fayraysayr ooma baybeeda]
> **yes, thank you** obrigado(a) [ohbreegadoo]
> **what would you like?** o que gostaria de beber? [oo kee gohstaree-a de baybayr]
> **a glass of red wine** um copo de vinho tinto [oong kopoo dee veen-yoo teentoo]

get back (return) voltar

get in (arrive) chegar [shaygar]

get off descer [daysayr], desembarcar [daysaymbarkar]
where do I get off? onde desço? [ohndee daysoo]

get on (to train etc) subir [soobeer], embarcar [aymbarkar]

get out (of car etc) sair [sa-eer]

get up (in the morning) levantar-se [layvantarsee]

gift o presente [prayzayntee]

gift shop a loja de presentes [loJa dee praysayntees]

gin o gim [Jeeng]
a gin and tonic, please um gim-tônica, por favor [oong Jeeng tohneeka poor favohr]

girl a menina [mayneena]

girlfriend a namorada

give* dar

can you give me some change? pode me dar um pouco de dinheiro trocado? [**p**odee mee dar oong p**oh**koo dee deen-y**ay**roo trohk**a**do]

I gave it to him dei a ele [day a **ay**lee]

will you give this to...? pode dar isto para...? [**ee**stoo]

dialogue

how much do you want for this? quanto quer por isto? [kw**a**ntoo kehr poor **ee**stoo]

20 reais vinte reais [**v**eentee Hay-**ī**s]

I'll give you 15 eu lhe dou quinze [**ay**-oo l-yi doh k**ee**nzee]

give back devolver [dayvohlv**ayr**]
glad contente [kohnt**ay**ntee]
glass (material) o vidro [**vee**droo]
(for drinking) o copo [k**o**poo]
a glass of wine um copo de vinho [oong – dee v**ee**n-yoo]
glasses os óculos [**o**kooloos]
gloves as luvas [**loo**vas]
glue a cola
go* ir [eer]

we'd like to go to the Museu de Arte Moderna queremos ir ao Museu de Arte Moderna [kayr**ay**moos eer ow mooz**ay**-oo dee **a**rtee mohd**eh**rna]

where are you going? aonde vai? [a-**oh**ndee vī]

where does this bus go? para onde vai este ônibus? [**a**ystee **oh**neeboos]

let's go! vamos! [v**a**moos]

she's gone (left) ela foi embora [**eh**la f**oh**-i aymbora]

where has he gone? onde ele foi? [**oh**ndee **ay**lee foh-i]

I went there last week fui lá na semana passada [fwee la na saym**a**na]

hamburger to go hambúrguer para viagem

go away ir embora [eer aymb**o**ra]

go away! vá embora!

go back (return) voltar

go down (the stairs etc) descer [days**ayr**]

go in entrar [aynt**rar**]

go out* (in the evening) sair [sa-**eer**]

do you want to go out tonight? quer sair esta noite? [kehr – **eh**sta n**oh**-itee]

go through atravessar

go up (the stairs etc) subir [soob**eer**]

goat a cabra

goat's cheese o queijo de cabra [k**ay**ʃoo dee]

God Deus [d**ay**-oos]

goggles os óculos de proteção [**o**kooloos dee prohtays**ow**ng]

gold o ouro [**oh**roo]

golf o golfe [g**o**lfee]

golf course o campo de golfe [k**a**mpoo dee]

good bom [bohng]

good! bom!
it's no good não presta
[nowng prehsta]
goodbye até logo [ateh logoo]
good evening boa-noite
[boh-a noh-itee]
Good Friday Sexta-Feira Santa
[saysta fayra]
good morning bom-dia
[bohng dee-a]
good night boa-noite
[boh-a noh-itee]
goose o ganso [gansoo]
got: we've got to leave temos
que ir [taymoos kee eer]
have you got any...? tem...?
[tayng]
government o governo
[gohvayrnoo]
gradually gradualmente
[gradwalmayntee]
grammar a gramática
[gramateeka]
gram(me) o grama
granddaughter a neta
[nehta]
grandfather o avô [avoh]
grandmother a avó [avaw]
grandson o neto [nehtoo]
grapefruit a grapefruit
grapefruit juice o suco de
grapefruit [sookoo dee]
grapes as uvas [oovas]
grass a grama [Hehlva]
grateful agradecido
[agradayseedoo]
gravy o molho [mohl-yoo]
great (excellent) ótimo [oteemoo]
that's great! isso é ótimo!

[eesoo eh]
a great success um grande
sucesso [oong grandee soosehsoo]
Great Britain a Grã-Bretanha
[grang braytan-ya]
Greece a Grécia [grehs-ya]
greedy (for food) guloso
[goolohzoo]
Greek (adj, language) grego
[graygoo]
green verde [vayrdee]
greengrocer's a quitanda
[keetanda]
grey cinza [seenza]
grill a grelha [grayl-ya]
grilled grelhado [grayl-yadoo]
grocer's a mercearia [mayrs-
yaree-a]
ground o chão [showng]
on the ground no chão [noo]
ground floor o térreo [teh-Hy-oo]
group o grupo [groopoo]
guarantee a garantia [garantee-a]
is it guaranteed? tem
garantia? [tayng]
guest (man/woman) o/ hóspede
[ospeedee]
guesthouse a hospedaria
[ohspaydaree-a]
guide (person; man/woman) o/a
guia [gee-a]
guidebook o guia (livro)
[leevroo]
guided tour a visita guiada
[veezeeta gee-ada]
guitar a guitarra [geetaHa]; o
violão [vee-oh-lowng]
gum (in mouth) a gengiva
[JaynJeeva]

gun a arma de fogo [dee **foh**goo]
gym o ginásio [Jeen**az**-yoo]

H

hair o cabelo [kab**ay**loo]
hairbrush a escova de cabelo [eesk**oh**va dee]
haircut o corte de cabelo [**kor**tee]
hairdresser's (unisex, women's) o cabeleireiro [kabaylayr**ay**roo] (men's) o barbeiro [barb**ay**roo]
hairdryer o secador de cabelo [saykad**ohr** dee kab**ay**loo]
hair gel o gel para cabelo [Jehl para]
hairgrips o grampo de cabelo [**gram**poo]
hair spray o spray para cabelo
half* a metade [mayt**a**dee], meio/meia [**may**-oo]
half an hour meia hora [**may**-a]
half a litre meio litro [**may**-oo **lee**troo]
about half that cerca de metade disso [**say**rka dee mayt**a**dee d**ee**soo]
half board a meia pensão [**may**-a payns**ow**ng]
half-bottle a meia garrafa [gaH**a**fa]
half fare a meia tarifa [**may**-a tar**ee**fa]
half price metade do preço [mayt**a**dee doo pr**ay**soo]
ham o presunto [prayz**oo**ntoo]
hamburger o hambúrguer [amb**oo**rgayr]

hammer o martelo [mart**eh**loo]
hand a mão [mowng]
handbag a mala de mão [dee]
handbrake o freio de mão [fr**ay**-oo]
handkerchief o lenço [**layn**soo]
handle (on door) a maçaneta [masan**ay**ta] (on suitcase etc) o fecho [**fay**shoo]
hand luggage a bagagem de mão [bag**a**Jayng]
hang-gliding a asa-delta [**a**za-**deh**lta]
hangover a ressaca [Hays**a**ka]
I've got a hangover estou de ressaca [eest**oh** dee]
happen acontecer [akohntays**ayr**]
what's happening? o que está acontecendo? [oo keest**a** akohntays**ayn**doo]
what has happened? o que aconteceu? akohntays**ay**-oo]
happy contente [kohnt**ayn**tee]
I'm not happy about this não estou contente com isso [nowng eest**oh** – kohng **ee**soo]
harbour o porto [**poh**rtoo]
hard duro [**doo**roo] (difficult) difícil [deef**ee**sil]
hard-boiled egg o ovo cozido [**oh**voo kohz**ee**doo]
hard lenses as lentes de contato rígidas [**layn**tees dee kohnt**a**too ree**Jee**das]
hardly mal
hardly ever quase nunca [**kwa**zee n**oo**nka]
hardware shop a loja de ferragens [**lo**Ja dee fay-Ha**Jayng**s]

hat o chapéu [shapeh-oo]

hate detestar, [daytaystar] odiar [ohd-yar]

have* ter [tayr]

can I have a...? pode me dar...? [podee mee dar]

do you have...? tem...? [tayng]

what'll you have? o que vai beber? [oo kee vī baybayr]

I have to leave now tenho de ir agora [tayn-yoo deer]

do I have to...? tenho de...?

can we have some...? pode nos dar...? [podee noos dar]

hayfever a febre do feno [fehbree doo faynoo]

hazelnut a avelã [avaylang]

he* ele [ay-lee]

head a cabeça [kabaysa]

headache a dor de cabeça [dohr dee]

headlights o farol

headphones os fones de ouvido [fohnees dee ohveedoo]

health food shop a loja de produtos naturais [loja dee prohdootoos natooris]

healthy saudável [sowdavil]

hear ouvir [ohveer]

dialogue

can you hear me? você pode me ouvir? [vohsay podee mee ohveer]

I can't hear you, could you repeat that? não, poderia repetir? [nowng pohdayree-a Haypayteer]

hearing aid o aparelho auditivo [aparayl-yoo owdeeteevoo]

heart o coração [kohrasowng]

heart attack o infarto [infartoo]

heat o calor [kalohr]

heater o aquecedor [akaysaydohr]

heating o aquecimento [akayseemayntoo]

heavy pesado [payzadoo]

heel (of foot) o calcanhar [kalkan-yar]

(of shoe) o salto

could you put new heels on these? poderia trocar o salto? [pohdayree-a trohkar oo]

heel bar a sapataria rápida [sapataree-a Hapeeda]

height (of person) a altura [altoora]

(mountain) a altitude [alteetoodee]

helicopter o helicóptero [ay-leekoptayroo]

hello alô [aloh]

helmet (for motorcycle) o capacete [kapasaytee]

help a ajuda [aJooda]

(verb) ajudar

help! socorro! [sohkoh-Hoo]

can you help me? pode me ajudar? [podee mee ajudar]

thank you very much for your help (said by man/woman) muito obrigado(a) pela ajuda [mweengtoo ohbreegadoo payla aJooda]

helpful prestativo [praystateevoo]

hepatitis a hepatite [aypateetee]

her*: I haven't seen her não a vi [nowng a vee]

to her para ela [**ehl**a]

with her com ela [kohng]

for her para ela

that's her é ela [eh]

that's her towel essa é a toalha dela [**eh**sa eh a twal-ya d**ehl**a]

herbal tea o chá de ervas [sha dee **ehr**vas]

herbs as ervas

here aqui [a**kee**]

here is/are... aqui está/estão... [eesta/eesto**wng**]

here you are aqui está

hers* dela [d**ehl**a]

that's hers isso é dela [**ee**soo eh]

hey! ei!

hi! (hello) oi! [ohla]

hide esconder [eeskohnd**ayr**]

high alto [**al**too]

highchair o cadeirão de bebê [kadayr**ow**ng dee bayb**ay**]

highway a rodovia [Hohdoh-**vee**-a]

hill a colina [koh**lee**na]

him*: I haven't seen him não o vi [nowng oo vee]

to him a ele [**ayl**ee]

with him com ele [kohng]

for him para ele

that's him é ele [eh]

hip o quadril

hire alugar [aloo**gar**]

for hire para alugar

where can I hire a bike? onde posso alugar uma bicicleta? [**ohn**dee **po**soo]

his*: it's his car é o carro dele [eh oo ka**Hoo** d**ayl**ee]

that's his isso é dele [**ee**soo eh d**ay**lee]

hit bater [ba**tayr**]

hitch-hike pedir carona [payd**eer** karo**hn**a]

hobby o passatempo [pasat**aym**poo]

hold segurar [saygoo**rar**]

hole o buraco [boo**ra**koo]

holiday as férias [**fehr**-yas]

on holiday em férias

Holland Holanda [oh**land**a]

home a casa [**ka**za]

at home (in my house etc) em casa [ayng]

(in my country) no meu país [noo may-oo pa-**ees**]

we go home tomorrow vamos embora amanhã [**va**moos aymb**o**ra aman-yang]

honest honesto [ohn**eh**stoo]

honey o mel [mehl]

honeymoon a lua-de-mel [**loo**-a dee]

hood (US: of car) o capô [kap**oh**]

hope esperar [eespay**rar**]

I hope so espero que sim [aysp**eh**roo kee seeng]

I hope not espero que não [nowng]

hopefully: hopefully... espero que...

horn (of car) a buzina [boo**zee**na]

horrible horrível [oh-**Hee**vil]

horse o cavalo [ka**va**loo]

horse riding andar a cavalo

hospital o hospital [ohspee**tal**]

hospitality a hospitalidade [ohspeetaleed**a**dee]

thank you for your hospitality
(said by man/woman) obrigado(a)
por sua hospitalidade
[ohbreegadoo pohr soo-a]

hot quente [kayntee]
(spicy) apimentado
[apeemayntadoo]
I'm hot estou com calor [tayn-
yoo kalohr]
it's hot today hoje está quente
[ohJee eesta]

hotel o hotel [ohtehl]
hotel room o quarto de hotel
[kwartoo doo ohtehl]
house a casa [kaza]
house wine o vinho da casa
[veen-yoo]
how como [kohmoo]
how many? quantos?
[kwantoos]
how do you do? como vai?
[kohmoo vī]

dialogues

how are you? como vai?
fine, thanks, and you?
(said by man/woman) bem,
obrigado(a), e você? [bayng
ohbreegadoo – ee vohsay]

how much is it? quanto é?
[kwantweh]
it's 20 reais são vinte reais
[sowng veentee Hay-īs]
I'll take it vou levar [voh]

humid úmido [oomeedoo]
hunger a fome [fomee]

hungry: are you hungry? está
com fome? [aysta kohng]
hurry apressar-se [apraysarsee]
I'm in a hurry estou com
pressa [aystoh kohng prehsa]
there's no hurry não há pressa
[nowng a]
hurry up! ande logo! [andee
logoo]
hurt doer [dwayr]
it really hurts dói muito [doy
mweengtoo]
husband o marido [mareedoo]
hydrofoil o hidrofólio
[eedrohfol-yoo]
hypermarket hipermercado
[eepayrmayrkadoo]

I

I* eu [ay-oo]
ice gelo [Jayloo]
with ice com gelo [kohng]
no ice, thanks (said by man/
woman) sem gelo, obrigado(a)
[sayng – ohbreegadoo]
ice cream o sorvete [sohrvaytee]
ice-cream cone o sorvete de
casquinha [dee kaskeen-ya]
iced coffee o café gelado
[kafeh Jayladoo]
ice lolly o picolé [peekohle]
ice rink o rinque de patinação
[Heenkee dee pateenasowng]
ice skates os patins de gelo
[pateens dee Jayloo]
idea a idéia [eedeh-ia]
idiot o idiota [eed-yota]

if se [see]
ill doente [dwayntee]
I feel ill eu me sinto mal [ay-oo mee seentoo]
illness a doença [dwaynsa]
imitation (leather etc) a imitação [eemeetasowng]
immediately imediatamente [eemayd-yatamayntee]
important importante [impohrtantee]
it's very important é muito importante [eh mweengtoo]
it's not important não é importante [nowng]
impossible impossível [impohseevil]
impressive impressionante [immprays-yohnantee]
improve melhorar [mayl-yorar]
I want to improve my Portuguese quero melhorar o meu português [kehroo – oo may-oo pohrtoogays]
in*: it's in the centre fica no centro [feeka noo sayntroo]
in my car no meu carro [noo may-oo kaHoo]
in Manaus em Manaus [ayng manows]
in two days from now daqui a dois dias [dakee a doh-is dee-as]
in five minutes em cinco minutos [ayng seenkoo meenootoos]
in May em maio [mī-oo]
in English em inglês [inglays]
in Portuguese em português [pohrtoogays]

is he in? ele está? [aylee eesta]
inch* a polegada [pohlaygada]
include incluir [inklweer]
does that include meals? isso inclui as refeições? [eesoo inklwee as Hayfaysoyngs]
is that included? isso está incluído no preço? [aysta [inklweedoo noo praysoo]
inconvenient inconveniente [inkohnvayn-yayntee]
incredible inacreditável [eenakraydeetavil]
Indian (adj) índio [ind-yanoo]
indicator o indicador [indeekadohr]
indigestion a indigestão [indeeJayshtowng]
indoor pool a piscina coberta [peeseena kohbehrta]
indoors dentro de casa [dayntroo dee kaza], em recinto fechado [ayng Hayseentoo fayshadoo]
inexpensive barato [baratoo]
infection a infecção [infeksowng]
infectious infeccioso
inflammation a inflamação [inflamasowng]
informal informal [infohrmal]
information a informação [infohrmasowng]
do you have any information about...? tem alguma informação sobre...? [tayng algooma – sohbree]
information desk o balcão de informações [balkowng dinfohrmasoyngs]

injection a injeção [inJehs**ow**ng]

injured ferido [fayr**ee**doo]

 she's been injured ela foi ferida [**eh**la foh-i fayr**ee**da]

in-laws os parentes por afinidade [par**ay**ntees poor afeeneed**a**dee]

inner tube (for tyre) a câmara de ar [k**a**mara dee ar]

innocent inocente [eenohs**ay**ntee]

insect o inseto [ins**eh**too]

insect bite a picada de inseto [peek**a**da dins**eh**too]

 do you have anything for insect bites? tem alguma coisa para picada de insetos? [tayng alg**oo**ma k**oh**iza – ins**eh**toos]

insect repellent o repelente de insetos [Haypayl**ay**ntee]

inside dentro [d**ay**ntroo]

 inside the hotel dentro do hotel [dwoht**ehl**]

 let's sit inside vamos nos sentar dentro [**va**moos noos sent**ar**]

insist insistir [inseest**eer**]

 I insist insisto [ins**ee**stoo]

insomnia a insônia [ins**on**-ya]

instant coffee o café solúvel [kaf**eh** sohl**oo**vil]

instead em vez [ayng vays]

 give me that one instead dê-me este em vez daquele [d**ay**mee **ay**ste ayng – dak**ay**lee]

 instead of... em vez de...

insulin a insulina [insool**ee**na]

insurance o seguro [sayg**oo**roo]

intelligent inteligente [intaylee**J**ayntee]

interested: I'm interested in... (said by a man/woman) estou muito interessado/interessada em... [ayst**oh** m**wee**ngtoo intayrays**a**doo – ayng]

interesting interessante [intayrays**a**ntee]

 that's very interesting isso é muito interessante [**ee**soo eh m**wee**ngtoo]

international internacional [intayrnas-yoh**nal**]

Internet internet [intayrn**eh**tee]

interpret interpretar [intayrpr**ay**tar]

interpreter (man/woman) o/a intérprete [int**ehr**praytee]

intersection o cruzamento [kroozam**ay**ntoo]

interval (at theatre) o intervalo [intayrv**a**loo]

into para

 I'm not into... não me interesso por... [nowng mintayr**eh**soo poor]

introduce apresentar [aprayzent**ar**]

 may I introduce...? posso apresentar...? [**p**oso]

invitation o convite [kohnv**ee**tee]

invite convidar [kohnveed**ar**]

Ireland a Irlanda [eerl**a**nda]

Irish irlandês [eerland**ays**]

 I'm Irish (man/woman) sou irlandês(esa) [soh – eerland**ay**za]

iron (for ironing) o ferro de

passar [feh-Hoo dee]
can you iron these for me?
pode passar estas roupas
para mim? [podee pasar ehstas
Hohpas para meeng]
is* é [eh]; está [aysta]
island a ilha [eel-ya]
it* o [oo], (f) a
it is... é... [eh]; está... [aysta]
is it...? é...?; está...?
where is it? onde é? [ohndee
eh]; onde está?
it's him é ele [aylee]
it was... era... [ehra]; estava...
[aystava]
Italian (adj, language) italiano
[eetal-yanoo]
Italy Itália [eetal-ya]
itch: it itches isso coça [eesoo
kosa]

J

jack (for car) o macaco
[makakoo]
jacket o paletó [paleeto]; a
jaqueta [Jakayta]
jam a geléia [Jayleh-ia]
jammed: it's jammed
está emperrado [aysta
aynkravadoo]
January janeiro [Janayroo]
jar o jarro
jaw o maxilar [makseelar]
jazz o jazz
jealous ciumento
[s-yoomayntoo]
jeans os jeans

jellyfish a água-viva [agwa
veeva]
jersey a malha [mal-ya]
jetty o píer [peer]
jeweller's a joalheria [Jwal-
yayree-a]
jewellery as jóias [Jo-yas]
Jewish judeu [Jooday-oo]
job o trabalho [trabal-yoo]
jogging o jogging
to go jogging fazer jogging
joke a piada [p-yada]
journey a viagem [v-yaJayng]
have a good journey! boa
viagem! [boh-a]
jug a jarra [JaHa]
a jug of water uma jarra de
água [ooma – dee agwa]
juice o suco [sookoo]
July julho [Jool-yoo]
jump pular [poolar]
jumper o pulôver
jump leads o cabo para ligar
duas baterias [kaboos – doo-as
batayree-as]
junction o cruzamento
[kroozamayntoo]
June junho [Joon-yoo]
just (only) só [saw]
just two só dois/duas
just for me só para mim
[meeng]
just here aqui mesmo [akee
maysmoo]
not just now agora não
[nowng]
we've just arrived nós
acabamos de chegar
[akabamoos dee shaygar]

K

keep ficar [**feek**ar], manter
[man**tayr**]
 keep the change fique com o
 troco [**feek**ee kohng oo tr**oh**koo]
 can I keep it? posso ficar com
 ele/ela? [**p**osoo feekar kohng
 aylee/**eh**la]
 you can keep it pode ficar
 com ele/ela [**p**odee]
ketchup o ketchup
kettle a chaleira [shal**ay**ra]
key a chave [sh**a**vee]
 the key for room 201, please
 a chave do quarto duzentos
 e um, por favor [doo kwartoo
 dooz**ay**ntooz-yoong poor fav**ohr**]
keyring o chaveiro [shav**ay**roo]
kidneys (in body, food) os rins
 [reengs]
kill matar
kilo* o quilo [**keel**oo]
kilometre* o quilômetro
 [keel**ohm**aytroo]
 how many kilometres
 is it to...? são quantos
 quilômetros até...? [sowng
 kwantoos – at**eh**]
kind (generous) am**á**vel
 that's very kind é muito
 amável [eh m**wee**ngtoo]

dialogue

which kind do you want?
que tipo deseja? [kee **teep**oo
days**ay**Ja]

I want this/that kind desejo
este/aquele tipo [**ay**stee/
a**kay**lee]

king o rei [Hay]
kiosk o quiosque [k-y**o**skee]
kiss o beijo [**bay**Joo]
 (verb) beijar [bay**J**ar]
kitchen a cozinha
 [kohz**een**-ya]
kitchenette a quitinete
Kleenex® o lenço de papel
 [**layn**soo dee pap**ehl**]
knee o joelho [Jwayl-yoo]
knickers a calcinha
 [a kowseen-ya]
knife a faca [**f**aka]
knock bater [bat**ayr**]
knock down atropelar
 [atrohpayl**ar**]
 he's been knocked down
 ele foi atropelado [**ay**lee f**oh**-i
 atrohpayl**ad**oo]
knock over (object) derrubar
 [dayHoobar]
 (pedestrian) atropelar
 [atropayl**ar**]
know* (somebody, a place)
 conhecer [kohn-yays**ay**r]
 (something) saber [sab**e**r]
 I don't know não sei
 [nowng say]
 I didn't know that não
 sabia disso [nowng sab**ee**-a
 d**ee**soo]
 do you know where I can
 find...? sabe onde posso
 encontrar...? [**s**abee **oh**ndee
 poswaynkohntrar]

L

label (on clothes) a etiqueta [ayteek**ay**ta]
(on bottles etc) o rótulo [H**o**tooloo]
ladies' room, ladies' (toilets) o banheiro feminino [ban-y**ay**roo faymeen**ee**noo]
ladies' wear as roupas femininas [H**oh**pas]
lady a senhora [sayn-y**o**ra]
lager a cerveja clara [sayrv**ay**-Ja]
lake o lago [l**a**goo]
lamb (meat) o cordeiro [kohrd**ay**roo]
lamp a lâmpada [l**a**mpada]
lane (motorway) a faixa [f**ī**sha]
(small road) a viela [v-y**eh**la]
language o idioma [eed-y**oh**ma]
language course o curso de idiomas [k**oo**rsoo dee eed-y**o**mas]
large grande [gr**a**ndee]
last último [**oo**lteemoo]
  last week semana passada [saym**a**na]
  last Friday sexta-feira passada [s**ay**sta-f**ay**ra]
  last night ontem à noite [**oh**ntayng a n**oh**-itee]
  what time is the last bus to Rio? a que horas sai o último ônibus para o Rio? [a ky**o**ras sī oo **oo**lteemoo **oh**neeboos – Hee-oo]
late tarde [t**a**rdee]
  sorry I'm late desculpe o atraso [deesk**oo**lpee oo atr**a**zoo]
  the bus was late o ônibus estava atrasado [ayst**a**va atraz**a**doo]

we must go – we'll be late temos de ir – chegaremos atrasados [t**ay**moos deer – shaygar**ay**moos atraz**a**doos]
it's getting late está ficando tarde [ayst**a** feek**a**ndoo]
later, later on mais tarde [mīs]
  I'll come back later volto mais tarde [v**o**ltoo]
  see you later até mais tarde [at**eh**]
latest o último [**oo**lteemoo]
  by Wednesday at the latest na quarta-feira o mais tardar [na kw**a**rta-f**ay**ra oo mīs]
laugh rir [reer]
launderette a lavandaria automática [lavandayr**ee**-a owtohmat**ee**ka]
laundromat a lavanderia automática [lavandayr**ee**-a owtohmat**ee**ka]
laundry (clothes) a roupa para lavar [H**oh**pa]
(place) a lavanderia [lavandayr**ee**-a]
lavatory o lavabo [lav**a**boo]
law a lei [lay]
lawn o gramado [Haylv**a**doo]
lawyer (man/woman) o advogado [advohg**a**doo], a advogada
laxative o laxante [lash**a**ntee]
lazy preguiçoso [praygees**oh**zoo]
lead (electrical) o fio [f**ee**-oo]
(verb) liderar [leed**ay**rar]
  where does this lead to? até onde vai esta estrada? [at**eh** **oh**ndee vī **eh**sta eestr**a**da]
leaf a folha [f**oh**l-ya]

leaflet o folheto [fohl-**yay**too]

leak o vazamento [vazama**mayn**too]
(verb) vazar [va**zar**]

the roof leaks o telhado está com goteiras [tayl-**ya**doo eesta kohng goh**tay**ras]

learn aprender [aprayn**dayr**]

least: not in the least de maneira nenhuma [dee ma**nay**ra nayn-**yoo**ma]

at least pelo menos [**pay**loo **may**noos]

leather o couro [**koh**roo]

leave (depart) partir [par**teer**]
(behind) deixar [**day**shar]

I am leaving tomorrow vou partir amanhã [voh par**teer** aman-**yang**]

he left yesterday ele partiu ontem [**ay**lee par**tee**-oo **ohn**tayng]

may I leave this here? posso deixar isto aqui? [**po**soo – **day**shar **ee**stwakee]

I left my coat in the bar deixei meu casaco no bar [day**shay** may-oo kazakoo noo]

when does the bus for Curitiba leave? quando parte o ônibus para Curitiba? [**kwan**doo partee oo **oh**neeboos – kooree**tee**ba]

leek o alho-poró [**al**-yoo poro]

left esquerda [ays**kayr**da]

on the left, to the left à esquerda [a ees**kayr**da]

turn left vire à esquerda [**vee**ree]

there's none left não sobrou nenhum [nowng sohb**roh** nayn-**yoong**]

left-handed canhoto [kan-**yoh**too]

left luggage (office) guarda-volumes/bagagem [**gwar**da voh**loo**mees/baga**Jayng**]

leg a perna [**pehr**na]

lemon o limão [lee**mowng**]

lemonade a limonada [leemoh**na**da]

lemon tea o chá de limão [sha dee lee**mowng**]

lend emprestar [aympray**star**]

will you lend me your...? você me empresta seu...? [aympre**hs**ta **say**-oo]

lens (of camera) a objetiva [ohbJe**tee**va]

lesbian a lésbica [**leh**sbeeka]

less* menos [**may**nos]

less than menos do que [doo kee]

less expensive mais barato [mīs bara**too**]

lesson a lição [lee**sowng**]

let (allow) deixar [**day**shar]

will you let me know? você me conta depois? [voh**say** mee **kohn**ta daypoh-is]

I'll let you know depois eu lhe conto [**ay**-oo l-yi]

let's go for something to eat vamos comer alguma coisa [**va**moos koh**mayr** al**goo**ma koh-iza]

let off: will you let me off at...? o senhor me deixa descer em...? [oo sayn-yor mee **day**sha day**sayr** ayng]

letter a carta [**kar**ta]

do you have any letters for me? tem alguma carta para mim? [tayng alg**oo**ma – meeng]

letterbox a caixa do correio [k**ī**sha do koh-**Hay**-oo]

lettuce a alface [al**fa**see]

lever a alavanca

library a biblioteca [beebl-yoht**eh**ka]

licence a licença [lees**ay**nsa]

lid a tampa

lie (verb: tell untruth) mentir [maynt**eer**]

lie down deitar-se [dayt**ar**see]

life a vida [**vee**da]

lifebelt o cinto de segurança [**seen**too dee saygoo**ransa**]

lifeguard o salva-vidas [**vee**das]

life jacket o colete salva-vida [kohl**ay**tee]

lift (in building) o elevador [aylayvad**ohr**]

could you give me a lift? pode me dar uma carona? [**po**dee mee dar **oo**ma kar**oh**na]

would you like a lift? quer uma carona? [kehr]

light a luz [loos]

(not heavy) leve [**leh**vee]

do you have a light? (for cigarette) tem fogo? [tayng **foh**goo]

light green verde-claro [**vay**rdee kla**roo**]

light bulb a lâmpada

I need a new light bulb preciso de uma lâmpada nova [prays**ee**zoo dee **oo**ma]

lighter (cigarette) o isqueiro [eesk**ay**roo]

lightning o raio [Ha-y**oo**]; o relâmpago [Hayl**am**pagoo]

like gostar [goh**star**]

I like it gosto disso [**go**stoo]

I like going for walks gosto de caminhar [dee kameen-y**ar**]

I like you gosto de você [dee voh**say**]

I don't like it não gosto disso [nowng – **dee**soo]

do you like...? você gosta de...? [voh**say** – dee]

I'd like a beer queria uma cerveja [kay**ree**-a **oo**ma sayrv**ay**Ja]

I'd like to go swimming quero nadar [**keh**roo]

would you like a drink? quer beber algo? [kher bayb**ayr**]

would you like to go for a walk? quer dar um passeio? [kehr dar oong pas**ay**oo]

what's it like? como é? [**koh**moo eh]

I want one like this quero um como este [**keh**roo oong kohmw**ay**stee]

lime a lima [**lee**ma]

lime cordial o suco de lima [**soo**koo dee]

line a linha [**leen**-ya]

could you give me an outside line? pode me dar uma linha? [**po**dee mee – **oo**ma]

lips os lábios [**lab**-yoos]

lip salve o protetor labial [proht**ay**toh**r**]

lipstick o baton [bat**ohng**]

liqueur o licor [leek**ohr**]

listen escutar [ayskootar]
litre* o litro [leetro]
 a litre of white wine uma
 garrafa de vinho branco [ooma
 gaHafa dee veen-yoo brankoo]
little pequeno [paykaynoo]
 just a little, thanks só um
 pouco, por favor [saw oong
 pohkoo poor favohr]
 a little milk um pouco leite
 [laytee]
 a little bit more um pouco
 mais [oong pohkoo mis]
live (verb) viver [veevayr];
 morar [mohrar]
 we live together vivemos
 juntos [veevaymoos Joontoos]

dialogue

where do you live? onde
você mora? [ohndee vohsay]
I live in London em
Londres [ayng lohndrees]

lively animado [aneemadoo]
liver (in body, food) o fígado
 [feegadoo]
loaf o pão [powng]
lobby (in hotel) o saguão [sagoo-
 owng]
lobster a lagosta [lagohsta]
local local [lohkal]
 can you recommend a local
 food? pode recomendar uma
 comida da região? [podee
 Haykohmayndar ooma kohmeeda da
 HayJ-yowng]
 can you recommend a local

restaurant? pode recomendar
 um restaurante? [Haystawrantee]
lock a fechadura [fayshadoora]
 (verb) fechar à chave [fayshar a
 shavee]
 it's locked está trancado [aysta
 trankadoo]
lock out: I've locked myself
 out (of room) eu me fechei por
 fora [ay-oo mee fayshay poor fora]
locker (for luggage etc) o armário
 com cadeado [armar-yoo kohng
 kad-yadoo]
lollipop o pirulito [peerooleetoo]
London Londres [lohndrees]
long comprido [kohmpreedoo]
 how long will it take to
 fix it? quanto tempo vai
 demorar para consertar?
 [kwantoo taympoo vī daymohrar
 – kohnsayrtar]
 how long does it take?
 quanto tempo demora?
 [daymora]
 a long time muito tempo
 [mweengtoo]
 one day/two days longer
 mais um dia/dois dias [mīs
 oong dee-a/doh-is dee-as]
long-distance call o
 telefonema interurbano
 [taylayfonayma intayroorbanoo]
look: I'm just looking, thanks
 (said by man/woman) só estou
 olhando, obrigado(a) [saw
 eestoh ol-yandoo ohbreegadoo]
 you don't look well você não
 parece bem [vohsay nowng
 parehsee bayng]

look out! cuidado! [kwidadoo]

can I have a look? posso ver? [posoo vayr]

look after tomar conta (de) [tohmar kohnta]

look at olhar (para) [ol-yar]

look for procurar [prohkoorar]

I'm looking for... estou procurando... [prohkoorandoo]

loose (handle etc) solto [sohltoo]

lorry o caminhão [kameen-yowng]

lose perder [payrdayr]

I've lost my way eu me perdi [ay-oo mee payrdee]

I'm lost, I want to get to... (said by man/woman) estou perdido/perdida, quero ir para... [aytoh payrdeedoo – kehroo eer]

I've lost my bag perdi minha bolsa [payrdee meen-ya]

lost property (office) achados e perdidos (seção de) [ashodoos ee payrdeedoos]

lot: a lot, lots muito [mweengtoo]

not a lot não muito [nowng]

a lot of people muita gente [mweengta Jayntee]

a lot bigger muito maior [mī-or]

I like it a lot gosto muito [gostoo mweengtoo]

lotion a loção [lohsowng]

loud alto [altoo]

lounge (in house, hotel) o salão [salowng]

(in airport) a sala de espera [dee ayspehra]

love o amor [amohr]

(verb) amar

I love Brazil adoro o Brasil [adoroo brazeel]

lovely (meal, food) delicioso [daylees-yohzoo]

(view) encantador [aynkantadohr]

(weather) excelente [aysaylayntee]

(present) adorável

low baixo [bīshoo]

luck a sorte [sortee]

good luck! boa sorte! [boh-a]

luggage a bagagem [bagaJayng]

luggage trolley o carrinho de bagagem [kaHeen-yoo dee]

lump (on body) o inchaço [inshasoo]

lunch o almoço [almohsoo]

lungs os pulmões [poolmoyngs]

luxurious (hotel, furnishings) luxuoso [loosh-wohzoo]

luxury o luxo [looshoo]

M

machine a máquina [makeena]

mad (insane) doido [doh-idoo]

(angry) zangado [zangadoo]

Madeira wine o vinho Madeira [veen-yoo madayra]

magazine a revista [Hayveesta]

maid (in hotel) a camareira [kamarayra]

maiden name o nome de solteira [nohmee dee sohltayra]

mail o correio [koh-Hay-oo]

(verb) postar [pohstar]

is there any mail for me? há

alguma correspondência para mim? [a algooma – meeng]

mailbox a caixa do correio [kīsha]

main principal [preenseepal]

main course o prato principal [pratoo prinseepal]

main post office o correio central [koh-Hay-oo sayntral]

main road (in town) a rua principal [Hoo-a preenseepal] (in country) a estrada principal [aystrada]

main switch o disjuntor principal [deesJoontohr]

make* (brand name) a marca (verb) fazer [fazayr]
I make it 50 reais calculo que sejam cinquenta reais [kalkooloo kee sayJowng sinkwaynta Hay-īs]
what is it made of? de que é feito? [dee kee eh faytoo]

make-up a maquiagem [mak-yaJayng]

man o homem [omayng]

manager o gerente [Jayrayntee]
can I see the manager? pode chamar o gerente? [podee shamar]

manageress a gerente

manual manual [manwal]

many muitos [mweengtoos]
not many não muitos [nowng]

map o mapa

March março [marsoo]

margarine a margarina [margareena]

market o mercado [mayrkadoo]

marmalade a geléia de laranja [dee laranJa]

married: I'm married (said by a man/woman) sou casado/casada [soh kazadoo]
are you married? você é casado/casada? [vohsay eh]

mascara o rímel [Heemil]

match (football etc) a partida [parteeda]

matches os fósforos [fosfooroos]

material (fabric) o tecido [tayseedoo]

matter: it doesn't matter não faz mal [nowng faz mal]
what's the matter? qual é o problema? [kwaleh oo prohblayma]

mattress o colchão [kohlshowng]

May maio [mī-oo]

may: may I have another one? (different one) pode me servir outro/outra? [podee mee sayrveer ohtroo]
may I come in? posso entrar? [poswayntrar]
may I see it? posso vê-lo/vê-la? [posoo vayloo/vayla]
may I sit here? posso me sentar aqui? [posoo mee sayntar akee]

maybe talvez [talvays]

mayonnaise a maionese [mī-ohnehzee]

me* mim [meeng]
that's for me isto é para mim [eestweh para meeng]
send it to me mande para mim

me too eu também [**ay**-oo tamb**ay**ng]

meal a refeição [Hayfays**ow**ng]; a comida [koh**mee**da]

dialogue

did you enjoy your meal?
gostou da comida? [gohst**oh** da koh**mee**da]

it was excellent, thank you
(said by man/woman) estava
excelente, obrigado(a)
[eesta**va** aysayl**ay**ntee
ohbree**ga**doo]

mean: what do you mean? o
que quer dizer? [oo kee kehr
deez**ayr**]

dialogue

**what does this word
mean?** o que significa esta
palavra? [oo kee seegnee**fee**ka
ehsta]

it means... in English
significa... em inglês [ayng
ingl**ays**]

measles o sarampo [sa**ram**poo]
meat a carne [**kar**nee]
mechanic o mecânico
[may**ka**neekoo]
medicine o remédio [Haym**eh**d-
yoo]
Mediterranean o
Mediterrâneo [maydeetayHan-
yoo]

medium médio [**meh**d-yoo]
medium-dry meio-seco [**may**-
oo s**ay**koo]
medium-rare malpassado
medium-sized de tamanho
médio [dee taman-yoo]
meet conhecer; encontrar
[aynkohn**trar**]
nice to meet you muito
prazer [m**wee**ngtoo praz**ayr**]
where shall I meet you? onde
nos encontramos? [**oh**ndee
noozaynkohn**tra**moos]
meeting a reunião [Hay-oon-
y**ow**ng]
meeting place o ponto
de encontro [**poh**ntoo dee
ayn**koh**ntroo]
melon o melão [may**low**ng]
men os homens [**o**mayngs]
mend consertar [konsay**rtar**]
**could you mend this for
me?** poderia consertar isto?
[podayr**ee**-a kohnsayrtar **ee**stoo]
menswear a roupa masculina
[**Hoh**pa maskoo**lee**na]
mention mencionar [mayns-
yoh**nar**]
don't mention it não há de
quê [nowng a dee kay]
menu o cardápio [kar**dap**-yoo]
may I see the menu, please?
posso ver o cardápio, por
favor [**po**sso vayr – poor fav**ohr**]
see menu reader page 212
message o recado [Hayka**doo**]
**are there any messages for
me?** tem algum recado para
mim? [tayng alg**oong** – meeng]

I want to leave a message for... gostaria de deixar um recado para... [gohstar**ee**-a dee daysh**ar** oong]

metal o metal [m**ay**tal]

metre* o metro [m**eh**troo]

microwave (oven) o forno de microondas [meekroh-**oh**ndas]

midday o meio-dia [m**ay**-oo dee-a]

at midday ao meio-dia [ow]

middle: in the middle no meio [noo m**ay**-oo]

in the middle of the night no meio da noite [n**oh**-itee]

the middle one o/a do meio

midnight a meia-noite [m**ay**-a n**oh**-itee]

at midnight à meia-noite

might: I might go pode ser que eu vá [p**o**dee sayr kee **ay**-oo]

I might not go pode ser que eu não vá [nowng]

I might want to stay another day pode ser que eu queira ficar mais um dia [k**ay**ra feekar mīs oong dee-a]

migraine a enxaqueca [aynshak**ay**ka]

mild (taste) suave [soo-**a**vee] (weather) ameno [am**ay**noo]

mile* a milha [m**eel**-ya]

milk o leite [l**ay**tee]

milkshake o milkshake

millimetre* o milímetro [meel**ee**maytroo]

minced meat a carne moída [karnee moh-**ee**da]

mind: never mind não faz mal [nowng fas]

I've changed my mind mudei de idéia [mood**ay** deed**eh**-ia]

dialogue

do you mind if I open the window? importa-se se eu abrir a janela? [import**a**see see **ay**-oo abreer a jan**eh**la]

no, I don't mind não, não me importo [nowng mimp**or**too]

mine*: it's mine é meu/minha [eh m**ay**-oo/m**ee**n-ya]

mineral water a água mineral [**a**gwa]

mints as balas de hortelã [dee ohrtayl**ang**]

minute o minuto [meen**oo**too]

in a minute num minuto [noong]

just a minute só um minuto

mirror o espelho [aysp**ay**l-yoo]

Miss a Senhorita, Srta. [sayn-yor**ee**ta]

miss: I missed the bus perdi o ônibus [payrd**ee** oo **oh**neeboos]

missing que falta

there's a suitcase missing falta uma mala [**oo**ma]

mist a névoa [n**eh**vwa]

mistake o erro [**ay**-Hoo]

I think there's a mistake acho que houve um erro [**a**shoo k-y**oh**vee oong]

sorry, I've made a mistake

desculpe, cometi um erro [deeskoolpee kohmaytee]

misunderstanding o mal-entendido [malayntayndeedoo]

mix-up: sorry, there's been a mix-up desculpe, houve uma confusão [ohvee ooma kohnfoozowng]

mobile phone o celular [sayloolar]

modern moderno [mohdehrnoo]

modern art gallery a galeria de arte moderna [galayree-a dee artee mohdehrna]

moisturizer o creme hidratante [kraymeedratantee]

moment: I won't be a moment não demoro nada [nowng daymoroo]

monastery o mosteiro [mohstayroo]

Monday segunda-feira [saygoonda fayra]

money o dinheiro [deen-yayroo]

month o mês [mays]

monument o monumento [mohnoomayntoo]

moon a lua [loo-a]

Moor o mouro [mohroo]

Moorish mourisco [mohreeskoo]

moped a bicicleta motorizada [beeseeklehta mohtohreezada]

more* mais [mīs]

can I have some more water, please? mais água, por favor [mīs agwa poor favohr]

more expensive mais caro [maīs karoo]

more interesting mais interessante [mizintayraysantee]

more than 50 mais de cinquenta [mīs dee seenkwaynta]

more than that mais que isso [mīs kee eesoo]

a lot more muito mais [mweengtoo mīs]

dialogue

would you like some more? deseja um pouco mais? [daysayJa oong pohkoo mīs]

no, no more for me, thanks (said by man/woman) não, nada mais para mim, obrigado(a) [nowng – meeng ohbreegadoo]

how about you? e você? [ee vohsay]

I don't want any more, thanks (said by man/woman) não quero mais nada, obrigado(a) [nowng kehroo mīs]

morning a manhã [man-yang]

this morning esta manhã [ehsta]

in the morning de manhã [dee]

Morocco o Marrocos [maHokoos]

mosquito o mosquito [mohskeetoo]

mosquito repellent o repelente de mosquito [Haypaylayntee dinsehtoos]

most: I like this one most of all gosto mais deste [gostoo mīs daystee]

most of the time a maior
parte do tempo [a mī-or partee
doo taympoo]

most tourists a maioria
dos turistas [mī-ohree-a doos
tooreestas]

mostly principalmente
[preenseepalmayntee]

mother a mãe [mayng]

motorbike a motocicleta
[motohseeklehta]

motorboat o barco a motor
[barkwa mohtohr]

motorway a rodovia
[Hohdoh-vee-a]

mountain a montanha
[montan-ya]

in the mountains nas
montanhas [nas]

mountaineering o alpinismo
[alpeeneesmoo]

mouse o camundongo
[kamoondohngoo]
(de computador) o mouse

moustache o bigode [beegodee]

mouth a boca [bohka]

mouth ulcer a afta

move (one's car, house etc) mudar
[moodar]

he's moved to another room
ele se mudou para outro
quarto [aylee see moodoh para
ohtro kwartoo]

could you move your car?
poderia mudar seu carro de
lugar? [pohdayree-a – say-oo
kaHoo dee loogar]

could you move up a little?
poderia se afastar um pouco?

[pohdayree-a see afastar oong
pohkoo]

where has it moved to? para
onde se mudou? [ohndee see
moodoh]

movie o filme [feelmee]

movie theater o cinema
[seenayma]

Mr o Senhor, Sr. [sayn-yohr]

Mrs a Senhora, Sra. [sayn-yora]

much muito [mweengtoo]

much better/worse muito
melhor/pior [mayl-yor/pee-or]

much hotter muito mais
quente [mīs kayntee]

not (very) much não muito
[nowng]

I don't want very much não
quero muito [kehroo]

mud a lama

mug (for drinking) a caneca
[kanehka]

I've been mugged (said by man/
woman) fui assaltado/assaltada
[fwee asaltadoo]

mum a mamãe [mamayng]

mumps a caxumba [kashoomba]

museum o museu [moozay-oo]

mushrooms os cogumelos
[kohgoomehloos]

music a música [moozeeka]

musician (man) o músico
[moozeekoo]

Muslim (adj) muçulmano
[moosoolmanoo]

mussels os mexilhões
[maysheel-yoyngs]

must: I must... eu devo/tenho
de... [tayn-yoo dee]

I mustn't drink alcohol não devo beber álcool [nowng dayvoo baybayr alkohl]

mustard a mostarda [mohstarda]

my* o meu [may-oo], a minha [meen-ya], os meus [may-oos], as minhas [meen-yas]

myself: I'll do it myself (said by man/woman) eu mesmo/mesma faço isso [ay-oo maysmoo – fasoo eesoo]

by myself (said by man/woman) sozinho/sozinha [sawzeen-yoo]

N

nail (finger) a unha [oon-ya] (metal) o prego [prehgoo]

nailbrush a escova de unhas [ayskohva dee oon-yas]

nail varnish o esmalte de unhas [aysmaltee]

name o nome [nohmee]

my name's John o meu nome é John [oo may-oo nohmee eh]

what's your name? qual é seu nome? [kwaleh oo say-oo]

what is the name of this street? qual é o nome desta rua? [kawleh – dehsta Hoo-a]

napkin o guardanapo [gwardanapoo]

nappy a fralda

narrow (street) estreita (rua) [aystrayta (Hoo-a)]

nasty (person, weather) mau [mow], (f) má (accident) grave [gravee]

national nacional [nas-yohnal]

nationality a nacionalidade [nas-yohnaleedadee]

natural natural [natooral]

nausea a náusea [nowz-ya]

navy (blue) azul-marinho [azool mareen-yoo]

near perto

is it near the city centre? é perto do centro da cidade? [eh – doo sayntroo da seedadee]

do you go near the Pão de Açúcar? passa perto do Pão de Açúcar? [pehrto doo powng dee asookar]

where is the nearest...? onde fica o/a... mais próximo/próxima...? [ohndee feeka oo/a... mis proseemoo]

nearby perto daqui [pehrto dakee]

nearly quase [kwazee]

necessary necessário [naysaysar-yoo]

neck o pescoço [payskohsoo]

necklace o colar [kohlar]

necktie a gravata

need: I need... preciso... [prayseezoo]

do I need to pay? preciso pagar?

needle a agulha [agool-ya]

negative (film) o negativo [naygateevoo]

neither: neither (one) of them nenhum deles [nayn-yoong daylees]

neither... nor... nem... nem... [nayng]

nephew o sobrinho [sohbreen-yoo]
net (in sport) a rede [Haydee]
Netherlands os Países Baixos, a Holanda [ohlanda]
network map o mapa de rede [Haydee]
never nunca [noonka]

dialogue

have you ever been to Petrópolis? já esteve em Petrópolis? [Ja eestayvee ayng]
no, never, I've never been there não, nunca estive lá [nowng noonka eesteevee]

new novo [nohvoo]
news (radio, TV etc) as notícias [nohtees-yas]
newsagent's a banca de jornal [dee Johrnīs]
newspaper o jornal [Johrnal]
newspaper kiosk a banca de jornal
New Year Ano-Novo [anoo nohvoo]
Happy New Year! Feliz ano novo! [faylees]
New Year's Eve o Réveillon
New Zealand Nova Zelândia [nova zayland-ya]
New Zealander: I'm a New Zealander (man/woman) sou neo-zelandês(esa) [soh neh-o zaylandays/neh-o zaylandayza]
next próximo [proseemoo]
the next corner/street on the left a próxima esquina/rua à esquerda [ayskeena/Hoo-a]
at the next stop na próxima parada
next week na próxima semana [saymana]
next to ao lado de [ow ladoo dee]
nice (food, person) agradável (looks, view etc) bonito [bohneetoo]
niece a sobrinha [sohbreen-ya]
night a noite [noh-itee]
at night à noite
good night boa-noite [boh-a]

dialogue

do you have a single room for one night? tem um quarto de solteiro por uma noite? [tayng oong kwartoo dee sohltayroo poor ooma]
yes, madam sim, senhora [seeng sayn-yora]
how much is it per night? quanto custa por noite? [kwantoo koosta]
it's 200 reais for one night são duzentos reais por uma noite [sowng doozayntoos Hay-īs]
thank you, I'll take it (said by man/woman) obrigado(a), fico com ele [ohbreegadoo – feekoo kohng aylee]

nightclub a casa noturna [kaza nohtoorna]

nightdress a camisola
[kameezola]

night porter o porteiro da
noite [pohrtayroo da noh-itee]

no* não [nowng]

I've no change não tenho
troco [tayn-yoo trohkoo]

there's no... left não tem mais
nenhum... [mīs nayn-yoong]

no way! de jeito nenhum!
[dee Jaytoo nayn-yoong]

oh no! (upset) ah não! [nowng]

nobody* ninguém [neengayng]

there's nobody there não tem
ninguém lá [nowng]

noise o barulho [barool-yoo]

noisy: it's too noisy é muito
barulhento [eh mweengto
barool-yayntoo]

non-alcoholic sem álcool
[sayng alkohl]

none* nenhum [nayn-yoong]

nonsmoking room sala
para não-fumantes [nowng
foomantees]

noon o meio-dia [may-oo dee-a]

no-one* ninguém [neengayng]

nor: nor do I nem eu [nayng
ay-oo]

normal normal

north o norte [nortee]

in the north no norte [noo]

to the north ao norte [ow]

north of Salvador ao norte de
Salvador [dee salvadohr]

northeast o nordeste
[nohrdehstee]

northern setentrional [saytayntr-
yohnal]

Northern Ireland a Irlanda do
Norte [eerlanda doo nortee]

northwest o noroeste [noroh-
ehstee]

Norway a Noruega [nohrwehga]

Norwegian (adj) norueguês
[nohrwegays]

nose o nariz [narees]

nosebleed o sangramento
nasal [sangramayntoo nazal]

not* não [nowng]

no, I'm not hungry não, não
estou com fome [aystoh kohng
fomee]

I don't want anything, thank
you (said by man/woman) não
quero nada, obrigado(a)
[kehroo – ohbreegadoo]

it's not necessary não é
necessário [eh naysaysar-yoo]

I didn't know that eu não
sabia [ay-oo – sabee-a]

not that one – this one aquele
não – este [akaylee – aystee]

note (banknote) a nota, a cédula
[sehdoola]

notebook o caderno [kadehrnoo]

notepaper (for letters) o papel de
carta [papehl dee]

nothing* nada

nothing for me, thanks (said
by man/woman) nada para
mim, obrigado(a) [meeng
ohbreegadoo]

nothing else mais nada [mīs]

novel o romance [Hohmansee]

November novembro
[nohvaymbroo]

now agora

number o número [**noo**mayroo]
I've got the wrong number
disquei o número errado
[deess**kay** oo n**oo**mayroo ayH**a**doo]
what is your phone number?
qual é o número do seu
telefone? [**kwal**eh oo – doo **say**-
oo taylayf**oh**nee]
number plate a placa do carro
[doo ka**Hoo**]
nurse (man/woman) o enfermeiro
[aynfayrm**ay**roo], a enfermeira
nut (for bolt) a porca
nuts as nozes [n**o**zees]

O

occupied (toilet, telephone)
ocupado [ohkoop**a**doo]
o'clock* horas [**o**ras]
October outubro [oht**oo**broo]
odd (strange) estranho [aystr**an**-
yoo]
of* de [day]
off (lights) apagada [apag**a**da];
desligada [deessleeg**a**da]
it's just off Praça da
República bem ao lado da
Praça da República [bayng ow
l**a**doo da pr**a**sa da Haypoo**blee**ka]
we're off tomorrow partimos
amanhã [part**ee**moozaman-yang]
offensive (language, behaviour)
ofensivo [ohfayns**ee**voo]
office (place of work) o escritório
[ayskreet**or**-yoo]
officer (said to policeman) senhor
guarda [sayn-y**oh**r gw**a**rda]

often frequentemente [fray-
kwaynteem**ay**ntee]
not often não com frequência
[nowng kohn fraykw**ay**ns-ya]
how often are the buses?
qual a frequência dos ônibus?
[kwal a fraykw**ay**ns-ya doos
ohneeboos]
oil (for car, for cooking) o óleo
[**ol**-yoo]
ointment a pomada [pohm**a**da]
OK tudo bem [**too**doo bayng]
are you OK? tudo bem com
você? [bayng kohng voh**say**]
is that OK with you? está bem
para você? [ayst**a**]
is it OK to...? tudo bem se...?
that's OK thanks (said by man/
woman) tudo bem, obrigado(a)
[ohbreeg**a**doo]
I'm OK, thanks (I've got enough)
para mim chega, obrigado(a)
[meeng sh**ay**ga]
(I feel OK) eu estou bem [ayst**oh**
bayng]
is this bus OK for...? este
ônibus vai para... [**ay**stee
ohneeboos v**i**]
I'm sorry, OK? desculpe
[desk**oo**lpee]
old velho [**veh**l-yoo]
old-fashioned antiquado
[anteekw**a**doo]
old town (old part of town) a
cidade velha [seed**a**dee **veh**l-ya]
in the old town na cidade
velha
olive oil o azeite [az**ay**tee]
olive a azeitona [azayt**oh**na]

91

black/green olives as azeitonas pretas/verdes [azaytohnas praytas/vayrdees]

omelette a omelete [ohmaylehtee]

on* sobre/em(+o/a) [sohbree]

on the street/beach na rua [Hoo-a], na praia

is it on this road? é nesta rua? [eh nehsta]

on the plane no avião [nwav-yowng]

on Saturday no sábado [noo]

on television na televisao [taylayveezowng]

I haven't got it on me não o tenho comigo [nowng oo tayn-yoo kohmeegoo]

this one's on me (drink) esta bebida é por minha conta [ehsta baybeeda eh poor meen-ya kohnta]

the light wasn't on a luz não estava acesa [loos nowng eestava asayza]

what's on tonight? qual é o programa para esta noite? [kwaleh oo prohgrama para ehsta noh-itee]

once (one time) uma vez [ooma vays]

at once (immediately) imediatamente [eemaydyatamayntee]

one* um [oong], uma [ooma]

the white one o/a branco/a [oo/a brankoo]

one-way ticket o bilhete/a passagem de ida [beel-yaytee/pasaJayng deeda]

onion a cebola [saybohla]

only só [saw], somente [somayntee], apenas [apaynas]

only one apenas um/uma [oong/ooma]

it's only 6 o'clock são apenas seis horas [sowng – sayz oras]

I've only just got here acabei de chegar [akabay dee shaygar]

on/off switch o interruptor [intayHooptohr]

open* (adj) aberto [abehrtoo] (verb) abrir [abreer]

when do you open? quando abre? [kwandwabree]

I can't get it open não consigo abrir [nowng kohnseegwabreer]

in the open air ao ar livre [ow ar leevree]

opening times o horário de funcionamento [orar-yoo dee foons-yohnamayntoo]

open ticket o bilhete/a passagem aberto/aberta [beel-yaytee/pasaJayng abehrtoo]

opera a ópera [opayra]

operation (medical) a operação [ohpayrasowng]

operator (telephone: man/woman) o/a telefonista [taylayfohneesta]

opposite: the opposite direction no sentido oposto [saynteedoo ohpohstoo]

the bar opposite o bar em frente [oo – frayntee]

opposite my hotel em frente ao meu hotel [ayng frayntee ow may-oo ohtehl]

optician o oculista [ohkooleesta]

or ou [oh]
orange (fruit, colour) a laranja [laranJa]
orange juice (fresh) o suco de laranja [**soo**koo dee]
(fizzy) refrigerante de laranja com gás [HayfreeJayrantee]
(diluted) a laranjada
orchestra a orquestra [ohr**keh**stra]
order: can we order now? (in restaurant) podemos pedir agora? [poh**day**moos pay**deer**]
I've already ordered, thanks (said by man/woman) já pedi, obrigado(a) [Ja pay**dee** ohbree**ga**doo]
I didn't order this não pedi isto [nowng – **ee**stoo]
out of order enguiçado [ayngees**a**doo]
ordinary comum [koh**moon**]
other outro [**oh**troo]
the other one o outro [oo]
the other day o outro dia [**dee**-a]
I'm waiting for the others estou esperando os outros [ay**toh** eespayran**doo** oos **oh**troos]
do you have any others? você tem outros? [voh**say** tayng]
otherwise senão [say**nowng**]
our* nosso [**no**soo], nossa [**no**sa], nossos [**no**soos], nossas [**no**sas]
ours* nosso, nossa, nossos, nossas
out: he's out ele saiu [sa-**ee**-oo]
three kilometres out of

town a três quilômetros da cidade [trays keel**oh**maytroos da seed**a**dee]
outdoors ao ar livre [ow ar **lee**vree]
outside fora [**fo**ra]
can we sit outside? podemos nos sentar fora? [poh**day**moos noos sayn**tar**]
oven o forno [**foh**rnoo]
over: over here aqui [a**kee**]
over there ali [a**lee**]
over five hundred mais de quinhentos/quinhentas [mīs dee keen-**yayn**toos]
it's over acabou [akab**oh**]
overcharge: you've overcharged me você cobrou a mais [voh**say** kohb**roh** a mīs]
overcoat o sobretudo [sohbrayt**oo**doo]; o casacão [kazak**owng**]
overlooking: I'd like a room overlooking the courtyard gostaria de um quarto voltado para o pátio [gohsta**ree**-a dee oong kw**ar**too vohlt**a**do paroo pat-yoo]
overnight (travel) noturno [noht**oor**noo]v, not**ur**na
owe: how much do I owe you? quanto lhe devo? [kw**an**too l-yi **da**yvoo]
own: my own... o meu próprio... [oo **may**-oo pr**opr**-yoo]
are you on your own? (to man/woman) está sozinho/sozinha? [ays**ta** sawz**een**-yoo]
I'm on my own (said by man/

woman) estou sozinho/sozinha [aystoh]

owner (man/woman) o dono [dohnoo], a dona [dohna]

oysters as ostras [ohstras]

P

pack fazer as malas [fazayr as malas]

a pack of... um pacote de... [oong pakotee dee]

package (parcel) a encomenda [aynkohmaynda]

package holiday o pacote de férias [pakotee dee fehr-yas]

packed lunch a embalagem de comida industrializada [aymbalajayng dee kohmeeda indoostr-yaleezada]

packet: a packet of cigarettes um maço de cigarros [masoo dee segaHoos]

padlock o cadeado [kad-yadoo]

page (of book) a página [paJeena]

could you page Mr...? poderia chamar o Sr...? [pohdayree-a shamar oo sayn-yohr]

pain a dor [dohr]

I have a pain here estou com uma dor aqui [aystoh kohng ooma dohr akee]

painful doloroso [dohlohrohzoo]

painkillers os analgésicos [analJehzeekoos]

paint a tinta [teenta]

painting a pintura [peentoora]

pair: a pair of... um par de... [oong dee]

Pakistani (adj) paquistanês [pakeestanays]

palace o palácio [palas-yoo]

pale pálido [paleedoo]

pale blue azul-claro [azool klaroo]

pan a panela [panehla]

panties as calcinhas [kalseen-yas]

pants (underwear) as cuecas [kwehkas]

(US) a calça comprida [kalsa kohmpreeda]

pantyhose a meia-calça [may-a kalsa]

paper o papel [papehl]

(newspaper) o jornal [Johrnal]

a sheet of paper uma folha de papel [ooma fohl-ya dee]

paper handkerchiefs os lenços de papel [laynsoos]

paragliding o parapente [parapayntee]

parcel o pacote [pakotee]

pardon (me)? (didn't understand/hear) como? [kohmoo]

parents os pais [pīs]

parents-in-law os sogros [sohgroos]

park o parque [parkee]

(verb) estacionar [aystas-yohnar]

can I park here? posso estacionar aqui? [posoo – akee]

parking lot o estacionamento [aystas-yohnamayntoo]

part a parte [partee]

partner (boyfriend/girlfriend)

o companheiro [kohmpan-
yayroo], a companh**ei**ra
party (group) o grupo [gr**oo**poo]
(celebration) a festa [**feh**sta]
pass (in mountains) o
desfiladeiro [deesfeelad**ay**roo]
passenger (man/woman) o
passageiro [pasaJ**ay**roo], a
passag**ei**ra
passport o passaporte
[pasap**o**rtee]
past*: in the past no passado
just past the information
office assim que passar o
centro de informações
[as**ee**ng kee pas**a**r oo s**ay**ntroo dee
infohrmas**oy**ngs]
path o caminho [kam**ee**n-yoo]
pattern o desenho [dayz**ay**n-yoo]
pavement a calçada [kals**a**da]
on the pavement na calçada
[na]
pavement café o café em
terraço [kaf**eh** ayng tayH**a**soo]
pay pagar
can I pay, please? por favor,
queria pagar [poor fav**oh**r
kayr**ee**-a]
it's already paid for já está
pago [Ja eest**a** p**a**goo]

dialogue

who's paying? quem vai
pagar? [kayng vī]
I'll pay eu pago [**ay**-oo
p**a**goo]
no, you paid last time, I'll
pay não, você pagou da

última vez [nowng voh**say**
pag**oh** da **oo**ltima v**ays**]

pay phone o telefone público
[taylayf**oh**nee p**oo**bleekoo]
peaceful tranquilo [trank**wee**loo]
peach o pêssego [p**ay**saygoo]
peanuts os amendoins
[amaynd**wee**ns]
pear a pêra [p**ay**ra]
peas as ervilhas [ayrv**ee**l-yas]
peculiar (taste, custom) peculiar
[paycool-**yar**]
pedestrian crossing a
passagem de pedestres
[pasaJ**ay**ng dee payd**eh**strees]
pedestrian precinct a área
de pedestres [**ar**-ya dee]; o
calçadão [kalsad**ow**ng]
peg (for washing) o prendedor
de roupas [praynday**doh**r dee
H**oh**pas]
(for tent) o espeque [aysp**eh**kee]
pen a caneta [kan**ay**ta]
pencil o lápis [**la**pees]
penfriend (man/woman)
o/a correspondente
[kohHayspohnd**ay**ntee]
penicillin a penicilina
[payneeseel**ee**na]
penknife o canivete [kaneev**eh**tee]
pensioner (man/woman) o/a
aposentado/a [apohzaynt**a**doo]
people as pessoas [payss**oh**-as]
the other people in the hotel
as outras pessoas no hotel
[az**oh**tras payss**oh**-as nwoht**eh**l]
too many people muita gente
[J**ay**ntee]

pepper (spice) a pimenta [peemaynta]

(vegetable) o pimentão [peemayntowng]

peppermint (sweet) a bala de hortelã [ohrtaylang]

per: per night por noite [poor noh-itee]

how much per day? quanto custa por dia? [kwantoo koosta poor dee-a]

per cent por cento [sayntoo]

perfect perfeito [payrfaytoo]

perfume o perfume [payrfoomee]

perhaps talvez [talvays]

perhaps not talvez não [nowng]

period (of time) o período [payree-oodoo]/
(menstruation) a menstruação [maynstrwasowng]

perm (hair) a permanente [payrmanayntee]

permit a permissão [payrmeesowng]

person a pessoa [paysoh-a]

personal stereo o walkman®

petrol a gasolina [gazooleena]

petrol can a lata de gasolina [dee]

petrol station posto de combustível [pohstoo dee kohmboosteevil]

pharmacy a farmácia [farmas-ya]

phone o telefone [taylayfohnee]
(verb) telefonar [taylayfohnar]

phone book a lista telefônica [leesta taylayfohneeka]

phone box a cabine telefônica [kabeene]

phonecard o cartão de telefone [kartowng dee]

phone number o número de telefone [noomayroo]

photo a fotografia [fohtohgrafee-a]

excuse me, could you take a photo of us? por favor, poderia tirar uma foto de nós? [poor favohr pohdayree-a tirar ooma fotoo dee nos]

phrasebook o guia de conversação [gee-a dee kohnvayrsasowng]

piano o piano [p-yanoo]

pickpocket (man/woman) o/a trombadinha [trohmbadeen-ya]

pick up: will you be there to pick me up? você vem me pegar? [vohsay vayng mee paygar]

picnic o piquenique [peekeeneekee]

picture (drawing, painting) o quadro [kwadroo]
(photograph) a fotografia [fohtohgrafee-a]

pie a torta; o empadão [aympadowng]

piece o pedaço [paydasoo]
a piece of... um pedaço de... [oong paydasoo dee]

pill a pílula [peeloola]
I'm on the pill estou tomando pílula [aystoh tohmandoo]

pillow o travesseiro [travaysayroo]

pillow case a fronha [frohn-ya]

pin o alfinete [alfeen**ay**tee]

pineapple o abacaxi [abak**a**shee]

pineapple juice o suco de abacaxi [**soo**koo deee]

pink cor-de-rosa [kohr dee r**o**za]

pipe (for smoking) o cachimbo [kash**ee**mboo]

(for water) o cano [k**a**noo]

pipe cleaner o desentupidor de cachimbo [dayzayntoopeed**ohr** dee kash**ee**mboo]

pity: it's a pity que pena [kee **pay**na]

pizza a pizza

place o lugar [l**oo**gar]

at your place na sua casa [**soo**-a k**a**za]

at his place na casa dele [d**ay**lee]

plain (not patterned) liso [**lee**zoo]

plane o avião [av-y**ow**ng]

by plane de avião [dee av-y**ow**ng]

plant a planta

plaster cast o gesso [ʃ**ay**soo]

plasters os curativos [koorat**ee**voos]

plastic o plástico [pl**a**steekoo]

plastic bag o saco/a sacola de plástico [**sa**koo/sak**o**la dee pl**a**steekoo]

plate o prato [pr**a**too]

platform a plataforma

which platform is it for Campinas? qual é a plataforma para Campinas? [kwal**eh** – kamp**ee**nas]

play (verb) jogar [ʃoh**gar**]

(in theatre) a peça de teatro [**peh**sa dee ty-**a**troo]

playground o playground

pleasant agradável

please por favor [poor fav**ohr**]

yes please sim, por favor [seeng]

could you please...? por favor, poderia...? [poor fav**ohr**]

please don't por favor, não faça isso [nowng f**a**sa **ee**soo]

pleased: pleased to meet you (said to man/woman) prazer em conhecê-lo(la) [praz**ayr** ayng kohn-yays**ay**loo]

pleasure: my pleasure de nada/não há de quê [nowng a dee kay]

plenty: plenty of... muito... [m**wee**ngtoo]

there's plenty of time temos muito tempo [t**ay**moos – t**ay**mpoo]

that's plenty, thanks (said by man/woman) chega, obrigado(a) [sh**ay**ga ohbreeg**a**doo]

pliers o alicate [aleek**a**tee]

plug (electrical) a tomada [toh**ma**da]

(for car) a vela [**veh**la]

(in sink) a tampa do ralo [doo ʃ**a**loo]

plumber o encanador [aynkanad**ohr**]

p.m.* da tarde [**tar**dee]

poached egg o ovo pochê [**oh**voo posh**ay**]

pocket o bolso [**bohl**soo]

point: two point five dois vírgula cinco [d**oh**-is v**eer**goola s**ee**nkoo]

there's no point não vale a pena [nowng v**al**-ya p**ay**na]

points (in car) os platinados
[plateenadoos]
poisonous venenoso
[vaynaynohzoo]
police a polícia [pohlees-ya]
  call the police! chame a
  polícia! [shamee a]
policeman o policial [pohlees-yal]
police station a delegacia de
  polícia [daylaygasee-a dee
  pohlees-ya]
policewoman a policial
polish (for shoes) a graxa de
  sapato [grasha dee sapatoo]
polite educado [aydookadoo]
polluted poluído [pohloo-eedoo]
pool (for swimming) a piscina
  [peeseena]
poor (not rich) pobre [pobree]
  (quality) de má qualidade [dee
  ma kwaleedadee]
pop music a música pop
  [moozeeka]
pop singer (man/woman) o
  cantor pop [kantohra], a
  cantora pop
popular popular [pohpoolar]
population a população
  [pohpoolasowng]
pork a carne de porco [karnee
  dee pohrkoo]
port (for boats) o porto [pohrtoo]
  (drink) o vinho do Porto [veen-
  yoo doo]
porter (in hotel) o porteiro
  [pohrtayroo]
portrait o retrato [raytratoo]
Portugal Portugal [pohrtoogal]
Portuguese (adj) português
  [pohrtoogays]

(language) português
(man) o português
(woman) a portuguesa
  [pohrtoogayza]
posh (restaurant, people) chique
  [sheekee]
possible possível [pohseevil]
  is it possible to...? é
  possível...? [eh]
  as... as possible tão/tanto...
  quanto possível [towng...
  kwantoo]
post (mail) o correio [koh-Hay-
  oo]
  (verb) postar [pohstar]
  could you post this for me?
  poderia postar isto para mim?
  [pohdayree-a – eestoo para meeng]
postbox a caixa do correio
  [kīsha doo koh-Hay-oo]
postcard o cartão-postal
  [kartowng pohstal]
postcode o código postal
  [kodeegoo pohstal]
poster (for room) o pôster
  (in street) o cartaz [kartas]
poste restante a posta-restante
  [posta Haystantee]
post office agência do correio
  [aJayns-ya doo koh-Hay-oo]
potato a batata [batata]
potato chips as batatas fritas
  [batatas freetas]
pots and pans as panelas
  [panehlas]
pottery (objects) a cerâmica
  [sayrameeka]
pound* (money, weight) a libra
  [leebra]

power cut a falta de luz [dee loos]

power point a tomada [tohmada]

practise: I want to practise my Portuguese quero praticar o meu português [kehroo prateekaroo may-oo pohrtoogays]

prawn o camarão grande [kamarowng grandee]

prefer: I prefer... prefiro... [prayfeeroo]

pregnant grávida

prescription (for medicine) a receita [Haysayta]

present (gift) o presente [prayzayntee]

president (of country: man/woman) o/a presidente [prayzeedayntee]

pretty bonito [bohneetoo]
it's pretty expensive é muito caro [mweengtoo karoo]

price o preço [praysoo]

priest o padre [padree]

prime minister o primeiro-ministro [preemayroo meeneestroo]

printed matter os impressos [imprehsoos]

priority (in driving) a preferencial [prayfayrayns-yal]

prison a prisão [preezowng]

private particular, privado [preevadoo]

private bathroom o banheiro privativo [ban-yayroo preevateevoo]

probably provavelmente [prohvavilmayntee]

problem o problema [prohblayma]

no problem! sem problema! [sayng prohblayma]

program(me) o programa [prohgrama]

promise: I promise prometo [prohmaytoo]

pronounce: how is this pronounced? como se pronuncia? [kohmoo see prohnoonsee-a]

properly (repaired, locked etc) bem [bayng]

protection factor (of suntan lotion) o fator de proteção solar [fatohr dee prohtaysowng]

Protestant protestante [prohtaystantee]

public convenience o banheiro público [ban-yayroo poobleekoo]

public holiday o feriado [fayr-yadoo]

pudding (dessert) o pudim [poodeeng]

pull puxar [pooshar]

pullover o pulôver

puncture o furo [fooroo]

purple roxo [Hohshoo]

purse (for money) a carteira [kartayra]
(US) a bolsa

push empurrar [aympooHar]

pushchair o carrinho de bebê [kaHeen-yoo dee baybay]

put* pôr [pohr]
where can I put...? onde posso pôr...? [ohndee posoo]
could you put us up for the night? poderia nos hospedar

por uma noite? [pohdayree-a nooz ohspaydar poor ooma noh-itee]

pyjamas o pijama [peeJama]

Q

quality a qualidade [kwalidadee]

quarantine a quarentena [kwarayntayna]

quarter a quarta parte [kwarta partee]

quayside: on the quayside no cais [noo kis]

question a pergunta [payrgoonta]

queue a fila [feela]

quick rápido [Hapeedoo]

that was quick! que rápido! [kee]

what's the quickest way there? qual é o caminho mais rápido para lá? [kwaleh oo kameen-yoo mīs Hapeedoo]

quickly depressa [dayprehsa]

quiet (place, hotel) calmo [kalmoo], tranquilo [trankweeloo]

quiet! cale-se! [kaleesee]

quite (fairly) bastante [bastantee]

(very) muito [mweengtoo]

that's quite right está certo [aysta sehrtoo]

quite a lot bastante

R

rabbit o coelho [kwayl-yoo]

race (for runners, cars) a corrida [koh-Heeda]

100

racket (tennis, squash) a raquete [Hakehtee]

radiator (of car) o radiador [Had-yadohr]

(in room) o aquecedor [akaysaydohr]

radio o rádio [Had-yoo]

on the radio no rádio [noo]

rail: by rail de trem [dee trayng]

railway a ferrovia [fayHohvee-a]

rain a chuva [shoova]

in the rain na chuva

it's raining está chovendo [aysta shohvayndoo]

raincoat a capa de chuva [kapa dee shoova]

rape o estupro [aystooproo]

rare (uncommon) raro [Haroo]

(steak) malpassado [pasadoo]

rash (on skin) a erupção [ayroopsowng]

raspberry a framboesa [frambwayza]

rat o rato [Hatoo]

rate (for changing money) a taxa de câmbio [tasha dee kamb-yoo]

rather: it's rather good é muito bom/boa [eh mweengtoo bohng/boh-a]

I'd rather... prefiro... [prayfeeroo]

razor (electric) o barbeador [barb-yadohr]

razor blades as lâminas de barbear [laminas dee barb-yar]

read ler [layr]

ready pronto [prohntoo]

are you ready? (said to man/woman) você está pronto/pronta? [aysta prohntoo]

I'm not ready yet (said by man/woman) ainda não [a-**ee**nda nowng]

dialogue

when will it be ready? quando ficará pronto? [kwandoo feekara]

it should be ready in a couple of days deve ficar pronto em dois dias [dehvee feekar – ayng doh-is dee-as]

real verdadeiro [vayrdad**ay**roo]
really realmente [Hay-alm**ay**ntee]
I'm really sorry sinto muito [seentoo m**wee**ngtoo]
that's really great isso é fantástico [ees**weh** fant**a**steekoo]
really? (doubt) é mesmo? [eh m**ay**smoo]
(polite interest) ah é?
rear lights lanternas traseiras [lant**eh**rnas traz**ay**ras]
rearview mirror o espelho retrovisor [ayspayl-yoo Haytrohveez**ohr**]
reasonable (prices etc) razoável [Haz**wa**vil]
receipt o recibo [Hays**ee**boo]
recently recentemente [Haysaynteem**ay**ntee]
reception (in hotel, for guests) a recepção [Haysepsowng]
at reception na recepção
reception desk o balcão de recepção [balk**owng**]
receptionist (man/woman)

o/a recepcionista [Haysayps-yohn**ee**sta]
recognize reconhecer [Haykohn-yays**ayr**]
recommend: could you recommend...? poderia recomendar...? [pohdayr**ee**-a Haykohmayndar]
record (music) o disco [d**ee**skoo]
red vermelho [vayrm**a**yl-yoo]
red wine o vinho tinto [veen-yoo t**ee**ntoo]
refund o reembolso [Hay-aymb**oh**lsoo]
can I have a refund? pode me reembolsar? [p**oo**dee mee Hay-aymboh**lsar**]
region a região [HayJ-y**owng**]
registered: by registered mail carta registrada [k**a**rta HayJeestr**a**da]
registration number número de licença [n**oo**mayroo dee lees**ay**nsa]
relative (noun: man/woman) o/a parente [par**ay**ntee]
religion a religião [HayleeJ-y**owng**]
remember: I remember eu lembro [l**ay**mbroo]
I don't remember não lembro [nowng]
do you remember? você lembra? [vos**ay** la**y**mbra]
rent (noun: for apartment etc) o aluguel [aloog**ehl**]
(verb: car etc) alugar [aloog**ar**]
to rent para alugar
rented car o carro alugado [k**a**Hoo aloog**a**doo]

repair consertar [kohnsayrtar]
can you repair this? pode consertar isto? [podee – eestoo]
repeat repetir [haypayteer]
could you repeat that? pode repetir?
reservation a reserva [hayzehrva]
I'd like to make a reservation gostaria de fazer uma reserva [gohstaree-a dee fazayr ooma]

dialogue

I have a reservation tenho uma reserva [tayn-yoo ooma]
yes sir, what name please? sim, senhor, em nome de quem? [seeng sayn-yohr ayng nohmee dee kayng]

reserve (verb) reservar [Hayzayrvar]

dialogue

can I reserve a table for tonight? posso reservar uma mesa para esta noite? [posoo – ooma mayza ehsta noh-itee]
yes madam, for how many people? sim, senhora, para quantas pessoas? [seeng sayn-yora – kwantas paysoh-as]
for two para duas [doo-as]
and for what time? e para que horas? [ee – k-yoras]
for eight o'clock para as 20 horas [veentee]
and could I have your

name, please? qual o seu nome, por favor? [kwal oo say-oo nohmee poor favohr]
cer alphabet for spelling

rest: I need a rest preciso descansar [prayseezoo deeskansar]
the rest of the group o resto do grupo [Hehstoo doo groopoo]
restaurant o restaurante [Haystowrantee]
restaurant car o vagão-restaurante [vagowng]
rest room o banheiro [ban-yayroo]
see **toilet**
retired: I'm retired (said by man/woman) sou aposentado/aposentada [soh apohzayntadoo]
return: a return to... um bilhete/uma passagem de ida e volta para... [oong beel-yaytee/pasaJayng deeda ee]
return ticket o bilhete/a passagem de ida e volta
see **ticket**
reverse charge call a chamada a cobrar [shamada kohbrar]
reverse gear a marcha ré [marsha Heh]
revolting asqueroso [askayrohzoo]
rib a costela [koshtehla]
rice o arroz [aHohs]
rich (person) rico [Heekoo] (food) substanciosa [soobstans-yoza]
ridiculous ridículo [Heedeekooloo]
right (correct) certo [sehrtoo]

(not left) direito [deer**ay**too]

you were right você tinha razão [voh**say** teen-ya Ha**zow**ng]

that's right está certo [a**ys**ta **seh**rtoo]

this can't be right isto não pode estar certo [**ees**too nowng **po**dee eestar]

right! certo!

is this the right road for...? esta é a estrada certa para...? [**eh**sta eh a eestrada]

on the right à direita [deer**ay**ta]

turn right vire à direita [**vee**ree]

right-hand drive com volante à direita [vohlantee a deer**ay**ta]

ring (on finger) o anel [a**neh**l]

I'll ring you eu telefono para você [**ay**-oo taylayf**oh**noo – voh**say**]

ring back voltar a telefonar [taylayfoh**nar**]

ripe (fruit) maduro [mad**oo**roo]

rip-off: it's a rip-off isso é um roubo [**ee**soo eh oong **roh**boo]

rip-off prices os preços exorbitantes [**pray**sooz ayzohrbeet**an**tees]

risky arriscado [aH**ees**kadoo]

river o rio [**Hee**-oo]

road (in town) a rua [**Hoo**-a]

(in country) a estrada [ay**stra**da]

is this the road for...? é esta a estrada para...? [**eh**sta]

it's just down the road é nesta rua [eh **neh**sta **Hoo**-a]

road accident o acidente automobilístico [aseed**ay**ntee owtohmohbeel**ee**steekoo]

road map o mapa rodoviário [Hohdohvee-**ar**-yoo]

roadsign a placa de sinalização [**pla**ka dee seenaleezas**ow**ng]

rob: I've been robbed (said by man/woman) fui roubado/roubada [fwee Hoh**ba**doo]

rock a rocha [**Ho**sha]

(music) o rock

on the rocks (with ice) com gelo [kohng J**ay**loo]

roll (bread) o pãozinho [powngz**een**-yoo]

roof o telhado [tayl-y**a**doo]

(of car) o teto [**teh**too]

roof rack o bagageiro de carro [bagaJayroo dee ka**Hoo**]

room o quarto [**kwar**too]

in my room no meu quarto [noo **may**-oo]

room service o serviço de quarto [sayrv**ee**soo dee **kwar**too]

rope a corda

rosé (wine) vinho rosé [Hoh**zay**]

roughly (approximately) aproximadamente [aprohseemadam**ay**ntee]

round: it's my round essa rodada é minha [Hoh**da**da eh **meen**-ya]

roundabout (for traffic) a rotatória [Hohtat**or**-ya]

round trip ticket o bilhete/a passagem de ida e volta [beel-y**ay**tee/pasaJayng d**ee**da ee]

see **ticket**

route o percurso [payrk**oor**soo]

what's the best route? qual é

o melhor percurso? [kwal**eh** oo mayl-y**or**]

rubber (material, eraser) a borracha [boh-H**a**sha]

rubber band o elástico [ayl**a**steekoo]

rubbish (waste) o lixo [l**ee**shoo]
(poor quality goods) o refugo [Hayf**oo**goo]

rubbish! (nonsense) que absurdo! [kee abs**oo**rdoo]

rucksack a mochila [moosh**ee**la]

rude grosseiro [grohs**ay**roo]

ruins as ruínas [H**wee**nas]

rum o rum [Hoong]
a rum and Coke® uma cuba-libre [**oo**ma k**oo**ba l**ee**bree]

run (verb: person) correr [koh-H**ay**r]
how often do the buses run? os ônibus passam com que frequência? [oos **oh**neeboos p**a**sowng kohng kee fraykw**ay**nsya]
I've run out of money estou sem dinheiro [ayst**oh** sayng din-y**ay**roo]

rush hour o horário de pico [ohr**ar**-yoo dee p**ee**koo]

S

sad triste [tr**ee**stee]

saddle a sela [s**eh**la]

safe (adj) seguro [sayg**oo**roo]

safety pin o alfinete de segurança [alfeen**ay**tee dee saygoor**a**nsa]

sail a vela [v**eh**la]
(verb) velejar [vaylayJ**ar**]

sailboard a prancha de windsurfe [pr**a**nsha dee]

sailboarding praticar windsurfe [prateek**ar**]

salad a salada

salad dressing o tempero de salada [taymp**ay**roo]

sale: for sale à venda [v**ay**nda]

salmon o salmão [salm**ow**ng]

salt o sal

same: the same o mesmo [m**ay**smoo]
the same as this igual a este [eegw**al** a **ay**stee]
the same again, please o mesmo outra vez, por favor [m**ay**smoo **oh**tra vays poor fav**ohr**]
it's all the same to me para mim tanto faz [meeng t**a**ntoo fas]

sand a areia [ar**ay**-a]

sandals as sandálias [sand**al**-yas]

sandwich o sanduíche [sandw**ee**shee]

sanitary napkin/towel o absorvente higiênico [absohrv**ay**ntee eeJ-y**ay**neekoo]

sardine a sardinha [sard**ee**n-ya]

Saturday sábado [s**a**badoo]

sauce o molho [m**oh**l-yoo]

saucepan a panela [pan**eh**la]

saucer o pires [p**ee**rees]

sauna a sauna [s**ow**na]

sausage a salsicha [sals**ee**sha]; a linguiça [leengw**ee**sa]

say* dizer [diz**ay**r]
how do you say... in Portuguese? como se diz...

em português? [**koh**moo see dees... ayng pohrtoog**ays**]
what did he say? o que ele disse? [oo kee **ay**lee d**ee**see]
he said... ele disse...
could you say that again? poderia repetir? [pohdayr**ee**-a Haypayt**eer**]
scarf (for neck) a echarpe [aysh**arp**ee]
(for head) o lenço de cabeça [**layn**soo dee kab**aysa**]
scenery a paisagem [pīza**Jayng**]
schedule (US) o horário [orar-yoo]
scheduled flight o vôo regular [**voh**-oo Haygoo**lar**]
school a escola [ays**ko**la]
scissors: a pair of scissors a tesoura [tayz**oh**ra]
scooter a motoneta [mohtohn**ay**ta]
scotch o uísque [w**ee**skee]
Scotch tape® a fita adesiva [**fee**ta aday**zee**va]
Scotland a Escócia [esk**os**-ya]
Scottish escocês [eeskohs**ays**]
I'm Scottish (man/woman) sou escocês/escocesa [soh eeskohs**ays**]
scrambled eggs os ovos mexidos [**o**voos maysh**ee**doos]
scratch o arranhão [a**Han**-yownq]
screw o parafuso [para**foo**zoo]
screwdriver a chave de fenda [sh**a**vee dee f**ayn**da]
sea o mar
by the sea à beira-mar [b**ay**ra]
seafood os frutos-do-mar [fr**oo**toos doo]

seafood restaurant o restaurante de frutos-do-mar [Haystowr**ant**ee dee]
seafront a orla da praia [**orla** da prī-a]
on the seafront na orla da praia [na]
seagull a gaivota [gī**vo**ta]
search procurar [prohko**orar**]
seashell a concha do mar [**koh**nsha doo]
seasick: I feel seasick (said by man/woman) estou enjoado/enjoada [ayst**oh** aynJ**wa**doo]
I get seasick enjôo sempre [aynJ**oh**-oo s**ay**mpree]
seaside: by the seaside à beira-mar [b**ay**ra]
seat o assento [as**ayn**too]
is this seat taken? este lugar está ocupado? [**ay**stee loog**ar** eest**a** ohkoop**a**doo]
seat belt o cinto de segurança [**seen**too dee saygoo**ran**sa]
sea urchin o ouriço-do-mar [ohr**ee**soo doo]
seaweed a alga marinha
secluded isolado [eezohl**a**doo], afastado [afast**a**doo]
second (adj) segundo [sayg**oon**doo]
(of time) o segundo
just a second! espere um segundo! [aysp**ay**ree oong sayg**oon**doo]
second class (travel) segunda classe [sayg**oon**da kl**a**see]
second floor o segundo andar [sayg**oon**doo]

(US) o primeiro andar
[pree**may**roo]

second-hand de segunda mão
[dee say**goo**nda mowng]

see* ver [vayr]

can I see? posso ver? [**po**soo]

have you seen the...? viu
o/a...? [**vee**-oo]

I saw him this morning eu o
vi esta manhã [**ay**-oo vee **eh**sta
man-yang]

see you! até mais! [at**eh** mis]

I see (I understand) entendo
[aynt**ay**ndoo]

self-catering apartment o
apart-hotel [apartoht**ehl**]

self-service self-service

sell vender [vaynd**ayr**]

do you sell...? vocês
vendem...? [**vay**ndayng]

Sellotape® a fita adesiva [**fee**ta
aday**zee**va]

send mandar

I want to send this to England
quero mandar isto para a
Inglaterra [**keh**roo – **ees**too
– inglat**eh**-Ha]

senior citizen (man/woman) o
cidadão da terceira idade
[seedad**ow**ng da tayrs**ay**ra
eed**a**dee], a cidadã da terceira
idade [seedad**ang**]

separate separado [saypar**a**doo]

separated: I'm separated (said
by man/woman) sou separado/
separada [soh]

separately (pay, travel)
separadamente [saypar**a**da-
mayntee]

September setembro
[sayt**aym**broo]

septic séptico [**seh**pteekoo]

serious sério [**seh**r-yoo]

service charge (in restaurant)
a taxa de serviço [**ta**sha dee
sayrv**ee**soo]

service station o posto de
combustível [**poh**stoo dee
kohmboost**ee**vil]

serviette o guardanapo
[gwardan**a**poo]

set menu o menu de preço
fixo [may**noo** dee pr**ay**soo
feeksoo]

several vários [var-yoos]

sew costurar [kohstur**ar**]

could you sew this back
on? poderia costurar isto?
[pohday**ree**-a – **ees**too]

sex o sexo [**seh**ksoo]

sexy sexy [**seh**ksee]; sensual
[sayn**swal**]

shade: in the shade à sombra
[**soh**mbra]

shallow (water) raso [Ha**zoo**]

shame: what a shame! que
pena! [kee p**ay**na]

shampoo o xampu [shamp**oo**]

shampoo and set lavar e
pentear [lavar e paynt-yar]

share (room, table etc) dividir
[deeveed**eer**], partilhar [parteel-
yar]

sharp (knife) afiado [af-yadoo]
(taste) ácido [**a**seedoo]
(pain) agudo [ag**oo**doo]

shattered (very tired) exausto
[ayz**ow**stoo]

shaver o barbeador [barb-yadohr]

shaving foam o creme de barbear [kraymee]

shaving point a tomada para barbeador [tohmada – barb-yar]

she* ela [ehla]
is she here? ela está aqui? [aysta akee]

sheet (for bed) o lençol [laynsol]

shelf a prateleira [prataylayra]

shellfish os mariscos [mareeskoos]

sherry o vinho xerez [veen-yoo shayrays]

ship o navio [navee-o]
by ship de navio [dee]

shirt a camisa [kameeza]

shit! merda! [mehrda]

shock o choque [shokee]
I got an electric shock from the... levei um choque elétrico do... [layvay oong – elehtreekoo doo]

shock-absorber o amortecedor [amohrtaysaydohr]

shocking chocante [shohkantee]

shoes os sapatos [sapatoos]
a pair of shoes um par de sapatos [oong par dee]

shoelaces os cordões de sapato [kohrdoyngs]

shoe polish a graxa de sapatos [grasha dee sapatoos]

shoe repairer o sapateiro [sapatayroo]

shop a loja [loJa]

shopping: I'm going shopping vou às compras [voh as kohmpras]

shopping centre o shopping center

shop window a vitrine [veetreenee]

shore (of sea, lake) a margem [marJayng]

short (person) baixo [bishoo]
(time, journey) curto [koortoo]

shortcut o atalho [atal-yoo]

shorts os shorts

should: what should I do? o que devo fazer? [kee dayvoo fazayr]
he should be back soon ele deve voltar logo [aylee dehvee vohltar logoo]
you should... você deveria... [vohsay dayvayree-a]
you shouldn't... você não deveria... [nowng]

shoulder o ombro [ohmbroo]

shout gritar

show (in theatre) o espetáculo [ayspaytakooloo]; o show
could you show me? poderia me mostrar? [pohdayree-a mee mostrar]

shower (in bathroom) o chuveiro [shoovayroo]
(of rain) o aguaceiro [agwasayroo]
with shower com chuveiro [kohng shoovayroo]

shower gel o gel de banho [Jehl dee ban-yoo]

shrimp o camarão [kamarowng]

shut (verb) fechar [fayshar]
when do you shut? a que horas vocês fecham? [a kee oras vohsays fehshowng]

when does it shut? a que
horas fecha?

it's shut está fechado/fechada
[aysta fayshadoo]

I've shut myself out eu me
fechei por fora [ay-oo mee
fayshay poor fohra]

shut up! cale a boca! [kalee a
bohka]

shutter (on camera) o obturador
[ohbtooradohr]

(on window) a persiana [payrs-yana]

shy tímido [teemeedoo]

sick (unwell) doente [dwayntee]

I'm going to be sick (vomit)
vou vomitar [voh voomeetar]

side o lado [ladoo]

the other side of the street
o outro lado da rua [ohtroo
– Hoo-a]

sidelights as luzes laterais
[loozees latayrīs]

side salad a salada à parte
[partee]

side street a rua secundária
[Hoo-a saykoondar-ya]

sidewalk a calçada [kalsada]

sight: the sights of... as
atrações turísticas de...
[atrasoyngs tooreesteekas dee]

sightseeing: we're going
sightseeing vamos fazer
um passeio turístico
[vamoos fazayr oong pasayoo
tooreesteekoo]

sign (roadsign etc) a placa de
trânsito [plaka dee tranzeetoo]

signal: he didn't give a signal
(driver, cyclist) ele não fez

nenhum sinal [aylee nowng
fays nayn-yoong seenal]

signature a assinatura
[aseenatoora]

signpost a placa indicativa
[plaka indeekateeva]

silence o silêncio [seelayns-yoo]

silk a seda [sayda]

silly bobo [bohboo], tolo [tohloo]

silver a prata

silver foil o papel-alumínio
[papehl aloomeen-yoo]

similar similar [seemeelar],
parecido [parayseedoo]

simple (easy) simples [seemplees]

since: since last week desde
a semana passada [daysd-ya
saymana]

since I got here desde que
cheguei [daysdee kee shaygay]

sing cantar

singer (man/woman) o cantor
[kantohr], a cantora

single: a single to... um bilhete
/uma passagem simples
para... [oong beel-yaytee/
pasaJayng seemplees]

I'm single (said by man/woman)
sou solteiro/solteira [soh
sohltayroo]

single bed a cama de solteiro

single room o quarto de
solteiro [kwartoo dee]

single ticket o bilhete/a
passagem simples [beel-yaytee/
pasaJayng seemplees]

sister a irmã [eermang]

sister-in-law a cunhada [koon-
yada]

sit: can I sit here? posso me sentar aqui? [**po**soo mee sayn**tar** a**kee**]

is anyone sitting here? tem alguém sentado aqui? [tayng al**gay**ng sayn**ta**doo a**kee**]

sit down sentar-se [sayn**tar**see]

sit down sente-se [**sayn**teesee]

size o tamanho [taman-yoo]

skin a pele [**peh**lee]

skin-diving mergulhar sem equipamento [mayrgool-**yar** sayng aykeepa**mayn**too]

skinny magricela [magree**seh**la]

skirt a saia [**sī**-ia]

sky o céu [**seh**-oo]

sleep dormir [dohr**meer**]

did you sleep well? dormiu bem? [dohr**mee**-oo bayng]

sleeper (on train) o vagão-leito [vag**ow**ng **lay**too]

sleeping bag o saco de dormir [**sa**koo dee dohr**meer**]

sleeping car (on train) o vagão-leito

sleeping pill o comprimido para dormir [kohmpree**mee**doo – dohr**meer**]

sleepy: I'm feeling sleepy estou com sono [ays**toh** kohng **soh**noo]

sleeve a manga

slide (photographic) o diapositivo [d-yapohzeet**ee**voo]

slip (garment) a combinação [kohmbeena**sow**ng]

slippery escorregadio [ayskoh-Hayga**dee**-oo]

slow lento [**layn**too]

slow down! (driving) mais devagar! [mīs dayva**gar**]

slowly devagar

very slowly muito devagar [**mwee**ngtoo]

could you speak more slowly? pode falar mais devagar? [**po**dee – mīs]

small pequeno [pay**kay**noo]

smell: it smells (smells bad) isto cheira mal [**ee**stoo **shay**ra]

smile sorrir [soh-H**eer**]

smoke o fumo [**foo**moo]

do you mind if I smoke? importa-se se eu fumar? [**impor**tasee see **ay**-oo foo**mar**]

I don't smoke não fumo [nowng]

do you smoke? você fuma? [voh**say foo**ma]

snack: just a snack só um lanchinho [saw oong lan**sheen**-yoo]

sneeze o espirro [ays**pee**Hoo]

snorkel o snorkel

snow a neve [**neh**vee]

it's snowing está nevando [ays**ta** nay**van**doo]

so: it's so good! é tão bom! [eh towng bohng]

it's so expensive! é tão caro! [**ka**roo]

not so much não tanto [nowng **tan**too]

it's not so bad não é tão ruim [eh towng H**ween**]

so am I, so do I eu também [**ay**-oo tam**bay**ng]

so-so mais ou menos [mīzohm**ay**noos]

soaking solution (for contact lenses) a solução para lentes de contato [sohloosowng para layntees dee kohntatoo]

soap o sabonete, o sabão [sabohnaytee/sabowng]

soap powder o sabão em pó [ayng paw]

sober sóbrio [sobr-yoo]

sock as meias [may-as]

socket (electrical) a tomada [tohmada]

soda (water) a club soda

sofa o sofá [sohfa]

soft (material etc) mole [molee]

soft-boiled egg o ovo quente [ohvoo kayntee]

soft drink o refrigerante [Hayfreejayrantee], o refresco [Hayfrayskoo]

soft lenses as lentes gelatinosas [layntees Jaylateenozas]

sole (of shoe, of foot) a sola
could you put new soles on these? pode pôr solas novas nestes sapatos? [podee pohr – naystees sapatoos]

some: can I have some water? poderia me dar um pouco de água? [podayree-a mee – oong pohkoo dee]
can I have some of this? poderia me dar um pouco disto? [deestoo]

somebody, someone alguém [algayng]

something algo [algoo]
something to eat algo para comer [kohmayr]

sometimes às vezes [as vayzees]

somewhere em algum lugar [ayng algoong loogar]

son o filho [feel-yoo]

song a canção [kansowng]

son-in-law o genro [JaynHoo]

soon logo [logoo]
I'll be back soon volto logo [voltoo]
as soon as possible logo que possível [logoo kee pohseevil]

sore: it's sore está doendo [aysta dwayndoo]

sore throat a dor de garganta [dohr dee]

sorry: (I'm) sorry sinto muito [seentoo mweengtoo]
sorry? (didn't understand) como? [kohmoo]

sort: what sort of...? que tipo de...? [kee teepoo dee]

soup a sopa [sohpa]

sour (taste) ácido [aseedoo]; azedo [azaydoo]

south o sul [sool]
in the south no sul [noo]

South Africa a África do Sul [doo]

South African (adj) sul-africano [soolafreekanoo]
I'm South African (man/woman) sou sul-africano/africana [soh]

southeast o sudeste [soodehstee]

southwest o sudoeste [soodoh-ehstee]

souvenir a lembrança [laymbransa], o suvenir

Spain a Espanha [ayspan-ya]

Spanish espanhol [ayspan-yol]

110

spanner a chave inglesa [shavee inglayza]

spare part a peça sobressalente [pehsa sohbraysalayntee]

spare tyre o estepe [aystehpee]

spark plug a vela [vehla]

sparkling wine o vinho espumante [veen-yo eespoomantee]

speak: do you speak English? você fala inglês? [inglays]

I don't speak... eu não falo... [ay-oo nowng faloo]

dialogue

can I speak to Roberto? posso falar com Roberto? [posso – kohng]

who's calling? quem fala? [kayng fala]

it's Patricia é Patrícia [eh]

I'm sorry, he's not in, can I take a message? desculpe, ele não está, quer deixar recado? [deeskoolpee aylee nowng eesta kehr dayshar Haykadoo]

no thanks, I'll call back later não, obrigada, eu ligo mais tarde [leegoo mīs tardee]

please tell him I called por favor, diga-lhe que liguei [poor favohr deegal-yi kee leegay]

spectacles os óculos [okooloos]

speed a velocidade [vaylohseedadee]

speed limit o limite de velocidade [leemeetee dee]

speedometer o hodômetro [ohdohmaytroo]; o velocímetro [vaylohseemaytroo]

spell: how do you spell it? como se soletra? [kohmoo see sohlehtra]

see alphabet

spend gastar [gastar]

spider a aranha [aran-ya]

spin-dryer a secadora de roupa [saykadohra dee rohpa]

splinter a pua [poo-a]

spoke (in wheel) o raio [Hī-oo]

spoon a colher [kohl-yehr]

sport o esporte [ayspohrtee]

sprain: I've sprained my... eu torci o... [tohrsee oo]

spring (season) a primavera [preemavehra]

(of car, seat) a mola

square (in town) a praça [prasa]

squash o squash

stairs a escada [ayskada]

stale (bread) duro [dooroo]; amanhecido [aman-yayseedoo]

stall: the engine keeps stalling o motor está sempre falhando [mohtohr eesta saympre fal-yandoo]

stamp o selo [sayloo]

dialogue

a stamp for England, please um selo para a Inglaterra, por favor [oong sayloo para inglateh-Ha poor favohr]

what are you sending? o que vai enviar? [oo kee vī aynv-yar]

this postcard este cartão-postal [aystee kartowng pohstal]

standby standby

star a estrela [aystrayla]
(in film: man/woman) o ator principal [atohr preenseepal], a atriz principal [atrees]

start o começo [kohmaysoo]
(verb) começar [kohmaysar]

when does it start? quando começa? [kwandoo kohmehsa]

the car won't start o carro não pega [oo kaHoo nowng pehga]

starter (of car) o motor de arranque [mohtohr dee aHankee]
(food) a entrada [ayntrada]

starving: I'm starving (said by man/woman) estou morrendo de fome [aytoh moh-Hayndoo]

state (country) o estado [aystadoo]

the States (USA) os Estados Unidos [aystadooz ooneedoos]

station a estação [aystasowng]

statue a estátua [aystatwa]

stay: where are you staying? (to man/woman) onde está hospedado/hospedada? [ohndee eesta ohspaydadoo]

I'm staying at... (said by man/woman) estou hospedado/hospedada em... [aytoh – ayng]

I'd like to stay another two nights gostaria de ficar mais duas noites [gohstaree-a dee feekar mīs doo-as noh-itees]

steak o bife [beefee]

steal roubar [Hohbar]

my bag has been stolen roubaram minha mala [Hohbarowng meen-ya]

steep (hill) íngreme [ingreemee]

steering o volante [vohlantee]

step: on the step no degrau [daygrow]

stereo o aparelho de som [aparayl-yoo dee sohng]

sterling as libras esterlinas [leebraz eestayrleenas]

steward (on plane) o comissário de bordo [kohmeesar-yoo dee bordoo]

stewardess a comissária de bordo [kohmeesar-ya]

sticking plaster o esparadrapo [aysparadrapoo]

sticky tape a fita adesiva [feeta adayzeeva]

still: I'm still here ainda estou aqui [a-eenda eestoh akee]

is he still there? ele ainda está aí? [aylee – eesta a-ee]

keep still! fique quieto! [feekee k-yehtoo]

sting: I've been stung (said by man/woman) fui picado/picada [fwee peekadoo]

stockings as meias [may-as]

stomach o estômago [aystohmagoo]

stomach ache a dor de estômago [dohr distohmagoo]

stone (rock) a pedra [**peh**dra]

stop parar

please, stop here (to taxi driver etc) pare aqui, por favor [**paree** akee poor fa**vohr**]

do you stop near...? pára perto de...? [**pehr**too dee]

stop it! pare com isso! [kohng **ee**soo]

stopover a parada; a escala [ays**ka**la]

storm a tempestade [taympays**ta**dee]

straight (whisky etc) puro [**poo**roo]

it's straight ahead sempre em frente [**say**mprayng fr**ayn**tee]

straightaway em seguida [ayng say**gee**da]

strange (odd) estranho [ays**tran**yoo]

stranger (man/woman) o estrangeiro [aystran**Jay**roo], a estrangeira

I'm a stranger here sou de fora [soh dee]

strap (on watch) a pulseira [pool**say**ra]

(on dress) a alça [**al**sa]

(on suitcase) a correia [koh-**Hay**-a]

strawberry o morango [mo**hrang**oo]

stream o riacho [Hee-**a**shoo]

street a rua [**Hoo**-a]

on the street na rua

streetmap o mapa de ruas

string o barbante [bar**ban**tee]

strong forte [**for**tee]

stuck atolado [ato**hla**doo]; preso [**pray**zoo]

it's stuck está atolado [ay**sta**]

student (male/female) o/a estudante [aystoo**dan**tee]

stupid estúpido [ays**too**peedoo]

suburb o subúrbio [soo**boorb**-yoo]

subway (US) o metrô [may**troh**]

suddenly de repente [dee Hay**payn**tee]

suede a camurça [ka**moor**sa]

sugar o açúcar [a**soo**kar]

suit o terno [**tehr**noo]

it doesn't suit me (jacket etc) não fica bem em mim [nowng **fee**ka bayng ayng meeng]

it suits you fica bem em você [**fee**ka – voh**say**]

suitcase a mala; maleta [ma**layt**a]

summer o verão [vay**rowng**]

in the summer no verão [noo]

sun o sol

in the sun ao sol [ow]

out of the sun à sombra [**soh**mbra]

sunbathe tomar sol [to**hmar**]

sunblock (cream) o protetor solar [prohtay**tohr** soh**lar**]

sunburn a queimadura de sol [kaymad**oo**ra day sol]

sunburnt queimado de sol [kaym**a**doo]

Sunday domingo [doo**meen**goo]

sunglasses os óculos de sol [**o**kooloos dee]

sun lounger a espreguiçadeira [ayspraygee-sad**ay**ra]

sunny: **it's sunny** faz sol

sunroof o teto solar [**teh**too]

sunset o pôr-do-sol [pohr doo]

sunshade o guarda-sol [gwarda]

sunshine a luz do sol [loos doo]

sunstroke a insolação [insohlas**ow**ng]

suntan o bronzeado [bronz-y**a**doo]

suntan lotion bronzeador [bronz-yad**ohr**]

suntanned bronzeado

suntan oil o óleo de bronzear [ol-yoo dee]

super ótimo [**o**teemoo]

supermarket o supermercado [soopermayrk**a**doo]

supper o jantar [J**a**ntar]; a ceia [**say**-a]

supplement (extra charge) o suplemento [sooplaym**ay**ntoo]

sure: are you sure? tem certeza? [tayng sayrt**ay**za]

sure! claro! [kl**a**roo]

surname o sobrenome [sohbrayn**oh**mee]

swearword a besteira [bayst**ay**ra]

sweater o suéter

sweatshirt a camiseta [kameez**ay**ta]

Sweden a Suécia [swe**h**s-ya]

Swedish (adj, language) sueco [swe**h**koo]

sweet (taste) doce [d**oh**see] (dessert) a sobremesa [sohbreem**ay**za]

sweets as balas [b**a**las]

swelling o inchaço [insh**a**soo]

swim nadar

I'm going for a swim vou nadar [voh]

let's go for a swim vamos nadar [**va**moos]

swimming costume o maiô [mi-**oh**]

swimming pool a piscina [peese**e**na]

swimming trunks o calção de banho [kals**ow**ng dee ban-yoo]

Swiss (adj) suíço [sw**ee**soo]

switch o interruptor [intayrHoopt**ohr**]

switch off (engine, TV) desligar [deesleeg**ar**] (lights) apagar

switch on (engine, TV) ligar (lights) acender [asaynd**ayr**]

Switzerland a Suíça [sw**ee**sa]

swollen inchado [insh**a**doo]; inflamado [inflam**a**doo]

T

table a mesa [m**ay**za]

a table for two uma mesa para duas pessoas [**oo**ma – d**oo**-as pays**oh**-as]

tablecloth a toalha de mesa [twal-ya dee m**ay**za]

table tennis o tênis de mesa [t**ay**nees]

table wine o vinho de mesa [v**ee**n-yoo]

tailback (of traffic) a fila de carros [**fee**la dee kaHoos]

tailor o alfaiate [alfi-**a**tee]

take (lead) levar

(accept) aceitar [asay**tar**]

can you take me to the...?
pode me levar ao...? [**po**dee
mee lay**var** ow]

do you take credit cards?
aceita cartão de crédito?
[a**say**ta kar**tow**ng dee kr**eh**deetoo]

fine, I'll take it está bem, fico
com ele [ay**sta** bayng **fee**koo
kohng **ay**lee]

can I take this? (leaflet etc)
posso levar isto? [**po**soo
– **ee**stoo]

how long does it take?
quanto tempo leva? [**kwan**too
taympoo **leh**va]

it takes three hours leva três
horas [tray**zo**ras]

is this seat taken? este lugar
está ocupado? [**ay**stee loo**gar**
ee**sta** okoopa**doo**]

hamburguer to take away o
hambúrguer para viagem
[v-ya**Jayng**]

can you take a little off here?
(to hairdresser) pode cortar um
pouco aqui? [**po**dee koh**rtar** oong
pohkoo a**kee**]

talcum powder o talco [**tal**koo]

talk falar

tall alto [**al**too]

tampons os tampões
[tam**poy**ngs]

tan o bronzeado [bronz-**ya**doo]

to get a tan bronzear-se
[bronz-**yar**see]

tank (of car) o tanque
[**tan**kee]

tap a torneira [tohr**nay**ra]

tape (for cassette) a fita cassete
[**fee**ta]

tape measure a fita métrica
[**meh**treeka]

tape recorder o gravador de
fita [grava**dohr**]

taste o sabor [sa**bohr**]

can I taste it? posso provar?
[**po**soo]

taxi o táxi

will you get me a taxi? pode
me chamar um táxi? [**po**dee
mee sha**mar** oong]

where can I find a taxi? onde
posso encontrar um táxi?
[**oh**ndee po**sway**nkohntrar]

dialogue

**to the airport/Hotel...,
please** para o aeroporto/
Hotel..., por favor [**pa**roo
a-ehrohp**ohr**too/oh**tehl** poor
fa**vohr**]
how much will it be?
quanto vai custar? [**kwan**too
vī koos**tar**]
70 reais setenta reais
[say**tayn**ta Hay-**īs**]
**that's fine right here,
thanks** aqui está bem,
obrigado(a) [a**kee** ee**sta**
bayng ohbree**ga**doo]

taxi-driver o taxista [tak**see**sta]

taxi rank o ponto de táxi
[**poh**ntoo dee taxi]

tea (drink) o chá [sha]

tea for one/two, please chá

para um/dois, por favor [oong/doh-is poor favohr]

teabags os saquinhos de chá [sakeen-yoos dee sha]

teach: could you teach me? poderia me ensinar? [pohdayree-a mee aynseenar]

teacher (man/woman) o/a professor/professora [prohfesohr]

team o time [teemee]

teaspoon a colher de chá [kohl-yehr dee sha]

tea towel o pano de prato [panoo dee prato]

teenager o/a adolescente [adohlaysayntee]

telephone o telefone [taylayfohnee]
see phone

television a televisão [taylayveezowng]

tell: could you tell him...? poderia dizer a ele...? [pohdayree-a deezayr a aylee]

temperature (weather) a temperatura [taympayratoora]
(fever) a febre [fehbree]

tennis o tênis [taynees]

tennis ball a bola de tênis [dee]

tennis court a quadra de tênis [kwadra]

tennis racket a raquete de tênis [Hakehtee]

tent a barraca (para acampar) [baHaka]

term (at school) o semestre escolar [saymehstree eeskohlar]

terminus (rail) o terminal [tayrmeenal]

terrible terrível [tay-Heevil]

terrific (weather) fantástico [fantasteekoo]
(food, teacher) excelente [aysaylayntee]

text (message) a mensagem de texto [maynsaJayng dee taystoo]

than* do que [doo kee]
smaller than menor do que [maynor]

thanks, thank you (said by man/woman) obrigado(a) [ohbreegadoo]
thank you very much muito obrigado(a) [mweengtoo]
thanks for the lift obrigado(a) pela carona [payla karohna]
no thanks não, obrigado(a) [nowng]

dialogue

thanks (said by man/woman) obrigado(a)
that's OK, don't mention it tudo bem, não tem de quê [toodoo bayng nowng tayng dee kay]

that*: that... esse/essa... [aysee/ehsa]
(further away) aquele/aquela... [akaylee/akehla]
that one esse/essa/isso [eesoo]
(further away) aquele/aquela/ aquilo [akeeloo]
I hope that... espero que... [ayspehro kee]
that's nice! que bom! [bohng]

is that...? aquilo é...? [eh]

that's it (that's right) é isso [**ee**soo]

the* o [oo], a

(**pl**) os [oos], as [as]

theatre o teatro [t-**ya**troo]

their* deles [**day**lees], delas [**deh**las]

theirs* deles, delas

them* os [oos]

(feminine) as [as]

for them para eles/elas [**ay**lees/**eh**las]

with them com eles/elas [kohng]

to them para eles/elas

who? – them quem? – eles/elas [kayng]

then (at that time) então [aynt**owng**]

(after that) depois [day**poh**-is]

there ali [a**lee**], lá

over there ali adiante [ad-**yan**tee]

up there ali acima [a**see**ma]

is there/are there...? existe...? [ay**zee**stee]

there is/there are... existe...

there you are (giving something) aqui está [a**kee ee**sta]

thermometer o termômetro [tayr**moh**maytroo]

Thermos flask® a garrafa térmica [ga**Ha**fa **teh**rmeeka]

these*: these men estes homens [aysteez**o**mayngs]

these women estas mulheres [**eh**stas mool-**yeh**rees]

I'd like these queria estes/estas [kay**ree**-a **ay**stess/**eh**stas]

they* (male) eles [**ay**lees]

(female) elas [**eh**las]

thick espesso, grosso [ays**pay**soo]

(stupid) estúpido [ays**too**peedoo]

thief (man/woman) o ladrão [la**drowng**], a ladra

thigh a coxa [**koh**sha]

thin fino [**fee**noo]

(person) magro [**ma**groo]

thing a coisa [**koh**-iza]

my things as minhas coisas [**meen**-yas **koh**-izas]

think pensar [payn**sar**]

I think so acho que sim [**a**shoo kee seeng]

I don't think so acho que não [nowng]

I'll think about it vou pensar nisso [voh]

third party insurance o seguro contra terceiros [say**goo**roo **koh**ntra tayr**say**roos]

thirsty: I'm thirsty estou com sede [ay**stoh** kohng **say**dee]

this*: this boy este menino [**ay**stee may**nee**noo]

this girl esta menina [**eh**sta may**nee**na]

this one este [**ay**stee]/esta [**eh**sta]/isto [**ee**stoo]

this is my wife esta é a minha mulher [eh a **meen**-ya mool-**yehr**]

is this...? isto é...? [**ee**stweh]

those*: those... esses/essas... [**ay**sees/**eh**sas]

(further away) aqueles/aquelas... [a**kay**lees/a**keh**las]

which ones? – those quais? – esses/essas [kwīs]

(further away) quais?
– aqueles/aquelas

thread o fio [**fee**-oo]

throat a garganta

throat pastilles as pastilhas
para a garganta [pas**teel**-yas]

through por, através [atra**vehs**]
does it go through...? (train,
bus) passa por...? [pohr]

throw atirar [atee**rar**], jogar
[**Joh**gar]

throw away jogar fora

thumb o polegar [poh**layg**ar]

thunderstorm o temporal
[taympoh**ral**]

Thursday quinta-feira [**keen**ta
fayra]

ticket o bilhete [beel-**yay**tee], a
passagem [pasa**Jay**ng]

dialogue

> a ticket to São Paulo um
> bilhete para São Paulo
> [oong – sowng **pow**loo]
> coming back when?
> quando volta? [**kwan**doo]
> today/next Tuesday hoje/
> na próxima terça-feira
> [**oh**Jee/na **pro**sima **tayr**sa **fay**ra]
> that will be 90 reais são
> noventa reais [sowng
> noh**vayn**ta Hay-**ī**s]

ticket office (bus, rail) a
bilheteria [beel-yaytay**ree**-a]

tide a maré [ma**reh**]

tie (necktie) a gravata

tight (clothes etc) apertado

[apayr**ta**doo], justo [**Joo**stoo]
it's too tight está muito
apertado [aysta m**ween**gtoo]

tights a meia-calça [**may**-a **kal**sa]

till a caixa registradora [**kī**sha
HayJeestra**doh**ra]

time* o tempo [**taym**poo]
what's the time? que horas
são? [k-**yo**ras sowng]
this time esta vez [**eh**sta vays]
last time a última vez [**ool**teema]
next time a próxima vez
[**pro**seema]
three times três vezes [trays
vayzees]

timetable o horário [oh**rar**-yoo]

tin (can) a lata

tinfoil o papel-alumínio [pap**ehl**
aloom**een**-yoo]

tin-opener o abridor de lata
[abree**dohr**]

tiny minúsculo [meen**oo**skooloo]

tip (to waiter etc) a gorgeta
[gohr**Jay**ta]

tired cansado [kan**sa**doo]
I'm tired (said by man/woman)
estou cansado/cansada
[ays**toh**]

tissues os lenços de papel
[**layn**soos dee pap**ehl**]

to: to Rio/São Paulo para
Rio/São Paulo [Hee-oo/sowng
powloo]
to São Paulo/Rio para São
Paulo/Rio
we're going to the museum/
to the post office vamos ao
museu/ao correio [vam**ooz** ow
moo**zay**-oo/ow koh-**Hay**-oo]

toast (bread) a torrada [toh-Hada]

today hoje [ohJee]

toe o dedo do pé [daydoo doo peh]

together junto [Joontoo]
we're together (in shop etc) estamos juntos [aystaymoos Joontoos]

toilet o banheiro [ban-yayroo]
where is the toilet? onde fica o banheiro? [ohndee feeka]
I have to go to the toilet tenho de ir ao banheiro [tayn-yoo deer ow]

toilet paper o papel higiênico [papehl eeJ-yayneekoo]

tomato o tomate [tohmatee]

tomato juice o suco de tomate [sookoo dee tohmatee]

tomato ketchup o ketchup

tomorrow amanhã [aman-yang]
tomorrow morning amanhã de manhã [aman-yang dee man-yang]
the day after tomorrow depois de amanhã [daypoh-is dee aman-yang]

toner (cosmetic) o tônico [tohneekoo]

tongue a língua [leengwa]

tonic (water) a água tônica [agwa]

tonight esta noite [ehsta noh-itee]

tonsillitis a amigdalite [ameegdaleetee]

too (excessively) muito [mweengtoo]; demais [daymīs]
(also) também [tambayng]
too hot muito quente [kayntee]

too much demais [daymīs]

me too eu também [ay-oo tambayng]

tooth o dente [dayntee]

toothache a dor de dente [dohr dee dayntee]

toothbrush a escova de dentes [ayskohva]

toothpaste a pasta de dentes [pasta]

top: on top of... em cima de... [ayng seema dee]
at the top no alto [noo altoo]
at the top of... no topo de... [tohpoo dee]

top floor o último andar [oolteemoo andar]

topless topless

torch a lanterna [lantehrna]

total o total [tohtal]

tour a excursão [ayskoorsowng]
is there a tour of...? há alguma excursão/visita guiada a...? [algooma – veezeeta gee-ada]

tour guide (man/woman) o/a guia turístico/turística [gee-a tooreesteekoo]

tourist (man/woman) o/a turista [tooreesta]

tourist information office centro de informação turística [sayntroo dee infohrmasowng tooreesteeka]

tour operator agência de viagem [aJayns-ya dee v-yaJayng]

towards para, em direção a [ayng deeraysowng a]

towel a toalha [twal-ya]

town a cidade [seedadee]
in town na cidade
just out of town junto à
cidade [Joontwa]
town centre o centro da cidade
[sayntroo]
town hall a prefeitura
[prayfaytoora]
toy o brinquedo [breenkaydoo]
track (US) a plataforma
see platform
tracksuit a roupa de ginástica
[Hohpa dee Jeenasteeka]
traditional tradicional [tradis-
yohnal]
traffic o trânsito [tranzeetoo]
traffic jam o engarrafamento
[ayngaHafamayntoo]
traffic lights o semáforo
[saymafohroo]
trailer (for carrying tent etc) o
trailer
trailer park o acampamento de
trailer [akampamaynto dee]
train o trem [trayng]
by train de trem [dee]

dialogue

is this the train for...? é este
o trem para...? [eh ayste]
sure sim [seeng]
no, you want that platform
there não, você deve ir
para aquela plataforma
[nowng vohsay dehvee eer]

trainers (shoes) os tênis
[taynees]

train station a estação de trem
[aystasowng dee trayng]
tram o bonde [bohndee]
translate traduzir [tradoozeer]
could you translate that?
poderia traduzir isto?
[podayree-a – eestoo]
translation a tradução
[tradoosowng]
translator (man/woman) o
tradutor [tradootohr], a
tradutora
trash (waste) o lixo [leeshoo]
trashcan a lata de lixo [dee]
travel viajar [v-yaJar]
we're travelling around
estamos viajando por aí
travel agent's a agência de
viagens [aJayns-ya di v-yaJayngs]
traveller's cheque o cheque de
viagem [shehkee dee v-yaJayng]
tray a bandeja [bandayJa]
tree a árvore [arvohree]
tremendous tremendo
[traymayndoo]
trendy da moda
trim: just a trim, please (to
hairdresser) queria só cortar as
pontas, por favor [keeree-a saw
kohrtar as pontas poor favohr]
trip (excursion) a excursão
[ayskoorsowng]
I'd like to go on a trip to...
gostaria de fazer uma
excursão para... [gohstaree-a
dee fazayr ooma]
trolley o carrinho [kaHeen-yoo]
trouble: I'm having trouble
with... tenho tido problemas

com... [tayn-yoo teedoo prohblaymas kohng]
trousers a calça [kalsa]
true verdadeiro [vayrdadayroo]
  that's not true não é verdade [nowng eh vayrdadee]
trunk (US: of car) o porta-malas
trunks (swimming) o calção de banho [kalsowng dee ban-yoo]
try experimentar [ayspay-reemayntar], provar [prohvar]
  can I try it? posso experimentar? [posoo]
  (food) posso provar?
try on experimentar, provar
  can I try it on? posso experimentar?
T-shirt a camiseta [kameezayta]
Tuesday terça-feira [tayrsa fayra]
tuna o atum [atoong]
tunnel o túnel [toonil]
turn: turn left/right vire à esquerda/direita [veeree a eeskayrda/deerayta]
turn off: where do I turn off? onde devo virar? [ohndee dayvoo]
  can you turn the heating off? pode desligar o aquecimento? [podee deesleegar oo akayseemayntoo]
turn on: can you turn the heating on? pode ligar o aquecimento?
turning (in road) a curva [koorva]
TV TV [tay-vay]
tweezers a pinça [peensa]
twice duas vezes [doo-as vayzees]

twice as much o dobro [dohbroo]
twin beds as camas separadas [kamas sayparadas]
twin room o quarto com duas camas [kwartoo kohng doo-as]
twist: I've twisted my ankle torci o tornozelo [tohrsee oo tohrnohzayloo]
type o tipo [teepoo]
  a different type of... um tipo diferente de... [oong – deefayrayntee dee]
typical típico [teepeekoo]
tyre o pneu [pnay-oo]

U

ugly feio [fay-oo]
UK Reino Unido [Haynooneedoo]
ulcer a úlcera [oolsayra]
umbrella o guarda-chuva [gwarda shoova]
uncle o tio [tee-oo]
unconscious inconsciente [inkohns-yayntee]
under (in position) sob, embaixo, debaixo [sohb, aymbishoo, daybishoo]
  (less than) menos de [maynoos dee]
underdone (meat) malpassado [pasadoo]
underground (railway) o metrô [maytroh]
underpants as cuecas [kwehkas]
understand: I understand eu

compreendo [**ay**-oo kohmpr-**yayn**doo]
I don't understand não compreendo [nowng]
do you understand? você compreende? [vohs**ay** kompr-**yayn**dee]
unemployed desempregado [dayzaymprayg**a**doo]
United States os Estados Unidos [ayst**a**dooz oon**ee**doos]
university a universidade [ooneevayrseed**a**dee]
unleaded petrol a gasolina sem chumbo [gazool**ee**na sayng sh**oo**mboo]
unlimited mileage quilometragem ilimitada [keelohmaytr**a**Jayng eeleemeet**a**da]
unlock abrir [ab**ree**r]
unpack desfazer a mala [deesfaz**ay**r a m**a**la]
until até [at**eh**]
unusual incomum [inkohm**oo**ng]
up cima [**see**ma]
up there lá em cima [ayng **see**ma]
he's not up yet (not out of bed) ele ainda não se levantou [**ay**lee a-**ee**nda nowng see lav-ant**oh**]
what's up? (what's wrong?) o que há? [oo kee a]
upmarket sofisticado [sohfeesteek**a**doo]
upset stomach indisposição estomacal [indeespohzees**ow**ng eestohmak**a**l]

upside down de pernas para o ar [dee p**eh**rnas proo ar]
upstairs em cima [ayng **see**ma]
urgent urgente [oorJ**ay**ntee]
us* nós [nos]
with us conosco [kohn**oh**skoo]
for us para nós [nos]
USA os EUA, Estados Unidos [ayst**a**dooz oon**ee**doos]
use usar [ooz**ar**]
may I use...? posso usar...? [**po**soo]
useful útil [**oo**til]
usual comum [kohm**oo**ng], usual [**oo**zwal]
the usual (drink etc) o de sempre [oo dee **saym**pree]

V

vacancy: do you have any vacancies? (hotel) há vagas? [a v**a**gas]
vacation as férias [**feh**r-yas]
on vacation em férias [ayng]
vaccination a vacinação [vaseenas**ow**ng]
vacuum cleaner o aspirador de pó [aspeerad**oh**r dee paw]
valid (ticket etc) válido [v**a**leedoo]
how long is it valid for? até quando é válido? [at**eh** kw**a**ndoo eh]
valley o vale [v**a**lee]
valuable (adj) valioso [val-y**oh**zoo]
can I leave my valuables

here? posso deixar aqui meus objetos de valor? [**po**soo dayshar a**kee may**-oos ob**jeh**toos dee valohr]

value o valor

van a van

vanilla a baunilha [bow**nee**l-ya]

a vanilla ice cream um sorvete de baunilha [oong sohr**vay**tee dee]

vary: it varies isso depende [**ee**soo day**payn**dee]

vase o vaso [**va**zoo]

veal a vitela [vee**teh**la]

vegetables os legumes [lay**goo**mees]; as verduras [vayr**doo**ras]

vegetarian (man/woman) o vegetariano [vay**jay**tar-y**a**noo], a vegetariana

vending machine a máquina de vendas [**ma**keena dee **vayn**das]

very muito [m**ween**gtoo]

very little for me muito pouco para mim [**poh**koo para meeng]

I like it very much gosto muito disso [**gos**too – **dee**soo]

vest (under shirt) a camiseta [kamee**zay**ta]

via via [**vee**-a]

video (film) o vídeo [**veed**-yoo]

video recorder o gravador de vídeo [grava**dohr** dee]

view a vista [**vees**ta]

villa a mansão [man**sowng**]

vinegar o vinagre [vee**na**gree]

vineyard a vinha [**veen**-ya], o vinhedo [veen-**yay**doo]

visa o visto [**vees**too]

visit visitar [veezee**tar**]

I'd like to visit... gostaria de visitar... [gohsta**ree**-a dee]

vital: it's vital that... é vital que... [eh vee**tal** kee]

vodka a vodca [**vo**dca]

voice a voz [vos]

voltage a voltagem [voh**lta**jayng]

vomit vomitar [voomee**tar**]

W

waist a cintura [seen**too**ra]

waistcoat o colete [koh**lay**tee]

wait esperar [ayspay**rar**]

wait for me espere por mim [ayspe**hree** poor meeng]

don't wait for me não espere por mim [nowng]

can I wait until my wife/partner gets here? posso esperar até minha mulher/companheira chegar? [**po**soo eespay**rar** ateh meen-ya mool-**yehr**/kohmpan-**yay**ra shay**gar**]

can you do it while I wait? pode fazer isso enquanto espero? [**po**dee fa**zayr ee**soo aynk**wan**too eespe**hroo**]

could you wait here for me? poderia me esperar aqui? [poday**ree**-a mee ayspay**rar** a**kee**]

waiter o garçom [gar**sohng**]

waiter! garçom!

waitress a garçonete [garsoh-**neh**tee]

waitress! garçonete!

wake: can you wake me up at 5.30? pode me acordar às cinco meia? [podee mee akohrdar as seenkwee may-a]

wake-up call a chamada para despertar [shamada para deespayrtar]

Wales o País de Gales [pa-ees dee galees]

walk: is it a long walk? é uma caminhada longa? [eh ooma kameen-yada longa]

it's only a short walk é uma caminhada curta [koorta]

I'll walk vou a pé [voh a peh]

I'm going for a walk vou dar um passeio [oong pasay-oo]

Walkman o walkman

wall (outside) o muro [mooroo] (inside) a parede [paraydee]

wallet a carteira [kartayra]

wander: I like just wandering around gosto de perambular por aí [gostoo dee payramboolar poor a-ee]

want: I want a... queria um... [keeree-a oong]

I don't want any... não quero... [nowng kehroo]

I want to go home quero ir para casa [eer para kaza]

I don't want to não quero

he wants to ele quer [aylee kehr]

what do you want? o que você quer? [oo kee vohsay kehr]

ward (in hospital) a enfermaria [aynfayrmaree-a]

warm quente [kayntee]

I'm so warm estou com tanto calor [aystoh kohng tantoo kalohr]

was*: he was (ele) era [(ayle) ehra]; (ele) estava [aystava]

she was (ela) era [(ehla)]; (ela) estava

it was era; estava

wash lavar (oneself) lavar-se [–see]

can you wash these? pode lavar isto? [podee – eestoo]

washer (for bolt etc) a arruela [aHwehla]

washhand basin a pia [pee-a]

washing (clothes) a roupa para lavar [Hohpa]

washing machine a máquina de lavar roupas [makeena dee]

washing powder o detergente em pó [day-tayrJayntee]

washing-up liquid o detergente líquido [leekeedoo]

wasp a vespa [vayspa]

watch (wristwatch) o relógio (de pulso) [Hay-loJ-yoo (dee poolsoo)]

will you watch my things for me? pode dar uma olhada nas minhas coisas? [podee dar ooma ohl-yada nas meen-yas koh-izas]

watch out! cuidado! [kwidadoo]

watch strap a pulseira de relógio [poolsayra dee Hay-loJ-yoo]

water a água [**a**gwa]
  may I have some water?
  pode me dar um pouco
  de água? [**po**dee mee dar oong
  p**oh**koo dee **a**gwa]
waterproof (adj) impermeável
  [impayrmay-**a**vil]
waterskiing o esqui aquático
  [**a**yskee akwat**ee**koo]
wave (in sea) a onda [**oh**nda]
way: it's this way é por aqui
  [eh poor ak**ee**]
  it's that way é por ali [al**ee**]
  is it a long way to...? é muito
  longe até...? [m**wee**ngtoo
  l**oh**nJee at**eh**]
  no way! de jeito nenhum! [dee
  J**ay**too nayn-y**oo**ng]

dialogue

  could you tell me the way
  to...? pode me indicar o
  caminho para...? [**po**dee
  mind**ee**kar oo kam**ee**n-yoo]
  go straight on until you
  reach the traffic lights siga
  em frente até chegar ao
  semáforo [**see**gayng fr**ay**ntee
  at**eh** sh**ay**gar ow saymaf**oh**roo]
  turn left vire à esquerda
  [v**ee**ree a ayk**ay**rda]
  take the first on the right
  pegue a primeira à direita
  [**peh**gee a preem**ay**ra dir**ay**ta]
  see where

we* nós [nos]
weak fraco [fr**a**koo]

weather o tempo [**tay**mpoo]

dialogue

  what's the weather
  forecast? qual é a previsão
  do tempo? [kwal**eh** a
  prayveez**ow**ng doo **tay**mpoo]
  it's going to be fine vai
  fazer tempo bom [vi faz**ayr**
  – bohng]
  it's going to rain vai chover
  [shohv**ayr**]
  it'll brighten up later vai
  melhorar mais tarde [mayl-
  yohr**ar** m**ī**s t**a**rdee]

wedding o casamento
  [kazam**ay**ntoo]
wedding ring a aliança [al-y**a**nsa]
Wednesday quarta-feira
  [kwarta f**ay**ra]
week a semana [saym**a**na]
  a week (from) today de hoje
  a uma semana [dee **oh**Jee a
  ooma]
  a week (from) tomorrow de
  amanhã a uma semana [dee
  aman-y**a**ng]
weekend o fim de semana
  [feeng dee]
  at the weekend no fim de
  semana [noo]
weight o peso [**pay**zoo]
weird esquisito [ayskeez**ee**too]
  he's weird ele é esquisito
  [**ay**lee eh]
welcome: welcome to... bem-
  vindo a... [bayng v**een**doo]

you're welcome (don't mention it) não tem de quê [nowng tayng dee kay]

well: I don't feel well não me sinto bem [mee **see**ntoo bayng]

she's not well ela não está bem [**eh**la – eesta]

you speak English very well você fala inglês muito bem [vo**say** – ingl**ays** m**wee**ngtoo bayng]

well done! muito bem!

this one as well este também [**ays**tee tambayng]

well well! (surprise) veja só! [**vay**Ja saw]

dialogue

how are you? como vai? [**koh**mo vī]

very well, thanks, and you? (said by man/woman) muito bem, obrigado(a), e você? [m**wee**ngto bayng ohbreeg**a**doo – ee voh**say**]

well-done (meat) bem passado [bayng pas**a**doo]

Welsh galês [gal**ays**]

I'm Welsh (man/woman) sou galês(esa) [soh – gal**ay**za]

were*: we were éramos [**eh**ramoos]; estávamos [ayst**a**vamoos]

you were você era [voh**say eh**ra]; você estava [ayst**a**va]

they were eles/elas eram [aylees/**eh**las **eh**rowng]; eles/elas

estavam [ayst**a**vowng]

west o oeste [oh-**eh**stee]

in the west no oeste [noo]

West Indian (adj) caribenho [kareeb**ayn**-yoo]

wet molhado [mohl-y**a**doo]

what? o quê? [oo kay]

what's that? o que é isso? [oo k-yeh **ee**soo]

what should I do? o que devo fazer? [oo kee d**ay**voo faz**ayr**]

what a view! que vista! [kee v**ee**sta]

what bus do I take? que ônibus devo tomar? [kee **oh**neeboos d**ay**voo toh**mar**]

wheel a roda [**H**oda]

wheelchair a cadeira de rodas [kad**ay**ra dee h**o**das]

when? quando? [kw**a**ndoo]

when we get back quando nós voltarmos [nos vohlt**a**rmoos]

when's the ferry/train? quando sai o ferryboat/o trem? [sī o trayng]

where? onde? [**oh**ndee]

I don't know where it is não sei onde está [nowng say **oh**ndee eesta]

dialogue

where is the cathedral? onde fica a catedral? [**oh**ndee f**ee**ka]

it's over there fica para lá

could you show me where it is on the map? pode me mostrar onde está no

mapa? [**po**dee mee mohstrar
– e**es**ta noo mapa]
it's just here está bem aqui
[bayng ak**ee**]
see **way**

which: which bus? qual
ônibus? [kwal **oh**neeboos]

dialogue

which one? qual deles?
[kwal **day**lees]
that one aquele [ak**ay**lee]
this one? este? [**ays**tee]
no, that one não aquele ali
[nowng – al**ee**]

while: while I'm here enquanto
estou aqui [aynkw**a**ntoo eest**oh**
ak**ee**]
whisky o uísque [w**ee**skee]
white branco [br**a**nkoo]
white wine o vinho branco
[veen-yoo]
who? quem? [kayng]
who is it? quem é? [kayng eh]
the man who... o homem
que... [**o**mayng kee]
whole: the whole week a
semana toda [saym**a**na **toh**da]
the whole lot tudo isto [**too**doo
eestoo]
whose: whose is this? de
quem é isto? [dee kayng eh
eestoo]
why? por quê? [poork**ay**]
why not? por que não?
[nowng]

wide largo [**la**rgoo]
wife: my wife a minha mulher
[**meen**-ya mool-y**ehr**]
will*: will you do it for me?
você pode fazer isso para
mim? [vohs**ay** podee faz**ay**r
eesoo – meeng]
wind o vento [**vay**ntoo]
window a janela [Jan**eh**la]
(of shop) a vitrine [veetr**ee**nee]
near the window perto da
janela [**pehr**too]
in the window (of shop) na
vitrine
window seat o lugar na janela
[loog**ar** na Jan**eh**la]
windscreen o pára-brisa
[para-br**ee**za]
windscreen wiper o limpador
de pára-brisa [**lee**mpador dee
para br**ee**za]
windsurfing o windsurfe
windy: it's so windy está
ventando muito [ayst**a**
vaynt**a**ndoo mw**ee**ngtoo]
wine o vinho [**veen**-yoo]
can we have some more
wine? poderia nos trazer
mais vinho? [podar**ee**-a noos
traz**ay**r mis]
wine list a carta de vinhos
[**ka**rta de v**een**-yoos]
winter o inverno [inv**ehr**noo]
in the winter no inverno
[noo]
winter holiday as férias de
inverno [**fehr**-yas dinv**ehr**noo]
wire o arame [ar**a**mee]
(electric) o fio [**fee**-oo]

127

wish: best wishes com os melhores cumprimentos [kohng oos mayl-yorees koompreemayntoos]

with com [kohng]

I'm staying with... estou na casa de... [aystoh na kaza dee]

without sem [sayng]

witness a testemunha [taystaymoon-ya]

will you be a witness for me? quer ser minha testemunha? [kehr sayr meen-ya]

woman a mulher [mool-yehr]

wonderful (weather, holiday, person) maravilhoso [maraveel-yohzoo] (meal) excelente [aysaylayntee]

won't*: it won't start não pega [nowng pehga]

wood (material) a madeira [madayra]

woods (forest) o bosque [boskee]

wool a lã [lang]

word a palavra [palavra]

work o trabalho [trabal-yoo] it's not working não funciona [nowng foons-yohna] I work in... trabalho em... [ayng]

world o mundo [moondoo]

worry: I'm worried (said by man/woman) estou preocupado/preocupada [aystoh pray-ohkoopadoo]

worse: it's worse está pior [aysta p-yor]

worst o pior [oo]

worth: is it worth a visit? vale uma visita? [valee ooma veezeeta]

would: would you give this to...? poderia dar isto a...? [pohdayree-a dar eestwa]

wrap: could you wrap it up? pode embrulhá-lo? [aymbrool-yaloo]

wrapping paper o papel de embrulho [papehl dee aymbrool-yoo]

wrist o pulso [poolsoo]

write escrever [ayskrayvayr] could you write it down? pode escrever isso? [podee – eesoo] how do you write it? como se escreve isso? [kohmoo see ayskrehvee]

writing paper o papel de carta [papehl dee]

wrong: it's the wrong key não é esta chave [nowng eh ehsta shavee] this is the wrong bus não é este ônibus [aystee ohneeboos] the bill's wrong a conta está errada [kohnta eesta ayHada] sorry, wrong number desculpe, disquei o número errado [deeskoolpee deeskay oo noomayroo ayHadoo] sorry, wrong room desculpe, eu me enganei de quarto [ay-oo mee aynganay dee kwartoo] there's something wrong with... há algo errado com... [a algoo ayHadoo kohng] what's wrong? o que está errado? [oo keesta]

128

X

X-ray os raios X [**Ha**-yoos shees]

Y

yacht o iate [**ya**tee]
yard* a jarda [**J**arda]
year o ano [**a**noo]
yellow amarelo [amar**eh**loo]
yes sim [seeng]
yesterday ontem [**oh**ntayng]
  yesterday morning ontem de
  manhã [dee man-**ya**ng]
  the day before yesterday
  anteontem [antee-**oh**ntayng]
yet ainda [a-**ee**nda], já [**J**a]

dialogue

is it here yet? já está aqui?
[**J**a eesta ak**ee**]
no, not yet não, ainda não
[nowng a-**ee**nda nowng]
you'll have to wait a little
longer yet ainda terá de
esperar um pouquinho
[tay**ra** dee ayspay**ra**r oong
pohk**ee**n-yoo]

yoghurt o iogurte [yohg**oo**rtee]
you* você [voh**say**]; tu [too]
(more formal: to man/woman) o
senhor [oo sayn-**yoh**r], a sen**h**ora
this is for you isto é para você
[**ee**stoo eh para voh**say**]; isto é
para ti

with you com você [kohng
voh**say**]; contigo [kohnt**ee**goo]
young jovem [**J**ovayng]
your* seu [**say**-oo], sua [**soo**-a];
teu [**tay**-oo], tua [**too**-a]
(more formal: to man/woman) do
senhor [sayn-**yoh**r], da senhora
[sayn-y**ora**]
yours* seu [**say**-oo], sua [**soo**-a];
teu [**tay**-oo], tua [**too**-a]
(more formal: to a man/woman)
do senhor [doo sayn-**yoh**r], da
senhora [sayn-y**ora**]
youth hostel o albergue
da juventude [alb**eh**rgee da
Joovaynt**oo**dee]

Z

zero zero [**zeh**roo]
zip o zíper [**zee**payr]
  could you put a new zip on?
  pode pôr um zíper novo?
  [**po**dee pohr oong – **no**hvoo]
zipcode o código postal (CEP)
[**ko**deegoo postal]
zoo o jardim zoológico
[Jard**ee**ng zoh-ohlo**J**eekoo]
zucchini a abobrinha
[abobr**ee**n-ya]

Zu

Portuguese

→

English

Colloquialisms

The following are words you might well hear. You shouldn't be tempted to use any of the stronger ones unless you are sure of your audience.

babaca [babaka] silly
biruta [beeroota] nutter
burro m [booHoo] thickhead
cai fora! [kī fora] go away!
cara/sujeito m [kara/sooJaytoo] bloke
chateação [shat-yasowng] bother
corta essa! [korta ehsa] don't be stupid!
de saco cheio [dee sakoo shayoo] pissed
está à vontade [eesta vohntadee] he's/she's in his/her element
estou me lixando [eestoh mee leeshandoo] I don't give a damn
excelente! [aysaylayntee] bloody good!
fantástico! [fantasteekoo] fantastic!
filho da mãe! [feel-yoo da mayng] bastard!
filho da puta! [da poota] son-of-a-bitch!
foda-se! [fohdasee] fuck off!
fora daqui! [fora dakee] get out of here!
imbecil [imbayseel] stupid
isso é bico [eesweh beekoo] piece of cake
maluco [malookoo] barmy, nuts
merda! [mehrda] shit!
não faz mal [nowng fas mal] it doesn't matter
não diga! [nowng deega] you don't say!
que absurdo! [kee absoordoo] rubbish!, nonsense!
que droga! [droga] blast!
que saco! [sakoo] oh no!, blast!
sacana! bastard!
vá para o diabo! [va paroo d-yaboo] go to hell!
vá para o inferno! [infehrno] go to hell!
vá se danar! [see danar] damn you!

A

a the; to; her; it; to it; you
à to the
a/c c/o
abaixo [abīshoo] below; down
  mais abaixo [mīs] further
  down
abcesso m [absehsoo] abscess
aberto [abehrtoo] open; opened
  aberto até as 19 horas open
  until 7 p.m.
  aberto das... às... horas open
  from... to... o'clock
abertura f [abayrtoora] opening
aborrecer [aboh-Haysayr] to
  bore
aborrecido [aboh-Hayseedoo]
  bored
abridor de garrafa m [abreedohr
  dee gaHafa] bottle-opener
abridor de lata m [abreedohr dee
  lata] can-opener, tin-opener
abril m [abreel] April
abrir [abreer] to open; to
  unlock
absorventes higiênicos mpl
  [absohrvayntees iJ-yayneekoos]
  sanitary towels
acabado [akabadoo] over;
  finished
acabar [akabar] to finish
acalmar-se [akalmarsee] to calm
  down
acampar [akampar] to camp
acaso: por acaso [poor akazoo]
  by chance

aceitar [asaytar] to accept; to
  take
acelerador m [asaylayradohr]
  accelerator
acender [asayndayr] to switch
  on; to light
  acenda o farol baixo switch
  on dipped headlights
  acenda o pisca-alerta switch
  on your parking lights
acento m [asayntoo] accent
aceso [asayzoo] on, switched
  on
acesso m [asehsoo] access
acetona f [asaytohna] nail
  polish remover
achados e perdidos mpl
  [ashadoos ee payrdeedoos] lost
  property, lost and found
acho: acho que não [ashoo kee
  nowng] I don't think so
  acho que sim [seeng] I think
  so
acidente m [aseedayntee]
  accident; crash
acidente rodoviário [Hohdohvee-
  ar-yoo] road accident
ácido [asidoo] sour; sharp
acima [aseema] up; above
acompanhar [akohmpan-yar] to
  accompany
aconselhar [akohnsayl-yar] to
  advise
acontecer [akohntaysayr] to
  happen
  o que aconteceu? [oo kee-akohn-
  taysay-oo] what has happened?,
  what's up?, what's wrong?

o que está acontecendo? [oo keesta akohntaysayndoo] what's happening?

acordado [akohrdadoo] awake

acordar [akohrdar] to wake, to wake up

ele já acordou? [aylee Ja akohrdoh] is he awake?

acordo: de acordo com [d-ya-kohrdoo kohng] according to

açougue m [asohgee] butcher's shop

acreditar [akraydeetar] to believe

acriano m [akree-ano] born or living at Acre

acrílico m [akreeleekoo] acrylic

adaptador m [adaptadohr] adapter

adega f [adehga] cellar; old-style bar

adeus [aday-oos] goodbye

adiantado [ad-yantadoo] in advance

adiante: fica ali adiante [feekalee ad-yantee] it's over there

adoecer [adwaysayr] to fall ill

adolescente m/f [adohlaysayntee] teenager

adorar [adohrar] to adore

adulta f [adoolta], **adulto** m [adooltoo] adult

advogada f [advohgada], **advogado** m [advohgadoo] lawyer

aeroporto m [a-ehrohpohrtoo] airport

afastado [afastadoo] secluded

afiado [af-yadoo] sharp

afogador m [afohgadohr] choke

África f Africa

África do Sul [doo sool] South Africa

africano m [afreekanoo] African

afta f mouth ulcer

afundar [afoondar] to sink

agência f [aJayns-ya] agency

agência de turismo [dee tooreesmoo] tour operator

agência de viagens [dee v-ya-Jayngs] travel agency

agência do correio [doo koh-Hay-oo] post office

agenda f [aJaynda] diary

agitar: agitar bem antes de usar shake well before using

agora [agora] now

agora não [nowng] not just now

agosto [agohstoo] August

agradável [agradavil] nice, pleasant

agradecer [agradaysayr] to thank

agradecido [agradayseedoo] grateful

agricultor m [agreekooltohr] farmer

água f [agwa] water

água-de-colônia [dee kohlohn-ya] eau de toilette

água destilada [agwa daysteelada] distilled water

água fria [free-a] cold water

água potável [pohtavil] drinking water

aguardar [agwardar] to wait for

água-viva f [**vee**va] jellyfish
agudo [a**goo**doo] sharp
agulha f [a**goo**l-ya] needle
aí [a-**ee**] there
aids f AIDS
ainda [a-**een**da] yet, still
 ainda mais... [mīs] even
 more...
 ainda não [nowng] not yet
 ainda são só... [sowng saw] it's
 only...
ajuda f [a**Joo**da] help
ajudar to help
alagoano m [alagwanoo] born or
 living at Alagoas
alarme m [a**lar**mee] alarm
alarme de incêndio [dinsaynd-
 yoo] fire alarm
alavanca f lever
alavanca de câmbio [dee kamb-
 yo] gear lever
albergue da juventude m
 [al**beh**rgee da Joovaynt**oo**dee]
 youth hostel
alça f [**al**sa] strap
aldeia f [al**day**-a] village
aldeia de pescadores [dee
 payskad**oh**rees] fishing village
além: além de [a**layng** dee] apart
 from
 para além de [paral**ayng**]
 beyond
alemã f [alaymang] German
Alemanha f [alayman-ya]
 Germany
alemão m [alaym**owng**] German
alérgico a... [a**lehr**Jeekoo]
 allergic to...
alfabeto m [alfab**eh**too] alphabet

alfaiataria f [alfi-atar**ee**-a],
 alfaiate m [alfi-**atee**] tailor
alfândega f [al**fan**dayga]
 Customs
alfinete m [alfeen**ay**tee] brooch;
 pin
alfinete de segurança [dee
 saygoo**ran**sa] safety pin
alga f seaweed
algodão m [algohd**owng**] cotton
algodão em rama [ayng Hama]
 cotton wool
alguém [alg**ayng**] anybody;
 somebody, someone
algum [alg**oo**ng] some; any
 em algum lugar [ayng loogar]
 somewhere
alguma [alg**oo**ma] some; any
 alguma coisa [koh-iza]
 something; anything
algumas [alg**oo**mas] some; any
alguns [alg**oo**ns] some; any
ali [al**ee**] (over) there
 ali adiante [ad-yantee] over
 there
 ali em cima [ayng seema] up
 there
 é por ali [eh poor] it's that way
aliança f [al-yansa] wedding
 ring
alicate m [alikatee] pliers
alicate de unhas [dee oon-yas]
 nail clippers
alimento m [aleem**ayn**too] food
almoçar [almohsar] to have
 lunch
almoço m [alm**oh**soo] lunch
almofada f [almohfada] cushion
alô! [al**oh**] hello!

alpinismo m [alpeen**ee**smoo] mountaineering

altitude f [alteet**oo**dee] height

alto [**al**too] high; tall; loud

no alto [noo] at the top

altura f [alt**oo**ra] height

altura máxima maximum headroom

alugar [aloo**gar**] to hire, to rent

aluga-se [al**oo**gasee] for hire, to rent

alugam-se quartos rooms to let, rooms for rent

aluguel m rent

aluguel de barcos [dee b**ar**koos] boat hire

aluguel de cadeiras [kad**ay**ras] beach chairs for hire

aluguel de carros [ka**Hoo**s] car hire, car rental

aluguel de guarda-sóis [gwarda soys] sunshades for hire

aluguel de pedalinhos [paydal**ee**n-yoos] pedal boat hire

alvejante m [alvay**Jan**tee] bleach

amamentar [amamayn**tar**] to breastfeed

amanhã [aman-**yang**] tomorrow

amanhã à tarde [**tar**dee] tomorrow afternoon

amanhã de manhã [dee man-**yang**] tomorrow morning

amanhecer m [aman-yays**ayr**] dawn

amapaense m/f [amapa-**ayn**see] born or living at Amapá

amar to love

amarelo [amar**eh**loo] yellow

amargo [a**mar**goo] bitter

amável [a**ma**vil] kind; generous

amazonense m/f [amazohn**ayn**see] born or living at Amazonas

ambos [**am**boos] both

ambulância f [amboo**lans**-ya] ambulance

ameno [a**may**noo] mild

América f [a**meh**reeka] America

americano m [amayreek**an**oo] American

amiga f [am**ee**ga] friend

amigdalite f [ameegdal**ee**tee] tonsillitis

amigo m [am**ee**goo] friend

amistoso [amees**toh**zoo] friendly

amor m [a**mohr**] love

amortecedor m [amohrtaysayd**ohr**] shock-absorber

ampères mpl [am**peh**rees] amps

ampliação f [ampl-yas**owng**] enlargement

analgésicos mpl [analJ**eh**zeekoos] painkillers

âncora f [**an**kohra] anchor

andar m floor, storey; surface

andar superior [soopayr-y**ohr**] top floor

andar (verb) to walk; to ride

andar a cavalo [ka**va**loo] horse-riding

andar a pé [peh] to walk

ande! go!, walk!

anel m [an**eh**l] ring

animado [anee**ma**doo] lively

aniversário m [aneevayrsar-yoo] birthday

aniversário de casamento m [dee kazam**ayn**too] wedding anniversary

ano m [**a**noo] year

Ano-Novo [**noh**voo] New Year

anteontem [antee-**oh**ntayng] the day before yesterday

antepassado [antaypa**s**ado] m ancestor

anterior: dia anterior m [**d**ee-a antayr-y**ohr**] the day before

antes [**a**ntees] before

antibióticos mpl [anteeb-**yo**teekoos] antibiotics

anticoncepcional m [antee-kohnsayps-yohna**l**] contraceptive

antidiarréico m [anteed-ya**H**aykoo] medicine for diarrhoea

antigo [ant**ee**goo] ancient, old

antiguidade f [anteegeed**a**dee] antique

anti-histamínicos mpl [–eestam**ee**neekoos] antihistamines

antiquado [anteekw**a**doo] old-fashioned

antiquário m [anteekw**a**r-yoo] antique shop

anti-séptico m [–**seh**pteekoo] antiseptic

anúncio m [an**oo**ns-yoo] advertisement

ao [ow] to the; at the
  ao norte de north of
  ao ar livre [**lee**vree] outdoors

aos [ows] to the; at the

apagar to switch off
  apagar o farol alto switch headlights off

apanhar [apan-**yar**] to get on, to catch

aparelho m [apar**ayl**-yoo] device

aparelho auditivo [owdeet**ee**voo] hearing aid

aparelho de som [dee sohng)] stereo; audio equipment

aparelho para a surdez [para soord**ays**] hearing aid

apartamento m [apartam**ay**ntoo] apartment, flat

apart-hotel m [apartee oht**ehl**] self-catering apartment

apelido m [apayl**ee**doo] nickname

apendicite f [apayndees**ee**tee] appendicitis

apertado [apayrt**a**doo] tight (for clothes)

apertar [apayrt**ar**]to hold tight; to fasten

apetite m [apayt**ee**tee] appetite

apimentado [peek**a**ntee] hot, spicy

apinhado [apeen-**ya**doo] crowded

aposentada f [apohz**a**ynt**a**da] pensioner; retired

aposentado m [apohz**a**ynt**a**doo] pensioner; retired

aprender [apraynd**ayr**] to learn

apresentar [aprayz**a**ynt**ar**] to introduce

apressar-se [apraysa**rsee**] to hurry
  ande logo! [andee l**o**goo] hurry up!

aproximadamente [aprohseemadam**ay**ntee] approximately, roughly

aquecedor m [akaysayd**oh**r] heater

aquecedor elétrico
[aylehtreekoo] electric fire

aquecimento m
[akayseemayntoo] heating

aquecimento central [sayntral]
central heating

aquela [akehla]**, aquele** [akaylee]
that, that one (further away)

aquelas [akehlas]**, aqueles**
[akaylees] those (further away)

aqui [akee] (over) here

aqui embaixo [aymbishoo]
down here

aqui está/estão... [eesta/
eestowng] here is/are...

aqui mesmo [maysmoo] just
here

bem aqui [bayng] just here

é por aqui [eh por] it's this way

aquilo [akeeloo] that; that one
(further away)

ar m air

árabe [arabee] Arab; Arabic

os árabes the Arabs

arame m [aramee] wire

aranha f [aran-ya] spider

arco-íris m [arkoo eerees]
rainbow

ar-condicionado m [kohndees-
yohnadoo] air conditioning

área [ar-ya] area

**área para não-fumantes
f** [nowng foomantees]
nonsmoking area

areia f [aray-a] sand

arma de fogo f [dee fohgoo] gun

armarinho f [armareen-yoo]
haberdasher

armário m [armar-yoo] cupboard

armário com chave m [kohng
shavee] locker

armazém m [armazayng]
warehouse

aroma artificial/natural
[arteefees-yal] artificial/natural
fragrance

arqueologia f [ark-yohloh-Jee-a]
archaeology

arquiteto m [arkeetehtoo]
architect

arranhão m [arran-yowng]
scratch

arrebentado [araybayntadoo]
burst

arredores mpl [aHaydorees]
suburb

arriscado [aHiskadoo] risky

arruela f [aHwehla] washer

arte f [artee] art

artesanato m [artayzanatoo]
handicrafts, crafts

artificial [arteefees-yal] artificial

artigos de cortiça [arteegoos dee
kohrteesa] cork goods

artigos de couro [kohroo]
leather goods

artigos de luxo [looshoo]
luxury goods

artigos de pele [pehlee] leather
goods

artigos de viagem [v-yaJayng]
travel goods

artigos esportivos
[eespohrteevoos] sports goods

artigos para bebês [baybays]
baby goods

artista m/f [arteesta] artist

árvore f [arvohree] tree

as [as] the; them; you

às to the; at the

asa f [**a**za] wing

asa-delta f [-d**eh**lta] hang-gliding

asma f asthma

aspirador de pó m [aspeerad**ohr** dee paw] vacuum cleaner

aspirina f [aspeer**ee**na] aspirin

assaltado [asalt**a**doo] mugged

assar to bake; to roast

assento m [as**ay**ntoo] seat

assim [as**ee**ng] this way

  assim está bem [eest**a** bayng] that'll do nicely

  assim está bem? is that OK?

assinado [aseen**a**doo] signed

assinar [asee**nar**]to sign

assinatura f [aseenat**oo**ra] signature

atadura f [atad**oo**ra] dressing (for wounds)

atalho m [at**a**l-yoo] shortcut

ataque m [at**a**kee] fit; attack

ataque cardíaco [kard**ee**-akoo] heart attack

até [at**eh**] until

  até amanhã [aman-y**a**ng] see you tomorrow

  até já [Ja] see you soon

  até logo! [**lo**goo] see you!, see you later!

  até mesmo... [m**ay**smoo] even...

atenção [ataynso**w**ng] please note; caution; warning

aterrissagem f [atay-Hee-sa**Ja**yng] landing

aterrissar [atay-Hee-s**ar**] to land

atirar [atee**rar**] to throw

Atlântico m Atlantic

atletismo m [atlayte**ee**smoo] athletics

ator m [at**ohr**] actor

atração noturna [atras**ow**ng noht**oo**rna] evening performance

atrações turísticas de... [atras**oy**ngs tooreest**ee**kas] the sights of...

atraente [atra-**ay**ntee] attractive

atrás [atr**a**s] at the back, behind

  atrás de... [dee] behind...

atrasado [atraz**a**doo] late, delayed

  estar atrasado [eest**ar**] to be late

atraso m [atr**a**zoo] delay

através de [atrav**eh**s dee] through

atravessar [atrav**ay**sar] to go through, to cross

atriz f [atr**ee**s] actress

atropelar [atropay**lar**] to knock over, to knock down

australiano m [owstral-y**a**noo] Australian

autêntico [owt**ay**nteekoo] genuine

automático [owtohm**a**teekoo] automatic

Automóvel Clube do Brasil Brazilian Motoring Organization

av. avenue

ave f [**a**vee] bird

avenida f [avayn**ee**da] avenue

avião m [av-yowng] plane, airplane

de avião [dee av-yowng] by plane; by air

aviso [aveezoo] warning; notice

avó f [avaw] grandmother

avô m [avoh] grandfather

azedo [azaydoo] sour

ácido [aseedoo] sour

azul [azool] blue

azul-marinho [-mareen-yoo] navy blue

B
—

babá f childminder

babaca silly

bagageiro de carro [bagaJayroo dee kaHoo] roof rack

bagagem f [bagaJayng] luggage, baggage

bagagem de mão f [dee mowng] hand luggage

baía f [ba-ee-a] bay

baiano [ba-yanoo] born or living at Bahia

bairro m [bīHoo] district

baixo [bīshoo] low; short

bala sweet, candy

bala de hortelã [dee ohrtaylang] mints

balcão [balkowng] balcony; counter

balcão de informações [dinfohrmasoyngs] information desk

balcão de recepção [dee Haysaypsowng] reception desk

balde [baldee] bucket

banca de jornal [dee Johrnal] newspaper kiosk

banco m [bankoo] bank; stool

banda f band

bandagem f [bandaJayng] bandage

bandeira f [bandayra] flag

bandeja m [bandayJa] tray

banheira f [ban-yayra] bathtub, bath

banheiro m [ban-yayroo] bathroom; toilet, rest room

banheiro feminino [faymeeneenoo] ladies' toilets, ladies' room

banheiro masculino [maskooleenoo] gents' toilet, men's room

banheiro privativo [preevateevo] private bathroom

banheiro público [poobleeko] public convenience

banho m [ban-yoo] bath

barata f cockroach

barato [baratoo] cheap, inexpensive

barba f beard

barbante m [barbantee] string

barbatanas fpl [barbatanas] flippers

barbeador elétrico [barby-adohr aylehtreekoo] electric shaver

barbeiro m [barbayroo] men's hairdresser's, barber's shop

barco m [barkoo] boat

barco a motor [barkwa mohtohr] motorboat

barco a remo [Haymoo] rowing boat

barco a vapor [vapohr] steamer

barco à vela [vehla] sailing boat

barcos de aluguel [dee aloogehl] boats for hire

barraca de camping f [baHaka dee] tent

barraca de praia f [prī-a] beach hut

barulhento [barool-yayntoo] noisy

barulho m [barool-yoo] noise

barzinho m [barzeen-yoo] pub

base [bazee] foundation cream

bastante [bastantee] fairly; rather; quite (a lot)

batedor de carteira m [bataydohr dee kartayra] pickpocket

bater [batayr] to hit; to knock

bateria f [batayree-a] battery

batom m [batohng] lipstick

bêbado [baybadoo] drunk

bebê m [baybay] baby

beber [baybayr] to drink

o que vai beber? [oo kee vī] what'll you have?

bebida f [baybeeda] drink

beco sem saída m [baykoo sayng sa-eeda] cul-de-sac, dead end

bege beige

beijar [bayJar] to kiss

beijo m [bayJoo] kiss

beira: à beira-mar [bayra] at/by the sea

belga m/f Belgian

Bélgica f [behlJeeka] Belgium

beliche m [bayleeshee] berth, bunk; couchette; bunk beds

bem [bayng] fine, well, OK; properly

bem aqui [akee] right here

está bem [eesta] that's fine

está bem? are you all right?

bem passado [pasadoo] well-done

bem-educado [bayng aydookadoo] polite

bem-vindo [veendoo] welcome

bem-vindo a... welcome to...

berço m [bayrsoo] cot

besteira f [baystayra] nonsense; swearword

bexiga f [beesheega] bladder

biblioteca f [beebl-yohtehka] library

bicicleta f [beeseeklehta] bicycle, bike

bicicleta motorizada f [mohtohreezada] moped

bifurcação f [beefoorkasowng] fork (in road)

bigode m [beegodee] moustache

bilhete m [beel-yaytee] ticket

(de excursão) [diskoorsowng] excursion ticket

(de loteria) [di lohteree-a] lottery ticket

um bilhete de ida [deeda] single ticket, one-way ticket

um bilhete de ida e volta [deeda ee] return ticket, round trip ticket

um bilhete aberto [abehrtoo] open ticket

um bilhete simples m [seemplees] single ticket, one-way ticket

bilheteria f [beel-yaytayree-a] box office, ticket office

biruta [beeroota] nutter

blusa f [blooza] blouse

boa [boh-a] good

boa-noite [noh-itee] good evening; good night

boa sorte! [sohrtee] good luck!

boa-tarde [tardee] good afternoon; good evening

boa viagem! [v-yaJayng] have a good journey!

boas festas! [boh-as fehstas] merry Christmas and a happy New Year!

bobagem f [bohbaJayng] nonsense; swearword

boca f [bohka] mouth

bóia f [bo-ya] buoy

bola f ball

bola de futebol [dee footaybol] football

bolha f [bohl-ya] blister

bolinha f [boleen-ya] ball (small)

bolsa [bohlsa] handbag, (US) purse

bolso m [bohlsoo] pocket

bom [bohng] good; fine

bom apetite! [apayteetee] enjoy your meal!

bomba f [bohmba] bomb; pump

bomba de ar air pump

bomba de gasolina [dee gazohleena] petrol pump

bombeiros mpl [bohmbayroos] fire brigade

bom-dia [bohng dee-a] good morning

bondinho m [bohndeen-yoo] cable car

bondinho do Pão de Açúcar Pão de Açúcar cable car

boné m [bohneh] cap, hat

boneca f [bohnehka] doll

bonito [bohneetoo] beautiful; nice; pretty

borboleta f [bohrbohlayta] butterfly

borda f edge

borracha f [boh-Hasha] rubber; eraser

bosque m [boskee] woods, forest

bota f boot (footwear)

bota de borracha [dee boh-Hasha] wellington

botão m [bohtowng] button

botijão de gás f [bohteeJowng dee gas] gas cylinder

BR national highway sign

braço m [brasoo] arm

branco [brankoo] white

Brasil m [brazeel] Brazil

brasileiro m [brazeelayroo] Brazilian, f [brazeelayra] Brazilian

brasiliense [brazeel-yaynsee] born or living at Brasília

breve [brehvee] brief

em breve soon

bricabraque m bric-a-brac

briga f [breega] fight

brigar to fight

brilhante [breel-yantee] bright; brilliant

brincadeira f [breenkadayra] joke

brincos mpl [**breen**koos] earrings

brinquedo m [breen**kay**doo] toy

brisa f [**bree**za] breeze

británico [breet**anee**koo] British

bronquite [brohn**kee**tee] bronchitis

bronzeado m [brohn-**ya**doo] tan; suntan; suntan

bronzeador m [brohnz-yad**ohr**] suntan lotion

bronzear [brohnz-**yar**] to tan

bule de chá m [**boo**lee] teapot

buraco m [boo**ra**koo] hole

burro m [**boo**Hoo] donkey; thickhead; stupid

buscar [boo**skar**] to collect; to fetch

bússola f [**boo**soola] compass

buzina f [boo**zee**na] horn

C

c/ with

c/c current account

cá here

cabeça f [ka**bay**sa] head

cabeleireiro m [kabaylay**rayr**oo] hairdresser's

cabeleireiro feminino [faymeen**ee**noo] ladies' hairdresser

cabeleireiro masculino [maskool**ee**noo] men's hairdresser

cabeleireiro unissex [oonees**ehks**] unisex salon

cabelo m [kab**ay**loo] hair

cabelo com ponta dupla [kohng **poh**nta **doo**pla] split ends

cabide m [ka**bee**dee] coathanger

cabine f [ka**bee**ne] cabin

cabine telefônica [ka**bee**ne tele**foh**nika] phone box, phone booth

cabo handle

cabos para ligar duas baterias mpl [**ka**boos – batay**ree**-as] jump leads

cabra f goat

caça f [**ka**sa] game (meat); hunting

cachimbo m [ka**shee**mboo] pipe (for smoking)

cachorro m [ka**shoh**-Hoo] dog

cada each; every

cadeado m [kad-**ya**doo] padlock

cadeira f [ka**day**ra] chair

cadeira de rodas [Hodas] wheelchair

cadeirão de bebê [kaday**row**ng dee bay**bay**] highchair

caderno notebook

caderno de endereços [de ayndayr**ay**soos] address book

café m [ka**feh**] café; coffee

café-da-manhã m [da man-**ya**ng] breakfast

cãibra f [**kay**ngbra] cramp

cair [ka-**eer**] to fall

caia fora! [**kī**a] get out of here!

cais m [**kīs**] quay; quayside

caixa m/f [**kī**sha] box; cash desk, till; cashier; cashpoint, ATM; savings bank; building society

caixa de câmbio [dee kamb-yoo] gearbox

caixa do correio [doo koh-**Hay**-oo] postbox; mailbox

caixa de fusíveis/disjuntores [di foozeevays/deesJoont**oh**rees] fusebox

caixa eletrônico [aylaytr**oh**neekoo] cashpoint, ATM

caixa fechado m [fayshadoo] till closed

calça comprida f [kalsa kohmpreeda] trousers, (US) pants

calçada f [kalsada] pavement, sidewalk; walk

calçado m [kalsadoo] footwear

calcanhar m [kalkan-yar] heel (of foot)

calção de banho [kalsowng dee ban-yoo] swimming trunks

calcinha f [kalseen-ya] panties

calculadora f [kalkooladohra] calculator

caldeira f [kaldayra] boiler

cale a boca! [kalee a bohka] quiet!; shut up!

calendário m [kalayndar-yoo] calendar

calmo [kalmoo] calm

calor m [kalohr] heat
estou com calor [eestoh kohng] to be hot
hoje está fazendo calor [ohjee eesta fazayndoo] it's hot today

cama f [kama] bed

cama de campanha [dee kampan-ya] campbed

cama de casal [kazal] double bed

cama de solteiro [sohltayroo] single bed

câmara de ar inner tube

camareira [kamarayra] chambermaid

camarim m [kamareeng] dressing room

camarote m [kamarotee] cabin

camas separadas fpl [kamas sayparadas] twin beds

câmbio [kamb-yoo] exchange rate; gearbox

câmbio do dia [doo dee-a] current exchange rate

câmera f camera

caminhão m [kameen-yowng] truck

caminhar [kameen-yar] to walk

caminho m [kameen-yoo] path

caminhonete f [kameen-yohnehtee] light truck

camisa f [kameeza] shirt

camisaria f [kameezaree-a] shirt shop

camiseta [kameezayta] vest (under shirt)

camisola f [kameezola] nightdress

campainha f [kampa-een-ya] bell

camping camping; campsite

camping de trailer caravan site, (US) trailer park

campo m [kampoo] field; countryside, country

campo de futebol [dee footaybol] football ground

campo de golfe [golfee] golf course

camundongo m
[kamoond**oh**ngoo] mouse

camurça f [kam**oo**rsa] suede

canadense m/f [kanad**ay**nsee]
Canadian

canal m canal; channel

canal da Mancha English
Channel

canção f [kans**ow**ng] song

cancelado [kansayl**a**doo]
cancelled

cancelar [kansayl**a**r] to cancel

caneca f [kan**eh**ka] mug

caneta f [kan**ay**ta] pen

caneta esferográfica [eesfayroh-
gr**a**feeka] ballpoint pen

caneta hidrográfica [eedroh-
gr**a**feeka] felt-tip pen

canhoto [kan-y**oh**too] left-
handed

canivete m [kaneev**eh**tee]
penknife

cano m [k**a**noo] pipe (for water)

cano de esgoto m [k**a**noo dee
aysg**oh**too] drain

canoa f [kan**oh**-a] canoe

canoagem f [kanoh-**a**-Jayng]
canoeing

cansado [kans**a**doo] tired

cantar to sing

cantina f [kant**ee**na] Italian food
restaurant

cantor m [kant**oh**r], **cantora** f
singer

cão de guarda [kowng dee
gw**a**rda] guard dog

capa de chuva f [dee sh**oo**va]
raincoat

capacete m [kapas**ay**tee] helmet

capaz: eu não seria capaz de...
[**ay**-oo nowng sayr**ee**-a kap**a**s dee]
I wouldn't be able to...

capela f [kap**eh**la] chapel

capixaba m/f [kapeesh**a**ba] born
or living at Espírito Santo

capô m [kap**oh**] bonnet (of car),
(US) hood

capota de carro f [dee kaH**oo**]
car roof

cápsula f capsule

cara m guy

caranguejo m [karang**ay**Joo] crab

carburador m [karboorad**oh**r]
carburettor

cardápio m [kard**a**p-yoo] menu

cardigã [kardeeg**a**ng] cardigan

careca [kar**eh**ka] bald

carga máxima maximum load

carimbar [kareemb**a**r] to stamp

carioca [kar-y**o**ka] born or
living at Rio de Janeiro city

carnaval m carnival

desfile de carnaval m
[deesf**ee**lee dee] carnival parade

caro [k**a**roo] expensive

carona f [kar**oh**na] lift; ride

dar (uma) carona a to give
a lift to

carpete m [karp**eh**tee] carpet

carrinho m [kaH**ee**n-yoo] trolley,
(US) cart

carrinho de bagagem [dee
bag**a**Jayng] luggage trolley,
(US) baggage cart

carrinho de bebê [bayb**ay**]
pushchair; pram

carrinho de mão [mowng]
barrow

carro **m** [kaHoo] car
 de carro [dee] by car
carro alugado **m** [kaHoo aloogadoo] rented car
carroceria **f** [kaHohsayree-a] bodywork
carta [karta] letter
carta expressa [esprehsa] express letter
carta registrada [HayJeestrada] registered mail
cartão **m** [kartowng] card; pass; identity card; business card; cardboard
cartão de crédito [dee krehdeetoo] credit card
cartão de débito [dehbeetoo] charge card
cartão de embarque [aymbarkee] boarding pass
cartão de telefone [taylayfohnee] phonecard
cartão de visitas [veezeetas] business card
cartão do banco [doo bankoo] cheque card
cartão-postal **m** [pohstal] postcard
cartaz **m** [kartas] poster
carteira **f** [kartayra] purse; wallet
carteira de identidade [dee eedentidadee] ID card
carteira de motorista [mohtohreesta] driver's licence
carteiro **m** postman [kartayroo]
casa **f** [kaza] home; house
 em casa [ayng] at home
 ficar na casa de [feekar na...

dee] to stay with
 ir para casa [eer] to go home
 na sua casa [soo-a] at your place
casa de câmbio **f** [dee kambyoo] bureau de change; exchange rate
casa de saúde [dee sa-oodee] clinic; hospital
casado [kazadoo] married
casal **m** [kazal] couple
casamento **m** [kazamayntoo] wedding
casa noturna **f** [kaza nohtoorna] nightclub; disco
casar(se) [kazarsee] to get married
caseiro [kazayroo] home-made
caso **m** [kazoo] case
 em caso de in case of
catapora **f** [katapohra] chickenpox
catarata **f** waterfall; cataract
catarinense **m/f** [katareenaynsee] born or living at Santa Catarina
catedral **f** [kataydral] cathedral
categoria **f** [kataygohree-a] category
católico **m** [katoleekoo] Catholic
catorze [katohrzee] fourteen
cauda **f** tail
causa **f** [kowza] cause
 por causa de [poor – dee] because of
cavaleiro **m** [kavalayroo] horseman
cavalheiro **m** [kaval-yayroo] gentleman

cavalo m [kavaloo] horse

cave f [kavee] cellar; basement

caveira f [kavayra] skull

caverna f [kavehrna] cave

caxumba f [kashoomba] mumps

CE f [say eh] EC

cearense [say-araynsee] born or living at Ceará

cedo [saydoo] early

mais cedo [mis] earlier

cego [sehgoo] blind

celular m [sayloolar] mobile phone

cem [sayng] hundred

cemitério m [saymeetehr-yoo] cemetery

centígrado m [senteegradoo] centigrade

centímetro m [senteemaytroo] centimetre

cento e... [sayntwee] one hundred and...

central [sayntral] central

centro m [sayntroo] centre

centro da cidade [da seedadee] city centre, town centre

centro de informação turística [dinfohrmasowng tooreesteeka] tourist information office

CEP m [cehp] postcode, zip code

cerâmicas fpl [sayrameekas] ceramics

cerca f [sayrka] fence

cerimônia f [sayreemohn-ya] ceremony

de cerimônia [dee] formal

certamente [sehrtamayntee] certainly

certeza [sayrtayza] certainty

com certeza [kohng] certainly, of course, sure

tem certeza? [tayng] are you sure?

certidão f [sayrteedowng] certificate

certo [sehrtoo] correct, right; sure

cervejaria f [sayrvayjaree-a] beer house serving food

cesto m [saystoo] basket

cesto de compras [dee kompras] shopping basket

céu m [seh-oo] sky

chaleira f [shalayra] kettle

chamada [shamada] call

chamada a cobrar collect call, reverse charge call

chamada local [lohkal] local call

chamada para despertar [shamada para deespayrtar] wake-up call

chamar(se) [see] to be called

como se chama? [kohmoo see shama] what's your name?

chão m [showng] ground; floor

no chão [noo] on the floor; on the ground

chapelaria f [shapaylare-a] cloakroom, checkroom

chapéu m [shapeh-oo] hat

charuto m [sharootoo] cigar

chateação f [shat-yasowng] bother

chateado [shat-yadoo] bored

chatear [shat-yar] to annoy; to bore

chato [shatoo] boring

chave f [shavee] key

chave de fenda [dee faynda]
screwdriver

chave inglesa [inglayza]
wrench; spanner

chaveiro m [shavayroo] keyring

check-in: fazer check-in
[fazayr] to check in

chefe m [shehfee] boss

chefe da estação m [da eestas-
owng] station master

chega [shayga] that's plenty;
that's enough

chegada f [shaygada] arrival

chegadas (at the airport) arrivals

chegar [shaygar] to arrive, to
get in; to reach

cheio [shay-oo] crowded; fed
up; full

cheirar [shayrar] to smell

cheiro m [shayroo] smell

cheque m [shehkee] cheque,
(US) check

cheque de viagem m [dee v-
yaJayng] traveller's cheque

chinelo m [sheenehloo] slippers

chinês m [sheenays] Chinese

chique [sheekee] posh; chic

chocante [shohkantee] shocking

choque m [shokee] shock

chorar [shohrar] to cry

chover [shohvayr] to rain

está chovendo [eesta
shohvayndoo] it's raining

chumbo m [shoomboo] lead

chupeta f [shoopayta] dummy

churrasco m [shooHaskoo]
barbecue

chuva f [shoova] rain

chuvarada f [shoovarada] shower

chuveiro m [shoovayroo] shower

com chuveiro [kohng] with
shower

ciclismo m [seekleesmoo] cycling

ciclista m/f [seekleesta] cyclist

cidadã/cidadão da terceira
idade f/m [seedadang/seedadowng
da tayrsayra eedadee] senior
citizen

cidade f [seedadee] town; city;
town centre

cidade antiga [anteega] old
town

ciência f [s-yayns-ya] science

cigarro m [seegaHoo] cigarette

cima: em cima de... [ayng seema
dee] on top of...

lá em cima up there; upstairs

cinco [seenkoo] five

cinquenta [seenkwaynta] fifty

cinto m [seentoo] belt

cinto de segurança [dee
saygooransa] lifebelt; seatbelt

cintura f [seentoora] waist

cinza (colour) [seenza] grey

cinzeiro m [seenzayroo] ashtray

círculo m [seerkooloo] circle

ciumento [s-yoomayntoo] jealous

claro [klaroo] pale; light; clear;
claro! sure!, of course!

claro que não [kee nowng] of
course not

é claro [eh] of course

classe f [klasee] class

classe econômica
[aykohnohmeeka] economy class

clima m [kleema] climate,
weather

clínica f [kleeneeka] clinic

clínica médica [mehdeeka] clinic

clínica veterinária [vaytayreenar-ya] veterinary clinic

clube m [kloobee] club

clube de golfe [dee golfee] golf club

clube de tênis [dee taynees] tennis club

cobertor m [kohbayrtohr] blanket

cobra f [kobra] snake

cobrar [kobrar] to cash

cobrir [kobreer] to cover

coceira f [kohsayra] itch

código m [kodeegoo] code

código de área m [dee ar-ya] dialling code, area code

código postal m [pohstal] postcode, zip code

coelho m [kwayl-yoo] rabbit

cofre m [kofree] safe

coisa f [koh-iza] thing

cola f glue

colar m [kohlar] necklace

colarinho m [kohlareen-yoo] collar

colchão m [kohlshowng] mattress

coleção f [kohlaysowng] collection

colete m [kohlaytee] waistcoat

colete salva-vidas [veedas] life jacket

colher f [kohl-yehr] spoon

colher de chá f [dee sha] teaspoon

colírio m [kohleer-yoo] eye drops

colisão f [kohleezowng] crash

com [kohng] with

com licença [leesaynsa] excuse me

comandante m [kohmandantee] captain

combinação f [kohmbeenasowng] combination; slip, underskirt

começar [kohmaysar] to begin, to start

começo m [kohmaysoo] start, beginning

comédia f [kohmehd-ya] comedy

comer [kohmayr] to eat

comerciante m/f [kohmayrs-yantee] business person

comida f [kohmeeda] food; meal

comida congelada [kohnJaylada] frozen food

comida de bebê f [dee baybay] baby food

comissão f [kohmeesowng] commission

comissária de bordo f [kohmeesar-ya dee bordoo] stewardess, air hostess

comissário de bordo m [kohmeesar-yoo] steward

como [kohmoo] how; like; since, as

como? what?, pardon (me)?, sorry?

como é? [eh] what's it like?

como este [kohmwaystee] like this

como vai? [vī] how are you?, how do you do?

companheira f [kohmpan-yayra] partner, girlfriend

companheiro m [kohmpan-yayroo] partner, boyfriend

compartimento m [kohmparteemayntoo] compartment

completamente [kohmplehtamayntee] completely

completo [kohmplehtoo] full

complicado [kohmpleekadoo] complicated

compra f [kohmpra] purchase
ir às compras [eer as] to go shopping

comprar [kohmprar] to buy

compreender [kohmpr-yayndayr] to understand

compreendo [kohmpr-yayndoo] I understand, I see

comprido [kohmpreedoo] long

comprimento m [kohmpreemayntoo] length

comprimido m [kohmpreemeedoo] tablet

comprimido para dormir m [dohrmeer] sleeping pill

computador m [kohmpootadohr] computer

comum [kohmoong] ordinary

Comunidade Européia European Community

concerto m [kohnsayrtoo] concert

concessionário m [kohnsaysyohnar-yoo] agent

concha f [kohnsha] shell
concha do mar [doo] seashell

concordar [kohnkoordar] to agree
eu concordo [ay-oo kohnkordoo] I agree

concussão m [kohnkoosowng] concussion

condicionador [kohndeesyohnadohr] conditioner

condições fpl [kohndeesoyngs] conditions, terms

condução f [kohndoosowng] driving; transport

confeitaria f [kohnfaytaree-a] sweet shop, candy store; cake shop, bakery selling cakes

conferência f [kohnfayrayns-ya] conference

confirmar [kohnfeermar] to confirm

confortável [kohnfohrtavil] comfortable

confusão f [kohnfoozowng] confusion, mix-up

congestionamento m [kohnJayst-yohnamayntoo] traffic congestion

conhecer [kohn-yaysayr] to know

conosco [kohnohskoo] with us

consciente [kohns-yayntee] conscious

consertar [kohnsayrtar] to fix, to mend, to repair

consertos mpl [kohnsayrtoos] repairs

constrangedor [kohnstranJaydohr] embarrassing

consulado m [kohnsooladoo] consulate

consulta f [kohnsoolta] appointment

consultório m [kohnsooltor-yoo] surgery, doctor's office

consultório dentário [dayntar-yoo] dental surgery

conta f [**koh**nta] bill; account
conta bancária [bankar-ya] bank account
contar to count; to tell
contatar to contact
contente [kohnt**ay**ntee] happy; glad, pleased
contigo [kohnt**ee**goo] with you
conto m [**koh**ntoo] tale, story
contra against
contra-indicações fpl contraindications
contrário [kohntrar-yoo] opposite
controle de passaporte [kohntr**oh**lee dee pasap**or**tee] passport control
controle de trânsito [dee tranz**ee**too] traffic warden
conveniente [kohnvayn-y**ay**ntee] convenient
convento m [kohnv**ay**ntoo] convent
conversação f [kohnvayrsas**ow**ng] conversation
convés m [kohnv**eh**s] deck
convidada f [kohnveed**a**da], convidado m [kohnveed**a**doo] guest
convidar [kohnveed**a**r] to invite
convite m [kohnv**ee**tee] invitation
copo m [**ko**poo] glass
cor f [kohr] colour
coração m [kohras**ow**ng] heart
corajoso [kohraJ**oh**zoo] brave
corda f rope
cordão de sapato m [kord**ow**ng dee sap**a**too] shoelace
cordeiro m [kohrd**ay**roo] lamb
cor-de-rosa [H**o**za] pink

corpo m [**koh**rpoo] body
corredor m [koh-Hayd**oh**r] corridor
correia f [koh-H**ay**-a] strap
correio m [koh-H**ay**-oo] post, post office
pôr no correio [pohr noo] to post, to mail
correio aéreo [a-**eh**r-yoo] airmail
correio central m [s**ay**ntral] main post office
correio expresso [eespr**eh**soo] express mail, special delivery
corrente f [koh-H**ay**ntee] chain; current
corrente de ar draught
correr [koh-H**ay**r] to run
correspondência f [koh-Hayspohnd**ayn**s-ya] mail
correspondente m/f [koh-Hayspohnd**ay**ntee] penfriend
corrida f [koh-H**ee**da] race
cortado [kohrt**a**doo] cut
cortar to cut
cortar e fazer escova [ee faz**ay**r eesk**oh**va] cut and blow-dry
corte m [**ko**rtee] cut; haircut
corte de energia [dee aynayrJ**ee**-a] power cut
cortiça f [kohrt**ee**sa] cork
cortina f [kohrt**ee**na] curtain
cosméticos mpl [kohsm**eh**teekoos] cosmetics, make-up
costas fpl [**ko**stas] back (of body)
costela f [kohst**eh**la] rib
costurar [kohstoor**a**r] to sew
cotação cambial f [kohtas**ow**ng

kamb-yal] exchange rate
cotovelo m [kohtohvayloo] elbow
couro m [kohroo] leather
coxa f [kohsha] thigh
cozinha f [kohzeen-ya] kitchen
cozinhar [kohzeen-yar] to cook
cozinheiro m [kohzeen-yayroo] cook
crédito m [krehdeetoo] credit
creme m [kraymee] cream, lotion
creme de barba f [dee barba] shaving foam
creme de barbear [barb-yar] shaving cream
creme hidratante [eedratantee] moisturizer
criança f [kr-yansa] child
crianças fpl children
cru(a) [kroo, kroo-a] raw
Cruz Vermelha Red Cross
cruzamento m [kroozamayntoo] junction, crossroads
cruzamento perigoso [payree-gohzoo] dangerous junction
cruzar [kroozar] to cross
cruzeiro m [kroozayroo] cruise
cueca fpl [kwehka] underpants; pants
cuidado [kwidadoo] caution; care
  cuidado! look out!, , watch out!, be careful!, take care!
  cuidado com o cachorro beware of the dog
  cuidado com o trem beware of the train
  cuidado: portas automáticas warning: automatic doors

cuidadoso [kwidadohzoo] careful
cujo [kooJoo] of which; whose
culpa f [koolpa] fault
  é culpa minha/dele it's my/his fault
culpado [koolpadoo] guilty
cumprimento m [koompreemayntoo] compliment
  com os melhores cumprimentos with best wishes
cunhada f [koon-yada] sister-in-law
cunhado m [koon-yadoo] brother-in-law
curar [koorar] to cure
curativo adesivo m [koorateevoo adayzeevoo] Bandaid®
curso m [koorsoo] course
curso de línguas [dee leengwas] language course
curto [koortoo] short
curva f [koorva] turning; bend
curva perigosa dangerous bend
custar [koostar] to charge; to cost
cutelaria f [kootaylaree-a] cutlery shop

D

dá he/she/it gives; you give
da of the; from the
damos [damoos] we give
dança f [dansa] dance
dança folclórica [fohlkloreeka] folk dancing

dançar [dansar] to dance
danificar [daneefeekar] to damage
dão [downg] they give; you give
daqui [dakee] from now
dar to give
das [das] of the; from the
dás you give
data f [data] date
data de validade [dee valeedadee] expiry date
de [day] from; of; by; in
  de avião [dee av-yowng] by air
  de carro [dee kaHoo] by car
  de manhã [dee man-yang] in the morning
  de ônibus [dee ohneeboos] by bus
  de repente [dee Haypayntee] suddenly
  de onde [dee ohndee] where from
  de onde é? [eh] where do you come from?
dê passagem give way, yield
decepcionado [daysayps-yohnadoo] disappointed
decepcionante [daysayps-yohnantee] disappointing
decidir [dayseedeer] to decide
décimo [dehseemoo] tenth
decisão f [dayseezowng] decision
declaração f [dayklarasowng] statement
decolagem f [daykohlaJayng] take-off
decolar [daykohlar] to take off, to unglue

dedo m [daydoo] finger
dedo do pé [doo peh] toe
defeito m [dayfaytoo] fault, defect
deficiente físico [dayfees-yayntee] disabled
degrau m [daygrow] step
deitar-se [daytarsee] to lie down; to go to bed
deixar [dayshar] to leave (behind); to let
  deixar cair [ka-eer] to drop
dela [dehla] her; hers
delas [dehlas] their; theirs
dele [daylee] his
delegacia de polícia f [daylaygasee-a dee pohlees-ya] police station
deles [daylees] their; theirs
delicatéssen f delicatessen
delicioso [daylees-yohzoo] delicious
demais [daymīs] too much
demaquilante para os olhos m [daymakeelantee para ooz ol-yoos] eye make-up remover
dê-me [daymee] give me
demora f [daymora] delay
dentadura f [dayntadoora] dentures
dente m [dayntee] tooth
dentista m/f [daynteesta] dentist
dentro [dayntroo] inside
  dentro de casa [dee kaza] indoors
  dentro de... dias [dee-as] in... days' time
  dentro de um momento [oong mohmayntoo] in a minute

departamento m [daypartama**ayn**too] department

depender [daypaynd**ayr**] depend

depende de... [day**payn**dee dee] it depends on...

depois [daypoh-is] then, after that; afterwards

depois de... [dee] after...

depois de amanhã [dee aman-**yang**] the day after tomorrow

depósito m [daypo**zee**too] deposit; tank

depósito de madeira f [dee ma**dayra**] timber yard

depósitos mpl deposits

depressa [day**preh**sa] quickly

deprimido [daypreem**ee**doo] depressed

derrame cerebral [day-Hamee sayraybral] stroke

derrubar [dayHoobar] to knock over

desaconselhável para menores de... anos not recommended for those under... years of age

desagradável [dayzagrad**a**vil] unpleasant

desaparecer [dayzaparays**ayr**] to disappear

desapontado [dayzapohnta**doo**] disappointed

desastre m [dayza**stree**] disaster

descansar [deeskan**sar**] to relax

descanso m [deeskan**soo**] rest

descer [days**ayr**] to go down; to get off

descobrir [dayskohb**reer**] to find out, to discover

descolar [deeskohlar] to unglue

descontar [deeskohntar] to cash

desconto m [deesk**ohn**too] discount

descrição f [deeskrees**owng**] description

desculpar-se [deeskoolpar**see**] to apologize

desculpas fpl [deesk**ool**pas] apologies

desculpe [deesk**ool**pee] I'm sorry, excuse me, pardon (me)

desde [days**dee**] since; from

desejar [daysa**y**Jar] to want

que deseja? [kee daysay**J**a] how can I help you?

desembarcar [dayzaymbarkar] to go down; to get off

desempregado [dayzaympraygadoo] unemployed

desenho m [day**zayn**-yoo] drawing; pattern

desenvolver [dayzaynvolvayr] to develop

desfazer a mala [deesfazayr a mala] to unpack

desfiladeiro m [deesfeelad**ayroo**] pass

desinfetante m [dayzeenfaytantee] disinfectant

desligado [deesleegadoo] off, switched off

desligar [deesleegar] to turn off; to switch off

desligue o motor switch off your engine

desmaiar [deesmī-ar] to faint; to collapse

desocupar antes das... vacate before...

desodorante m [dayzohdoorantee] deodorant

despertador m [deespayrtadohr] alarm clock

destinatário m addressee

destino m [daysteenoo] destination

desvio m [daysvee-oo] detour, diversion

detergente m [daytayrJayntee] soap powder, washing powder

detergente líquido [leekeedoo] washing-up liquid

detestar [daytaystar] to hate

detestável [daytaystavil] obnoxious

Deus [day-oos] God

devagar [dayvagar] slow; slowly

deve [dehvee] you must, you have to

dever m [dayvayr] duty; to owe; to have to

deveria [dayvayree-a] you should

devolver [dayvolvayr] to give back

dez [dehs] ten

dezembro [dayzaymbroo] December

dezenove [dayzaynovee] nineteen

dezesseis [dayzayssays] sixteen

dezessete [dayzaysehtee] seventeen

dezoito [dayzoh-itoo] eighteen

dia m [dee-a] day

o dia todo [tohdoo] all day

dia do aniversário m [doo aneevayrsar-yo] birthday

dia útil [ootil] weekdays

diabética (f) [d-yabehteeka]

diabético (m) [d-yabehteekoo] diabetic

dialeto m [d-yalehtoo] dialect

diamante m [d-yamantee] diamond

diapositivo m [d-yapohzeeteevoo] slide

diária f [d-yar-ya] cost per day

diariamente [d-yar-yamayntee] daily

diário (m) [d-yar-yo] diary
(adv) daily

diarréia f [d-yaHeh-ia] diarrhoea

dicionário m [dees-yoonar-yoo] dictionary

diesel m diesel

dieta f [d-yehta] diet

diferença f [deefayraynsa] difference

diferente [deefayrayntee] different

difícil [deefeesil] difficult, hard

dificuldade f [deefeekooldadee] difficulty

digite o número desejado dial the number you require

diluir num pouco de água dissolve in a little water

Dinamarca f [deenamarka] Denmark

dinamarquês m [deenamarkays] Danish

dinheiro m [deen-yayroo] money; cash

diploma m [deeplohma] degree

dirá [deera] he/she will say;
you will say

dirão [deerowng] they will say;
you will say

dirás [deeras] you will say

direi [deeray] I will say

direita [deerayta] on the right
à direita (de) [dee] on the
right (of)
vire à direita [veeree] turn right

direito [deeraytoo] straight;
right (not left)

direitos mpl [deeraytoos] rights

diremos [deeraymoos] we will
say

direto [deerehtoo] direct

dirigir [deereeJeer] to lead; to
drive
dirigir embriagado [aymbr-
yagadoo] drunken driving
dirija com cuidado [deereeJa
kohng kwidadoo] drive carefully

discagem direta [deeskaJayng
deerehta] direct dialling

discar (no telefone) to dial

disco m [deeskoo] disco; record

discoteca f [deeskohtehka] disco

disjuntor principal m
[deesJootohr preenseepal] mains
switch

disquete m [deeskehtee] disk,
diskette

disse [deesee] I/he/she/it/you
said

dissemos [deesaymoos] we said

disseram [deesehrowng] you/
they said

disseste [deesehstee] you said

distância f [deestans-ya] distance

distribuição f
[deestreebweesowng] delivery

distribuidor m [distreebweedohr]
distributor

dito [deetoo] said

DIU m [dee-oo] IUD, coil

diversos [deevehrsoos] several

divertido [deevayrteedoo] fun,
amusing, enjoyable

divertir-se [deevayrteersee] to
enjoy oneself

divorciado [deevohrs-yadoo]
divorced

dizer [dizayr] to say; to tell
o que quer dizer? [oo kee kehr]
what do you mean?

do of the; from the
do que [doo kee] than

dobro [dohbroo] twice as much

doce [dohsee] sweet

documento m [dohkoomayntoo]
document

doença f [dwaynsa] disease,
illness

doente [dwayntee] ill, sick,
unwell

doer [dwayr] to hurt

dois [doh-is] two

doloroso [dohlohrohzoo] painful

domingo m [dohmeengoo] Sunday

domingos e feriados Sundays
and public holidays

dona f [dohna] owner; respectful
way of addressing a woman,
precedes the first name
dona Mrs

dono m [dohnoo] owner

dor f [dohr] ache, pain

dor de cabeça [dee kabaysa]
headache

dor de dente [dayntee]
toothache

dor de estômago [eestohmagoo]
stomach ache

dor de garganta [garganta] sore
throat

dor de ouvido [ohveedoo] earache

dor nas costas [nas kostas]
backache

dormir [dohrmeer] to sleep
 adormecido asleep

dos of the; from the

dou [doh] I give

doutor m [dohtohr], **doutora f**
 [dohtora] doctor

doze [dohzee] twelve

droga f [droga] drugs, narcotics

drogaria f [drohgaree-a] drugs-
store, shop selling toiletries

duas vezes [doo-as vayzees]
twice

dunas fpl [doonas] sand dunes

duplo [dooploo] double

durante [doorantee] during

duro [dooroo] hard; stale

duzentas [doozayntas], **duzentos**
 [doozayntoos] two hundred

dúzia f [dooz-ya] dozen

E

e [ee] and

é [eh] he/she/it is; you are
 é...? is he/she/it...?; are you...?

echarpe [aysharpee] scarf (for
neck)

edifício m [aydeefees-yoo]
building

edredom m [aydraydohng] duvet

efervescente [ayfayrvaysayntee]
effervescent, sparkling

ei! hey!

eixo m [ayshoo] axle

ela [ehla] she; her; it

elas [ehlas] they; them

elástico m [aylasteekoo] elastic;
elastic band

ele [aylee] he; him; it

eles [aylees] they; them

eletricidade f [aylaytreeseedadee]
electricity

eletricista m [aylaytreeseesta]
electrician

elétrico [aylehtreekoo] electric

eletrodomésticos mpl
 [aylehtrohdomehshtikoosh]
electrical appliances

elevador m [aylayvadohr] lift,
elevator

em [ayng] in; at; on
 em férias [fehr-yas] on
holiday; on vacation

embaixada f [aymbīshada]
embassy

embaixo [aymbīshoo] down,
downstairs; underneath
 embaixo de... [dee] underneath...
 lá embaixo down there

**embalagem de comida
industrializada** packed lunch

embalagem econômica f
economy pack

embalagem familiar family
pack

157

embaraçoso [aymbaras**oh**zoo]
embarrassing

embora [aymb**o**ra] although
ir embora to go away

embreagem f [aymbray-a**J**ayng]
clutch

embrulhar [aymbrool-y**a**r] to
wrap

embrulho m [aymbrool-y**oo**]
parcel

emergência f [aymayrJ**ay**ns-ya]
emergency

emocionante [aymohs-yohn**a**ntee]
exciting

emperrado [aympay**H**adoo]
stuck; jammed

empoeirado [aympoh-ay**ra**doo]
dusty

empório m [aymp**o**r-yoo] grocery
store

empregada f [aympreg**a**da] maid

empregado m [aympreg**a**doo]
employee

emprego m [aympr**ay**goo] job

empresa [aympr**ay**za] company,
firm

empresa aérea [a-**eh**r-ya]
airline

emprestado: pedir emprestado
[payd**ee**r aympraystadoo] to
borrow

emprestar [aympraysta**r**] to lend

empurrar [aympoo**Ha**r] to push

encaminhar [aynkameen-y**a**r] to
forward

encanador m [aynkanad**ohr**]
plumber

encantador [aynkantad**ohr**]
lovely

encaracolado [aynkarakohl**a**doo]
curly

encher [aynsh**ayr**] to fill up,
to fill

encomenda f [aynkohm**ay**nda]
package; parcel

balcão de encomendas m
parcels, parcels counter

encontrar [aynkohntr**a**r] to find;
to meet

endereço m [ayndayr**ay**soo]
address

enevoado [aynayvw**a**doo] foggy;
misty; cloudy

enfermaria f [aynfayrmar**ee**-a]
hospital ward

enfermeira f [aynfayrm**ay**ra],
enfermeiro m [aynfayrm**ay**roo]
nurse

enganado [ayngan**a**doo] wrong

enganar(se) [ayngan**a**rsee] to be
wrong, to make a mistake

eu me enganei [aygan**ay**] I've
made a mistake

engarrafamento m
[aynga**H**afam**ay**ntoo] traffic jam

engolir [ayngohl**ee**r] to swallow

engraçado [ayngras**a**doo] funny,
amusing

engrenagem f [ayngrayn**a**Jayng]
gear(s)

enguiçado [ayngees**a**doo] faulty;
out of order

enjôo m [aynJ**oh**-oo] nausea

enorme [ayn**o**rmee] enormous

enquanto [aynkw**a**ntoo] while

ensinar [aynseen**a**r] to teach

ensino médio m [aynss**ee**noo
mehd-yoo] secondary school,

high school

então [ayntowng] then, at that time

entender [ayntayndayr] to understand

entrada f [ayntrada] entrance, way in; starter, appetizer; admission charge

entrada livre admission free

entrada proibida no entry

entrar [ayntrar] to go in, to enter

entre! come in!

entre [ayntree] among; between

entrega em domicílio delivery service

entregar [ayntraygar] to deliver

entrevista [ayntrayveesta] appointment

entupido [ayntoopeedoo] blocked

envelope m [aynvaylopee] envelope

envelope aéreo m [a-ehr-yo] airmail envelope

envergonhado [aynvayrgohn-yadoo] ashamed

enviar [aynv-yar] to send

enxaqueca f [aynshakayka] migraine

época f [ehpohka] season; age

equipamento m [aykeepamayntoo] equipment

equipamento de camping camping equipment

era [ehra] I was; he/she/it was; you were

eram [ehrowng] they were; you were

éramos [ehramoos] we were

eras [ehras] you were

errado [eHadoo] wrong

erro m [ayHoo] mistake, error

erupção f [ayroopsowng] rash

és [ehs] you are

escada f [eeskada] ladder; stairs

escada rolante [Hohlantee] escalator

escadaria [eeskadaree-a] stairs

escala f [eeskala] intermediate stop

escalar [eeskalar] to climb

escaler m [eeskaler] dinghy

escapamento m [eeskapamayntoo] exhaust pipe

escocês m [eeskohsays] Scottish; Scotsman

escocesa f [eeskohsayza] Scottish; Scots woman

Escócia f [eeskos-ya] Scotland

escola f [eeskola] school

escola de idiomas f [dee eed-yohmas] language school

escola de samba f samba schools are samba clubs

escolher [eeskohl-yayr] to choose

esconder [eeskohndayr] to hide

escorregadio [eeskoh-Haygadee-oo] slippery

escova f [eeskohva] brush

escova de cabelo [dee kabayloo] hairbrush

escova de dentes [dayntees] toothbrush

escova de unhas [oon-yas] nailbrush

escrever [eeskrayvayr] to write
escrito [eeskreetoo] written
  escrito por... [eeskreetoo poor]
  written by...
  por escrito in writing
escritório m [eeskreetor-yoo]
  office
escurecer [eeskooraysayr] to
  get dark
escuro [eeskooroo] dark
escutar [eeskootar] to listen (to)
esferográfica f [eesfayroh-
  grafeeka] ballpoint pen
esmalte de unha m [eesmaltee
  dee oon-ya] nail varnish
Espanha f [espan-ya] Spain
espanhóis: os espanhóis
  [espan-oys] the Spanish
espanhol [espan-yol] Spanish
esparadrapo m [eesparadrapoo]
  sticking plaster
especialidade f [eespays-
  yalidadee] speciality
especialmente [eespays-
  yalmayntee] especially
espelho m [eespayl-yoo] mirror
espelho retrovisor
  [Haytrohveezohr] rearview
  mirror
espeque f [eespehkee] tent peg
esperar [eespayrar] to expect;
  to hope; to wait
  espere! [eespehree] wait
  espere pelo sinal wait for
  the tone
  espero que não [eespehroo kee
  nowng] I hope not
  espero que sim [seeng] I
  hope so

esperto [eespehrtoo] clever
espesso [eespaysoo] thick
espetáculo m [eespaytakooloo]
  show
espingarda f [eespeengarda] gun
espirrar [eespeeHar] to sneeze
espirro m [eespeeHoo] sneeze
esplanada f [eesplanada]
  esplanade
esporte m [eespohrte] sport
esportes aquáticos mpl
  [eespohrtees akwateekoos] water
  sports
esposa f [eespohza] wife
espreguiçadeira
  [eespraygeesadayra] deckchair;
  sun lounger
esquecer [eeskaysayr] to forget
  eu esqueci [ay-oo eeskaysee]
  I forgot
esquerda [eeskayrda] left
  à esquerda on the left (of),
  to the left
  vire à esquerda [veeree] turn
  left
esqui aquático m [eeskee
  akwateekoo] waterskiing
esquina f [eeskeena] corner
  na esquina [na] in the corner
esquisito [eeskeezeetoo] weird,
  odd, strange
essa [ehsa] that; that one
essas [ehsas] those
esse [aysee] that
essencial [aysayns-yal] essential
esses [aysees] those
esta [ehsta] this; this one
está [eesta] he/she/it is; you are
  ele está? [aylee] is he in?

está... it is...

está...? is it...?

está bem [bayng] that's fine, all right

estação f [eestasowng] station; season

estação de trem [dee trayng] railway station

estacionamento [eestas-yohnamayntoo] car park, parking lot

estacionamento privado [preevadoo] private parking

estacionamento proibido [proh-eebeedoo] no parking

estacionamento reservado aos hóspedes parking reserved for patrons, patrons only

estacionamento subterrâneo [soob-tayHan-yoo] underground car park/parking lot

estacionar [eestas-yohnar] to park

estadia f [eestadee-a] stay

estádio m [eestad-yoo] stadium

estado m [eestadoo] state

Estados Unidos (da América) mpl [eestadooz ooneedoos] United States (of America)

estamos [eestamoos] we are

estão [eestowng] they are; you are

estar [eestar] to be

estará [eestara] he/she/it/you will be

estarão [eestarowng] you/they will be

estarás [eestaras] you will be

estarei [eestaray] I will be

estaremos [eestaraymoos] we will be

estas [ehstas] these

estás [eestas] you are

estátua f [eestatwa] statue

estava [eestava] I/he/she/it/ you used to be

estavam [eestavam] you/they used to be

estávamos [eestavamoos] we used to be

estavas [eestavas] you used to be

este [aystee] this; this one

esteira de praia [eestayra dee prī-a] beach mat

estepe [eestehpee] spare tyre

estes [aystees] these

esteve [eestayvee] he/she/it was; you were

estive [eesteevee] I was

estivemos [eesteevaymoos] we were

estiveram [eesteevehrowng] they were; you were

estiveste [eesteevehstee] you were

estômago m [eestohmagoo] stomach

estou [eestoh] I am

estrada f [eestrada] road

estrada principal [preenseepal] main highway

estragado [eestragadoo] damaged; faulty; out of order

estragar [eestragar] to damage

estrangeira f, estrangeiro

m [eestran**Jay**roo] foreign; foreigner

estranha f [eestran-ya], **estranho m** [eestran-yoo] stranger; peculiar; funny; strange

estréia f [eestreh-ia] first showing

estreito [eestray**too**] narrow

estrela f [eestra**yla**] star

estudante m/f [eestoo**dantee**] student

estúpido [eest**oo**peedoo] stupid

estupro m [eest**oo**proo] rape

etiqueta f [ayteek**ay**ta] label

eu [**ay**-oo] I

  eu mesmo [**may**smoo] myself

EUA USA

Europa f [ay-oor**o**pa] Europe

européia f [ay-oorohp**eh**-ia], **europeu m** [ay-ooroohp**ay**-oo] European

exagerar [ayza**Jay**rar] to exaggerate

exame m [ay**za**mee] exam, test

exame de sangue m [dee **san**gee] blood test

exatamente! [ayzatam**ay**ntee] exactly!

exato [ay**za**too] accurate, correct

exausto [ay**zow**stoo] shattered, exhausted

excelente [aysay**lay**ntee] excellent; lovely

excesso de bagagem m [ays**eh**soo dee baga**Jay**ng] excess baggage

exceto [ays**eh**too] except

  exceto aos domingos Sundays excepted

exclusivamente para adultos for adults only

exclusivamente para uso externo for external use only

excursão f [ayskoorso**w**ng] coach trip; trip

excursões fpl [ayskoors**oy**ngs] excursions

exemplo m [ayz**ay**mploo] example

  por exemplo [poor] for example

exigir [ayzee**Jee**r] to demand

Exmo. Sr. (Excelentíssimo Senhor) Dear Sir

experiente [eespayr-y**ay**ntee] experienced

experimentar [eespayreem**ay**ntar] to try; to try on

explicar [ayspl**ee**kar] to explain

exposição f [eespohzees**ow**ng] exhibition

extensão f [eestayns**ow**ng] extension; extension lead

exterior: no exterior [noo] abroad

extintor m [eesteent**oh**r] fire extinguisher

extraordinário [aystra-ohrdeenar-yoo] extraordinary

extremamente [eestraymam**ay**ntee] extremely

F

fábrica f [**fa**breeka] factory

fabricado em... made in...

faca f [**fa**ka] knife

face f [**fa**see] cheek
fácil [**fa**sil] easy
faço [**fa**soo] I do
faculdade f [fakooldadee] college
faixa f [**fí**sha] lane
faixa de pedestres f [dee paydehstrees] pedestrian crossing, (US) crosswalk
falar to speak; to talk
　não falo inglês I don't speak English
　você fala...? do you speak...?
falido [faleedo] broke; bankrupt
falso [**fal**soo] fake; false
falta missing
faltar to be lacking; to be missing
família f [fameel-ya] family
famoso [fam**oh**zoo] famous
fantástico [fanta**stee**koo] fantastic
fará [fara] he/she/it/you will do
farão [far**ow**ng] you/they will do
farás [faras] you will do
farei [fa**ray**] I will do
faremos [fara**ee**moos] we will do
farmácia f [farmas-ya] pharmacy, chemist's
farmácia de plantão [dee plant**ow**ng] emergency pharmacies, duty chemists
farol m [far**ol**] headlight; lighthouse
　farol alto [far**ol al**too] headlights
　farol baixo [far**ol bí**shoo] dipped headlights

luzes laterais [**loo**zees latay**rí**s] sidelights
fator de proteção solar m [fat**ohr** de prohte**sow**ng] protection factor
fatura f [fat**oo**ra] invoice
favor [fav**ohr**] favour
　por favor [poor] please
　por favor, feche a porta please close the door
　por favor, não incomode please do not disturb
favorito [favoh**ree**too] favourite
fazem-se chaves keys cut here
fazendeiro m [fazaynd**ay**roo] farmer
fazer [faz**ayr**] to do; to make
　fazer a barba to shave
　fazer amor [am**ohr**] to make love
　fazer as malas [**ma**las] to pack
　fazer baldeação [balday-as**ow**ng] to change (trains)
　fazer escova [eesk**oh**va] to blow-dry
　fazer fila [**fee**la] to queue, to stand in line
　fazer turismo [toor**ee**smoo] sightseeing
febre f [**feh**bree] temperature, fever
　febre do feno [**feh**bree doo **fay**noo] hayfever
febril [febr**ee**l] feverish
fechado [faysh**a**doo] closed, shut; reserved; overcast
　fechado à chave [a sh**a**vee] locked
　fechado até... closed until...

fechado para balanço closed
for stocktaking

fechado para férias closed for
holidays

fechado para obras closed
for repairs

fechadura f [fayshadoora] lock

fechar [fayshar] to close; to
shut

fechar à chave to lock

feio [fay-oo] ugly

feira f [fayra] funfair; trade fair

feito [faytoo] made; done

feito à mão [faytwa mowng]
hand-made

feliz [faylees] happy

feliz aniversário! [aneevayrsar-
yoo] happy birthday!

Feliz Ano Novo! [anoo nohvoo]
Happy New Year!

Feliz Natal! Merry Christmas!

felizmente [fayleesmayntee]
fortunately

feminista f [faymeeneesta]
feminist

feriado m [fayr-yadoo] public
holiday

férias fpl [fehr-yas] holiday;
vacation

férias de inverno fpl [dinvehrnoo]
winter holiday

férias de verão fpl [dee
vayrowng] summer holidays

ferida f [fayreeda] wound

ferido [fayreedoo] injured

ferragens fpl [fayHaJayngs]
ironmongery, hardware

ferramenta f [fayHamaynta] tool

ferro m [feh-Hoo] iron

ferro de passar m iron

ferrovia f [feh-Hohvee-a] railway

festa f [fehsta] party

boas festas! [boh-as fehstas]
merry Christmas and a
happy New Year

fevereiro [fayvayrayroo]
February

fez [fays] he/she/it did, he/
she/it has done; you did,
you have done

fibras naturais [feebras natoorīs]
natural fibres

ficar [feekar] to remain, to
stay

ficar com [kohng] to keep

onde fica...? [feeka] where is...?

fígado m [feegadoo] liver

fila f [feela] queue, line

filha f [feel-ya] daughter

filho m [feel-yoo] son

filho da mãe! [da mayng]
bastard!

filho da puta! [poota] son-of-
a-bitch!

filmadora [feelmadohra] f
camcorder

filme m [feelmee] film; movie

filme colorido m [kohlohreedoo]
colour film

filme de PVC m [dee pay-vay-
say] clingfilm

filtro m [feeltroo] filter

filtro de café [dee kafeh] filter
paper

fim m [feeng] end

no fim eventually

no fim de... [noo – dee] at the
end of...

fim de rodovia [dee Hodohvee-a] end of motorway/highway

fim de semana [saymana] weekend

fim de temporada end of season

finalmente [feenalmayntee] at last

fino [feenoo] thin; fine

fio m [fee-oo] lead; thread; wire

fio dental m [dental] dental floss

fiscal de trem m [feeskal dee trayng] ticket inspector

fita f [feeta] tape, cassette

fita adesiva f sticky tape, Sellotape®, Scotch tape®

fita métrica [mehtreeka] tape measure

fiz [fees] I did, I have done

fizemos [feezaymoos] we did, we have done

fizeram [feezehrowng] you/they did, they have done

fizeste [feezehstee] you did, you have done

flanela de limpeza [flanehla dee leempayza] flannel

flertar [flayrtar] to flirt

flor f [flohr] flower

floresta f [florehsta] forest

fluentemente [flwenteemayntee] fluently

fluminense m/f [floomeenaynsee] born or living at the state of Rio de Janeiro

fogão m [fohgowng] cooker

fogo m [fohgoo] fire

fogos de artifício mpl [fogoos dee arteefees-yoo] fireworks

fogueira f [fohgayra] fire, campfire

foi [foh-i] it was, he/she went, he/she has left

folha f [fohl-ya] leaf; sheet

folheto m [fohl-yaytoo] leaflet; brochure

fome [fohmee] hunger

estou com fome [eestoh kohng] I'm hungry

você está com fome? [vohsay eesta] are you hungry?

fomos [fohmoos] we were, we have been; we went, we have gone

fones de ouvido mpl [fohnees dee ohveedoo] headphones

fonte f [fohntee] fountain

fora outside

do lado de fora [doo ladoo dee] outside

fora da cidade out of town

fora daqui! get out of here!

foram [fohrowng] you/they were, you/they have been; you/they went, you/they have gone

forma: em forma [ayng forma] fit

de qualquer forma [dee kwalkehr] anyway

formiga f [fohrmeega] ant

formulário m [fohrmoolar-yoo] form

forno m [fohrnoo] oven

forte m [fortee] strong

fósforos mpl [foshfooroos] matches

foste [fohstee] you were, you have been; you went, you have gone

fotocópias **fpl** [fohtohkop-yas]
photocopies
fotografar [fohtohgrafar] to
photograph
fotografia, foto f [fohtohgrafee-a]
photograph; photographic
goods
fotógrafo m [fohtografoo]
photographer
fraco [frakoo] weak
frágil [fraJil] fragile
fralda f [fralda] nappy, diaper
fraldas descartáveis **fpl**
[deeskartavays] disposable
nappies/diapers
França f [fransa] France
francês m [fransays] French;
Frenchman
francesa f [fransayza] French;
French woman
fratura f [fratoora] fracture
frear [fray-ar] to brake
freezer m freezer
freio m [frayoo] brake
freio de mão [dee mowng]
handbrake
frente f [frayntee] front
em frente [ayng] in front
em frente a opposite; in
front of
na frente at the front
frequência f [fraykwayns-ya]
frequency
frequente [fraykwayntee] frequent
frequentemente [fraykwayn-
teemayntee] frequently
fresco [frayskoo] fresh; cool
frigideira f [freeJeedayra] frying
pan

frio [free-oo] cold
estou com frio [eestoh kohng]
I'm cold
fritar [freetar] to fry
fronha f [frohn-ya] pillow case
fronteira f [frohntayra] border,
frontier
fuga f [fooga] leak
fui [fwee] I went, I have gone;
I was, I have been
fumaça f [foomasa] smoke
fumantes **pl** [foomantees]
smokers, smoking
fumar [foomar] to smoke
eu não fumo [nowng] I don't
smoke
você fuma? [fooma] do you
smoke?
funcionar [foons-yonar] to work
não funciona [nowng] out of
order
fundo m [foondoo] deep;
bottom
funil m [fooneel] funnel
furado [fooradoo] flat (tyre)
furioso [foor-yohzoo] furious
furo m [fooroo] puncture
fusível m [foozeevil] fuse
futebol m [footaybol] football
futuro m [footooroo] future
no futuro [noo] in future

G

gado m [gadoo] cattle
galão m [galowng] gallon
galeria de arte f [galayree-a dee
artee] art gallery

galês m [galays] Welsh; Welshman

Gales m [galees] Wales

galesa f [galayza] Welsh; Welsh woman

galocha wellington

ganhar [gan-yar] to win; to earn

ganso m [gansoo] goose

garagem f [garaJayng] garage

garantia f [garantee-a] guarantee

garçom m [garsohng] waiter

garçonete f [garsohnehtee] waitress

garfo m [garfoo] fork

garganta f throat

garota f [garohta] young lady

garrafa f [gaHafa] bottle

garrafa térmica f [tehrmeeka] vacuum flask

gás m [gas] gas

gasolina f [gazooleena] petrol, gasoline

gasolina aditivada [adeeteevada] four-star petrol

gasolina comum [komoong] three-star petrol, regular gas

gasolina sem chumbo [sayng shoomboo] unleaded petrol

gastar [gastar] to spend

gato m [gatoo] cat

gaúcho m [ga-ooshoo] born or living at Rio Grande do Sul

gaveta f [gavayta] drawer

geada f [Jay-ada] frost

gel de banho m [Jehl dee ban-yoo] shower gel

gel para cabelo m [Jehl para kabayloo] hair gel

geladeira f [Jayladayra] fridge

gelo [Jayloo] ice

gêmeos mpl [Jaym-yoos] twins

gengiva f [JenJeeva] gum

genro m [Jaynroo] son-in-law

gente (povo) f [Jayntee] people

geral [Jayral] general

geralmente [Jayralmayntee] usually

gerente m/f [Jayrayntee] manager; manageress

gesso m [Jaysoo] plaster cast

ginásio m [Jeenaz-yoo] gym

goiano m [goh-yanoo] born or living at Goiás

gola f [gola] collar

golfe m [gohlfee] golf

goma de mascar f [gohma dee maskar] chewing gum

gordo [gohrdoo] fat

gorduroso [gohrdoorohzoo] greasy

gorgeta f [gohrJayta] tip

gostar [gohstar] to like

gosta de...? [gosta dee] do you like...?

gosto [gostoo] I like, I like it

gostoso [gohstohzoo] tasty; pleasant; nice

gota f [gohta] drop

governo m [gohvayrnoo] government

Grã-Bretanha f [gran braytan-ya] Great Britain

gradualmente [gradwalmayntee] gradually

grama f grass

grama m gram(me)

gramado m [gramadoo] lawn

gramática f [gramateeka] grammar

grampo de cabelo [grampoo dee kabayloo] hairgrip

grande [grandee] large, big
muito grande [mweengtoo] too big

granizo m [graneezoo] hail

grátis, gratuito [gratweetoo] free (of charge)

gravador de CD m [gravadohr dee say-day] CD recorder

gravador de DVD m [day-vay-day] DVD recorder

gravador de fita cassete m [kasehtee] tape recorder

gravador de vídeo m [veed-yoo] video recorder

gravata f tie, necktie

grave [gravee] serious

grávida [graveeda] pregnant

graxa de sapato f [grasha dee sapatoo] shoe polish

Grécia f [grehs-ya] Greece

grego m [graygoo] Greek

grelha f [grayl-ya] grill

gripe f [greepee] flu

gritar [greetar] to shout

grosseiro [grohsayroo] rude

grosso [grohsoo] thick

grupo m [groopoo] group, party

grupo sanguíneo [sangeen-yo] blood group

guarda m/f [gwarda] caretaker

guarda-chuva m [gwarda shoova] umbrella

guardanapo m [gwardanapoo] napkin, serviette

guardar [gwardar] to keep

guarda-sol [gwarda] beach umbrella, sunshade

guarda-volumes [vohloomees] left luggage (office)

guerra f [geh-Ha] war

guia m [gee-a] guidebook

guia de conversação [dee kohnvayrsasowng] phrasebook

guia m [gee-a] guide, courier

guia turística f [tooreesteeka], guia turístico m [tooreesteekoo] tour guide

guichê m [geeshay] window; ticket window

guloso [goolohzoo] greedy

H

h is not pronounced in Portuguese

H gent's, men's room

há... [a] there is..., there are...
há...? is there...?, are there...?

há pouco [pohkoo] recently

há uma semana [ooma saymana] a week ago

há vagas [vagas] vacancies, rooms free

hábito m [abeetoo] custom; habit

hematoma m [aymatohma] bruise

hepatite f [aypateetee] hepatitis

herbanário m [ayrbanar-yoo] herbalist

hidrofólio m [eedrohfol-yoo] hydrofoil

hipermercado m

[eepayrmerk**a**doo] hypermarket

hipertensão [eepayrtaynso**ow**ng] high blood pressure

história f [ee**stor**-ya] history; story

hodômetro m [od**oh**maytroo] speedometer

hoje [**oh**Jee] today

homem m [**o**mayng] man

homens mpl [**o**mayngs] men

honesto [one**hs**too] honest

hora f [**o**ra] hour; time

hora de chegada [dee shay**ga**da] arrival time

hora de partida [par**tee**da] departure time

hora local local time

hora marcada f [mar**ka**da] appointment

horário m [o**hrar**-yoo] timetable, (US) schedule

horário de consultas [dee konso**ol**tas] surgery hours, (US) office hours

horário de funcionamento m [foons-yonama**yn**too] opening times

horário de pico [**pee**koo] rush hour

horário de visita [vee**zee**ta] visiting hours

horas fpl [**o**ras] hours; o'clock

às seis horas [as sayz **o**ras] at six o'clock

que horas são? [k-y**o**ras sowng] what's the time?

horrível [oh-H**ee**vil] awful, dreadful, horrible

hortelã f [ortay**lang**] peppermint

hospedado [ohspayd**a**doo]: **estar hospedado em** [ee**star** – ayng] to be a guest at, to stay at

hospedagem m [ohspayda**Ja**yng] accommodation

hospedaria [ohspayda**ree**-a] guesthouse

hospedar-se [ohspayd**ar**see] to stay

hóspede m/f [**o**speedee] guest

hospitalidade f [ohspeetalee**da**dee] hospitality

hotel m [oh**tehl**] hotel

hotel de luxo m [dee **loo**shoo] luxury hotel

houve [**oh**vee] there has been

humor m [oom**oh**r] humour

I

iate m [**ya**tee] yacht

ida: bilhete de ida [beel-y**a**ytee **dee**da] single ticket, one-way ticket

idade f [ee**da**dee] age

que idade você tem?/quantos anos você tem? [kee**da**dee voh**say** tayng/kwant**oos a**noos] how old are you?

idéia f [ee**deh**-ia] idea

ignição f [eegnees**ow**ng] ignition

igreja f [eegr**ay**Ja] church

igual [eeg**wal**] same

ilha f [**eel**-ya] island

imediatamente [eemayd-yata-ma**yn**tee] immediately, at once

imitação f [eemeetas**ow**ng] imitation

impermeável [impayrmay-avil] waterproof

importante [impohrtantee] important

importar to matter, to be important; to import

importa-se de...? [importasee] will you...?

importa-se se...? do you mind if...?

não me importo [nowng mimportoo] I don't mind

importunar [impohrtoonar] to annoy

importuno [importoonoo] annoying

impossível [impohseevil] impossible

impostos: livre de impostos [leevree dee] duty-free

imprescindível [imprayseendeevil] vital

impressionante [imprays-yohnnantee] impressive

impressos mpl [imprehsoos] printed matter

inacreditável [eenakraydeetavil] incredible

inaugurar: inauguração em breve [eenowgoorar] open soon

incêndio m [insaynd-yoo] fire

inchaço m [inshasoo] lump, swelling

inchado [inshadoo] swollen

incluído [inklweedoo] included

incluir [inklweer] to include

incomodado [inkohmohdadoo] annoyed

inconsciente [inkohnsyayntee] unconscious

inconstante [inkohnstantee] changeable

incrível [inkreevil] amazing, astonishing

indiano m [ind-yanoo] Indian

indicações fpl [indeekasoyngs] indications

indicador m [indeekadohr] indicator

indigestão f [indeeJaystowng] indigestion

indisposição estomacal f [indeespohzeesownng eestohmakal] upset stomach

indústria f [indoostr-ya] industry

infarto m [infartoo] heart attack

infecção f [infayksownng] infection

infeccioso [infayks-yohzoo] infectious

infecto [infehktoo] septic

infelizmente [infayleesmayntee] unfortunately

inflamação f [inflamasownng] inflammation

inflamável inflammable

informação f [infohrmasownng] information, piece of information

informação turística [infohrmasownng tooreesteeka] tourist information

informações fpl [infohrmasoyngs] directory enquiries; information

Inglaterra f [inglateh-Ha] England

inglês m [inglays] English; Englishman

em inglês [ayng] in English

inglesa f [inglayza] English; English woman

ingleses: os ingleses mpl [inglayzees] the English

ingredientes mpl [ingraydyayntees] ingredients

íngreme [eengreemee] steep

ingresso m [ingrehsoo] admission ticket

iniciante m/f [eenees-yantee] beginner

início m [inees-yoo] beginning
no início [noo] at the beginning

início de rodovia [Hodovee-a] start of motorway/highway

injeção f [inJaysowng] injection

inocente [inohsayntee] innocent

inseto m [insehtoo] insect

insistir [inseesteer] to insist

insolação f [insohlasowng] sunstroke

insônia f [inson-ya] insomnia

inteiro [intayroo] whole

inteligente [intayleeJayntee] intelligent, clever

interditado [intayrdeetado] blocked

interessado [intayraysadoo] interested

interessante [intayraysantee] interesting

internacional [internas-yohnal] international

interpretar [intayrpraytar] to interpret

intérprete m/f [intehrpraytee] interpreter

interruptor m [intay-Hooptohr] switch

intervalo m [intayrvaloo] interval

intoxicação alimentar f [intohkseekasowng] food poisoning

introduza a moeda na ranhura insert coin in slot

inundação f [eenoondasowng] flood

inverno m [invehrnoo] winter

ir [eer] to go
ir buscar [booskar] to get, to fetch

Irlanda f [eerlanda] Ireland

Irlanda do Norte f [eerlanda doo nortee] Northern Ireland

irlandês m [eerlandays] Irish; Irishman

irlandesa f [eerlandayza] Irish; Irishwoman

irmã f [eermang] sister

irmão m [eermowng] brother

irritado [ee-Heetadoo] pissed

isolado [eezohladoo] secluded

isqueiro m [eeskayroo] cigarette lighter

isso [eesoo] that; that one
isso é... [eh] that's...
isso é...? is that...?

isto [eestoo] this; this one
isto é...? [eestweh] is this...?

Itália f [eetal-ya] Italy

italiana f [eetal-yana] Italian,
italiano m [eetal-yanoo] Italian

J

já [Ja] ever; already
já que [Ja kee] since

janeiro [Janayro] January
janela f [Janehla] window
jantar m [Jantar] evening meal, dinner; supper; to have dinner
jaqueta f [Jakayta] jacket; coat
jarda f [Jarda] yard
jardim m [Jardeeng] garden
jardim zoológico [zoh-ohloJeekoo] zoo
jarro m [JaHoo] jug; jar
joalheria f [Jwal-yayree-a] jeweller's
joelho m [Jwayl-yoo] knee
jogador de futebol m [Jogadohr dee footaybol] football player
jogar [Johgar] to play
jogar fora to throw away
jogo m [Johgoo] game, match
jóias fpl [Jo-yas] jewellery
jornal m [Johrnal] newspaper
jovem m/f [Jovayng] young
jovens mpl [Jovayngs] young people
judeu [Jooday-oo] Jewish
julho [Jool-yoo] July
junho [Joon-yoo] June
junto da... [Joontoo da] beside the...
juntos [Joontoos] together
justo [Joostoo] just, fair
justo [Joostoo] tight (for clothes)

K

kit de primeiros socorros m [primayroos sohkorroosh] first-aid kit

L

lã f [lang] wool
lá over there, there
lábios mpl [lab-yoos] lips
lado m [ladoo] side
  do outro lado [doo ohtroo] opposite
  do outro lado de... [doo ohtroo ladoo dee] across the...
ladra f, **ladrão** m [ladrowng] thief
lago m [lagoo] lake; pond
lama f mud
lamentar [lamayntar] to regret, to be sorry
lâminas de barbear fpl [lameenas dee barb-yar] razor blades
lâmpada f lamp, light bulb
lanterna f [lantehrna] torch, flashlight
lanternas trazeiras [trazayras] rear lights
lápis m [lapees] pencil
lápis de olho [lapees dee ol-yoo] eyeliner
lápis de sobrancelha [dee sohbransayl-ya] eyebrow pencil
laranja f [laranJa] orange
largo m [largoo] wide; square
lata f can; tin
lata de lixo [lata dee leeshoo] bin, dustbin, trashcan
lavagem a seco f [lavaJayng a saykoo] dry-cleaning
lava-louça f [lava lohsa] sink
lavanderia f [lavandayree-a] laundry (place)

lavanderia automática [owtohma**teeka**] launderette

lavar to wash

lavar a mão [mowng] to handwash

lavar a roupa [**Hoh**pa] to do the washing

lavar e pentear [lavar ee paynt-**yar**] shampoo and set

lavar na máquina [na ma**keena**] machine wash

lavar(se) [see] to wash (oneself)

lava-rápido [Ha**peedoo**] carwash

laxante m [la**shantee**] laxative

lei f [lay] law

leiteria f [laytar**ee**-a] shop selling dairy products

leitor de CD m [lay**tohr** dee say-day] CD player

lembrança f [laym**bransa**] gift; souvenir

lembrar(se) [see] to remember

lembra-se? [**laym**brasee] do you remember?

não me lembro [**nowng** mee **laym**broo] I don't remember

lenço m [**layn**soo] handkerchief

lenço de cabeça [dee ka**baysa**] headscarf

lençol m [layn**sol**] sheet

lenços de papel mpl [**layn**soos dee pa**pehl**] tissues, paper handkerchiefs, Kleenex®

lentes de contato fpl [**layn**tees dee kohn**tatoo**] contact lenses

lentes gelatinosas [Jaylatee**nozas**] soft lenses

lentes rígidas [**Hee**Jeedas] hard lenses

lentes semi-rígidas [**say**mee **Hee**Jeedas] gas permeable lenses

lento [**layn**too] slow

leque m [**leh**kee] fan (handheld)

ler [layr] to read

lésbica f [**lehs**beeka] lesbian

leste m [**leh**stee] east

no leste [noo] in the east

letra f [**lay**tra] letter

letra de imprensa [im**praynsa**] block letters

levantar-se [layvan**tarsee**] to get up

levar to take; to carry

leve [**leh**vee] light (not heavy)

lhe [l-yay] (to) him; (to) her; (to) you

lhes [l-yays] (to) them; (to) you

libra f [**leebra**] pound

libras esterlinas fpl [eestayr**lee**nas] pounds sterling

lição f [lee**sowng**] lesson

licença f [lee**saynsa**] licence; permit

ligação f [liga**sowng**] connection; call

ligação a cobrar collect call, reverse charge call

ligação internacional [intayrnas-yoh**nal**] international call

ligação interurbana [intayroor**bana**] long-distance call

ligação local [loh**kal**] local call

ligar [lee**gar**] to turn on, to switch on; to call

limite de velocidade m [leemeetee dee vaylohseedadee] speed limit

limpador de pára-brisa m [leempadohr dee parabreeza] windscreen wiper

limpar [leempar] to clean

limpeza a seco f [leempayza a saykoo] dry-clean; dry-cleaning

limpo [leempoo] clean

língua f [leengwa] language; tongue

linha f [leen-ya] line

liquidação f [leekeedasowng] sale

liquidação total clearance sale

liso [leezoo] plain

lista f [leesta] list

lista telefônica [taylayfohneeka] phone book, telephone directory

litoral m [leetohral] coast

no litoral on the coast

litro m [leetroo] litre

livraria f [leevraree-a] bookshop, bookstore

livre [leevree] free, vacant

livro m [leevroo] book

lixa de unhas f [leesha dee oon-yas] nailfile

lixo m [leeshoo] rubbish, trash; litter

locadora de carros f [lohkadohra dee KaHoos] car hire, car rental

localidade f [lohkaleedadee] place

loção f [lohsowng] lotion

loção pós-sol aftersun cream

loção de limpeza [dee leempayza] cleansing lotion

locomotiva f [lohkohmohteeva] engine

logo [logoo] immediately, at once

logo que possível [kee pohseevil] as soon as possible

loiro [loh-iroo] blond

loja f [loJa] shop

loja de antiguidades [dee anteegeedadees] antique shop

loja de artesanato [dee artayzanatoo] craft shop, handicrafts shop

loja de artigos de pele [arteegoos dee pehlee] furrier

loja de artigos fotográficos [fohtohgrafeekoos] camera shop

loja de brinquedos [breenkaydoos] toyshop

loja de chapéus f [shapeh-oos] hat shop

loja de departamentos f [daypartamayntoos] department store

loja de ferragens [fayHaJayngs] hardware store

loja de lembranças [laymbransas] gift shop

loja de malas [malas] handbag shop

loja de material esportivo [eespohrteevoo] sports shop

loja de produtos naturais [prohdootoos natooris] health food shop

Londres [lohndrees] London

longe [lohnJee] far

ao longe [ow] in the distance

fica longe? [**fee**ka] is it far away?

lotação esgotada [lohtasowng eesgot**a**da] all tickets sold

lotado [loh**ta**doo] crowded

louça f [**loh**sa] crockery
lavar a louça to wash the dishes

louça de cerâmica [dee sayra-**mee**ka] pottery, earthenware

louça vitrificada [veetreefeek**a**da] glazed earthenware

louco [**loh**koo] crazy, mad

lua f [**loo**-a] moon

lua-de-mel f [**loo**-a dee mehl] honeymoon

lugar m [loo**gar**] seat; place
em outro lugar [ayng **oh**troo] elsewhere, somewhere else
um lugar na janela [na Jan**eh**la] window seat
um lugar no corredor [noo koh-Hay**dohr**] aisle seat

lugares em pé standing room

lugares reservados para deficientes e idosos seats reserved for disabled and senior citizen

luvas fpl [**loo**vas] gloves

luxo [**loo**shoo] luxury
de luxo [dee] de luxe

luxuoso [loosh-w**oh**zoo] luxurious

luz f [loos] light

luz do sol f [doo] sunshine

M

má bad; nasty

macaco m [mak**a**koo] jack

maçaneta f [masan**ayta**] door knob

machão m [mash**owng**] macho

machista [mash**ee**sta] sexist

macio [mas**ee**-oo] soft

maço m [**ma**soo] packet

madeira f [mad**ayra**] wood

madrasta f [mad**ra**sta] stepmother

madrugada f [madroo**ga**da] dawn
de madrugada [dee] at dawn

maduro [mad**oo**roo] ripe

mãe f [mayng] mother

magricela [magree**seh**la] skinny

magro [**ma**groo] slim; thin

maiô [mī-**oh**] swimming costume

maio [mī-oo] May

maior [mī-**or**] greater; bigger, larger
a maior parte (de) [**par**tee (dee)] most (of)
o maior the biggest

maioria: a maioria dos... [mī-oh**ree**-a doos] most...

mais [mīs] more
mais alguma coisa? [mīs alg**oo**ma **koh**-iza] anything else?
mais de... [mīs dee] more than..., over...
mais... do que... [doo kee] more... than...
mais longe [mīs **lohn**Jee] further
mais nada no more; nothing else
mais ou menos [mīs oh **may**noos] about, approximately, more or less; average, so-so

Ma

mais tarde [mīs tardee] later,
later on

mais um(a) [mīs oong/**oo**ma] an
extra one

não tem mais [nowng tayng mīs]
there's none left

mal hardly; badly

mala f [malas] bag; suitcase;
handbag

fazer as malas [fazayr as] to
pack one's bags

mal-entendido m [malayntayn-
deedoo] misunderstanding

maleta f [mal**ay**ta] briefcase

malha f [mal-ya] jersey

malpassado not cooked,
undercooked

maluco [mal**oo**koo] barmy, nuts

mamadeira f [mamad**ay**ra]
baby's bottle

mamãe f [mam**ay**ng] mum

manauara m/f [manow**ara**]
born or living at Manaus,
Amazonas

mancha f [mansha] spot, stain

mandar to send

manga f sleeve; mango

manhã f [man-y**ang**] morning

às sete da manhã [as s**eh**tee]
at seven a.m.

de manhã [dee] in the morning

esta manhã [**eh**sta] this
morning

mansão f [mans**ow**ng] villa

mantenha a direita/a esquerda
keep right/left

mantenha-se à direita,
caminhe pela esquerda
(cars) keep to the right,
(pedestrians) walk on the left

manter em lugar fresco store
in a cold place

manter longe da luz solar
direta store away from direct
sunlight

mão f [mowng] hand

mão única [**oo**neeka] one way

mapa m map

mapa de ruas [dee H**oo**-as]
street map

mapa rodoviário m
[Hohdohvee**ar**-yoo] road map

maquiagem f [mak-ya**Jay**ng]
make-up

máquina f [ma**kee**na] machine

máquina de lavar roupa [dee
lav**ar**] washing machine

máquina de vendas [**vay**ndas]
vending machine

máquina fotográfica
[fohtohgr**a**fika] camera

mar m sea

maranhense m/f [maran-y**ay**nsee]
born or living at Maranhão

maravilhoso [maraveel-y**oh**zoo]
wonderful

marca f make, brand name

marca registrada [HayJeestr**a**da]
registered trademark

marcha a ré [marsha Heh]
reverse gear

março [m**a**rsoo] March

maré f [mar**eh**] tide

mareado [mar-yad**oo**] seasick

margem f [marJayng] shore

marido m [mar**ee**doo] husband

Marrocos m [maH**o**koos]
Morocco

marrom [ma**Hohng**] brown

martelo **m** [mar**teh**loo] hammer

mas but

matar to kill

material de escritório [matayr-
y**al** dee ayskreet**or**-yoo] **m** office
supplies

maternidade **f** [matayrneed**a**dee]
maternity hospital

mato-grossense **m/f** [matoh-
groh-s**ay**nsee] born or living at
Mato Grosso

mato-grossense-do-sul [doo]
born or living at Mato
Grosso do Sul

mau [mow] bad; nasty

maxilar **f** [mak**see**lar] jaw

me me; to me; myself

mecânico **m** [mayk**a**neekoo]
mechanic

média: em média **f** [ayng m**eh**d-
ya] on average

médica **f** [m**eh**deeka] doctor

medicamento **m**
[maydeekam**ay**ntoo] drug

médico **m** [m**eh**deekoo] doctor

médio [m**eh**d-yoo] medium;
medium-rare

de tamanho médio [dee taman-
yoo] medium-sized

Mediterrâneo **m** [maydeetay**Han**-
yoo] Mediterranean

medo **m** [m**ay**doo] fear

meia **f** [m**ay**-a] half

meia dúzia **f** [d**oo**z-ya] half a
dozen

meia hora **f** [**o**ra] half an hour

meia pensão **f** [payns**ow**ng] half
board, American plan

meia-calça **f** [k**al**sa] tights,
pantyhose

meia-noite **f** [n**oh**-itee]
midnight

meias **fpl** [m**ay**-as] stockings;
socks

meias de náilon [dee] hosiery

meio **m** [m**ay**-oo] middle; half

no meio [noo] in the middle

meio bilhete **m** [beel-y**ay**tee]
half fare

meio-dia **m** [m**ay**-oo d**ee**-a]
midday, noon

ao meio-dia [ow] at midday

mel **m** [mehl] honey

melhor [mayl-y**or**] best; better

melhorar [mayl-yor**ar**] to
improve

mencionar [mayns-yohn**ar**] to
mention

menina **f** [mayn**ee**na] girl

menino **m** [mayn**ee**noo] boy

menor [mayn**or**] smaller

menos [m**ay**noos] less

menos de [dee] under, less
than

menos do que [doo kee] less
than

pelo menos [**pay**loo] at least

menstruação **f** [maynstroo-
as**ow**ng] period

mentir [maynt**eer**] to lie

menu de preço fixo **m** [dee
pr**ay**soo f**ee**ksoo] fixed-price
menu

menu turístico [tooreesteekoo]
tourist menu

mercado **m** [mayrk**a**doo] market

mercearia **f** [mayrs-yar**ee**-a]

grocery store
merda! [**meh**rda] shit!
mergulhar [mayrgool-**yar**] to dive
mergulho sem equipamento
m [mayrgool-yoo sayng
aykeepa**mayn**too] skin-diving
mês m [mays] month
mesa f [**may**za] table
mesma [**may**sma], **mesmo**
[**may**smoo] same; myself
é mesmo? really?
ele mesmo himself [**ay**lee]
mesmo se... [see] even if...
o mesmo/a mesma the same
metade do preço [doo **pray**soo]
half price
metade f [may**ta**dee] half
metro m [**meh**troo] metre
metrô m [may**troh**]
underground, (US) subway
meu [**may**-oo] my; mine
meu próprio... [**propr**-yoo] my
own...
meus [**may**-oos] my; mine
mexer [may**shayr**] to move
microondas m [meekroh-**oh**ndas]
microwave (oven)
mil [meel] thousand
milha f [**meel**-ya] mile
milhão m [meel-**yowng**] million
milímetro m [meelee**may**troo]
millimetre
mim [meeng] me
mineiro [mee**nay**roo] born or
living at Minas Gerais
minha [**meen**-ya], **minhas** [meen-
yas] my; mine
ministério m [meenee**stehr**-yoo]
ministry

minúsculo [meen**oo**skooloo] tiny
minuto m [mee**noo**too] minute
míope [**mee**-oopee] shortsighted
missa m [**mee**sa] mass
misturar [meestoo**rar**] to mix
mobília f [moh**beel**-ya] furniture
moça f [**moh**sa] young girl
mochila f [moh**shee**la] rucksack,
backpack
moda f fashion
na moda fashionable
moda feminina [faymee**nee**na]
ladies' fashions
moderno [moh**dehr**noo] modern
moeda f [moh-**eh**da] coin
moeda estrangeira
[eestran**Jay**ra] foreign currency
moinho m [moo-een-yoo] mill
moisés m [moh-i**zehs**] carry-cot
mola f [**mo**la] spring (in seat)
mole [**mo**lee] soft
molhado [mohl-**ya**doo] wet
momento m [moh**mayn**too]
moment
um momento [oong] hold on,
just a moment
montanha f [mohn**tan**-ya]
mountain
montar a cavalo [ka**va**loo] to go
horse-riding
monte m [**mohn**tee] hill
monumento m [mohnoo**mayn**too]
monument
monumento nacional [nas-
yohna] national monument
morar [moh**rar**] to live
mordida f [mohr**dee**da] bite
morno [**mohr**noo] lukewarm
morrer [moh-**Hayr**] to die

morte f [**mor**tee] death
morto [**moh**rtoo] dead
  morto de fome [dee **foh**mee]
  starving
mosca f [**moh**ska] fly
mosquito m [mohs**kee**too]
  mosquito
mosteiro m [mohs**tay**roo]
  monastery
mostrar [mohs**trar**] to show
moto f, **motocicleta** f
  [mohtohseek**leh**ta] motorbike
motoneta f [mohtoh**nay**ta]
  scooter
motor m [moh**tohr**] engine
motor de arranque [dee
  a**Han**kee] starter motor
motor home f caravan, (US)
  trailer
motorista m/f [mohtoh**rees**ta]
  driver; motorist
móveis de cozinha mpl [**mo**vays
  dee koh**zeen**-ya] kitchen
  furniture
movimentado [mohveemayn**ta**doo]
  busy
muçulmano [moosool**ma**noo]
  Muslim
mudar [moo**dar**] to move
  mudar de roupa [dee **Hoh**pa] to
  get changed
  mudar em... change at...
muitas vezes [**mween**gtas
  vayzees] often
muito [**mween**gtoo] a lot, lots;
  plenty of; much; very
  (much); quite
  muito bem [**bayng**] very well
  muito bem! well done!

muito mais [**mīs**] a lot more
muito prazer [pra**zayr**] nice to
  meet you
**muito prazer em conhecê-
lo** [ayng kohn-yay**say**loo] very
  pleased to meet you
muito tempo [**taym**poo] a long
  time
não muito [nowng] not (very)
  much; not a lot; not too
  much
muitos mpl [**mween**gtoos] many
muletas fpl [moo**lay**tas] crutches
mulher f [mool-**yehr**] woman;
  wife
multa f [**mool**ta] fine
multa por uso indevido [pohr
  oozoo inday**vee**doo] penalty for
  misuse
multidão f [mooltee**down**g] crowd
mundo m [**moon**doo] world
muro m [**moo**roo] wall
músculo m [**moos**kooloo] muscle
museu m [moo**zay**-oo] museum
música f [**moo**zeeka] music
música folclórica [fohl**klo**reeka]
  folk music
música pop pop music
músico m [**moo**zeekoo] musician

N

na in the; at the; on the
  na casa do Francisco at
  Francisco's
  na quinta-feira by Thursday
  na televisão on television
nacional [nas-yohna**l**] national

nacionalidade f [nas-yohnalidadee] nationality

nada nothing

de nada my pleasure, don't mention it

mais nada [mis] nothing else

nada a declarar nothing to declare

nadar to swim

namorada f [namohrada] girlfriend

namorado m [namohradoo] boyfriend

não [nowng] no; not

não beber do not drink

não congelar do not freeze

não contém... does not contain...

não diga! [deega] you don't say!

não engolir do not swallow

não exceder a dose indicada do not exceed the dose indicated

não faz mal [fas mal] it doesn't matter, never mind; it's OK

não fumar no smoking

não funciona out of order

não há vagas no vacancies

não mexer do not touch

não passar a ferro do not iron

não pendurar no varal do not hang, dry flat

não pisar na grama please keep off the grass

não secar na máquina do not spin-dry

não sei [say] I don't know

não tem de quê [tayng dee kay] don't mention it, you're welcome

não torcer do not wring

não... nada nothing; not... anything

não... nenhum [nayn-yoong] none; not... any

não... ninguém [neengayng] nobody, no-one; not... anybody, not... anyone

não... nunca [noonka] never

nariz m [narees] nose

nas [nas] in the; at the; on the

nascer [nasayr] to be born

nasci em... [nasee ayng] I was born in...

natação f [natasowng] swimming

Natal m Christmas

natural [natooral] natural

natureza f [natoorayza] nature

náusea f [nowz-ya] nausea

navio m [navee-o] ship

de navio [dee] by ship

neblina m [naybleena] fog

necessário [naysaysar-yoo] necessary

negativo m [naygateevoo] negative

negócio m [naygos-yoo] deal; business

nem eu [nayng ay-oo] nor do I

nem... nem... [nayng] neither... nor...

nenhum [nayn-yoong], **nenhuma** [nayn-yooma] none; no...

de jeito nenhum! [dee Jaytoo] no way!

de nenhum modo [**mo**doo] not in the least

nenhum deles [**day**lees] neither of them

neozelandês m [**neh**-o zaylandays], **neozelandesa f** [zaylandayza] New Zealander

nervoso [nayrvoh**zoo**] nervous

neta f [**neh**ta] granddaughter

neto m [**neh**too] grandson

nevar [nay**var**] to snow

neve f [**neh**vee] snow

névoa f [**neh**vwa] mist

nevoeiro m [nayvway**roo**] fog

ninguém [neeng**ayng**] nobody, no-one

nível do óleo m [**nee**vil doo ol-yoo] oil level

no [noo] in; in the; at the; on the

no alto [**al**too] at the top

no fundo de [**foon**doo] at the bottom of

no hotel [ohte**hl**] at the hotel

no sábado on Saturday

nº number

noite f [**noh**-itee] evening; night

à noite in the evening; at night

de noite [dee] at night

esta noite [**eh**sta] this evening; tonight

Noite de Natal f Christmas Eve

noite de Santo Antônio [santoo anto**hn**-yoo] 13th June: Saint's day with music, fireworks and campfires

noite de São João [sowng Joo-owng] 24th June: Saint's day with music, fireworks and campfires

noite de São Pedro [sowng pay**droo**] 29th June: Saint's day with music, fireworks and campfires

noiva f [**noh**-iva] engaged; fiancée

noivo m [**noh**-ivoo] engaged; fiancé

nojento [nohJ**ayn**too] disgusting; filthy

nome m [**noh**mee] name

nome de solteira [dee soh**l**tayra] maiden name

nono [**noh**noo] ninth

nora f daughter-in-law

nordeste m [nohrde**h**stee] northeast

noroeste m [noroh-e**h**stee] northwest

norte m [**nor**tee] north

ao norte [ow] to the north

no norte [noo] in the north

Noruega f [nohr**weh**ga] Norway

norueguês m [nohrweg**ays**], **norueguesa f** [noorweg**ay**za] Norwegian

nos [noos] in the; at the; on the; us; to us; ourselves

nós [nos] we; us

nossa, nossas [**no**sas], **nosso** [**no**soo], **nossos** [**no**soos] our; ours

Nossa Senhora [**no**sa sayn-**yo**ra] Our Lady

Nosso Senhor [**no**soo sayn-**yohr**] Our Lord

nota f note; banknote, (US) bill

notas falsas fpl [notas falsas] forged banknotes

notícias fpl [nohtees-yas] news

Nova Zelândia [zayland-ya] New Zealand

nove [novee] nine

novecentas [noveesayntas], **novecentos** [noveesayntoos] nine hundred

novembro [nohvaymbroo] November

noventa [nohvaynta] ninety

novidades fpl [nohveedadees] news

novo [nohvoo] new

novo endereço m [ayndayraysoo] forwarding address

nu [noo], **nua** [noo-a] naked

num [noong], **numa** [nooma] in a

número m [noomayroo] number

número de licença [dee leesaynsa] registration number

número de telefone [taylayfohnee] phone number

número do vôo [doo voh-oo] flight number

nunca [noonka] never

nuvem f [noovayng] cloud

O

o [oo] the; him; it; to it; you

o que [oo kay] what

o que é isso? [oo k-yeh eesoo] what's this?

objetiva f [objaytee-va] lens (of camera)

objetos de vime mpl [objehtoos dee veemee] wicker goods

objetos perdidos lost property, lost and found

obra f work

obras (na estrada) fpl roadworks

obrigado/obrigada [ohbreegadoo] thanks, thank you

muito obrigado/obrigada [mweengtoo] thank you very much

observar [obsayrvar] to watch

obturador m [obtooradohr] shutter

óbvio [obv-yoo] obvious

Oceano Atlântico [ohs-yanoo atlanteekoo] Atlantic Ocean

oculista m [okooleesta] optician

óculos mpl [okooloos] glasses, spectacles

óculos de sol [dee] sunglasses

óculos protetores [prohtaytohrees] goggles

ocupado [okoopadoo] engaged; busy; occupied

oeste m [oh-ehstee] west

no oeste [noo] in the west

ofender [ohfayndayr] to offend

ofensivo [ohfaynseevoo] offensive

oferecer [ohfayraysayr] to offer

oferta especial f [ohfehrta eespays-yal] special offer

oitavo [oh-itavoo] eighth

oitenta [oh-itaynta] eighty

oito [oh-itoo] eight

oitocentas [oh-itoosayntas],

oitocentos [oh-itoos**ayn**toos] eight hundred

olá! [oh**la**] hi!, hello!

óleo m [**ol**-yoo] oil

óleo de bronzear [dee brohnz-**yar**] suntan oil

oleoso [ol-y**oh**zoo] oily

olhar para [ol-**yar**] to look at

olho m [**ohl**-yoo] eye

ombro m [**ohm**broo] shoulder

onda f [**ohn**da] wave

onde [**ohn**dee] where

  aonde você vai? [vi] where are you going?

  de onde você é? [dee **ohn**dee voh**say** eh] where are you from?

  de onde? where from?

  onde está? [e**sta**] where is it?

  onde/onde é? [**ohn**dee eh] where/where is it?

ônibus m [**ohn**eeboos] coach, bus

ônibus para o aeroporto [**p**aroo a-ehroh**pohr**too] airport bus

ontem [**ohn**taynģ] yesterday

  ontem à noite [**n**oh-itee] last night

  ontem de manhã [dee man-**yanģ**] yesterday morning

onze [**ohn**zee] eleven

operação f [ohpayras**owng**] operation

oposto [oh**pohs**to] opposite

orelha f [oh**rayl**-ya] ear

orelhão m [ohrayl-**yowng**] payphone

organizar [ohrganee**zar**] to organize

orgulhoso [ohrgool-**yoh**zoo] proud

orquestra f [ohrkeh**stra**] orchestra

os [oos] the; them; you

osso m [**ohs**soo] bone

otimista [ohteem**eesta**] optimistic

ótimo [**oteem**oo] super

ótimo! great!, good!, excellent!

otorrinolaringologista [ohtoh-Heenoo-laringoh-loJ**eesta**] ear, nose and throat specialist

ou [oh] or

  ou... ou... either... or...

ouço [**ohs**oo] I hear

ouriço-do-mar m [ohreesoo doo] sea urchin

ouro m [**ohr**oo] gold

ousar [oh**zar**] to dare

outono m [ohtoh**noo**] autumn, (US) fall

  no outono [noo] in the autumn, in the fall

outro [**ohr**too] different, another; other

  em outro [aynģ] in another; on another

  outra coisa [**ohr**ta koh-iza] something else

  outra vez [vays] again

  outras localidades [**ohr**tras lohkaleed**adees**] other places

outubro [ohtoo**broo**] October

ouvir [ohv**eer**] to hear

  ao ouvir o sinal... [ow ohveer oo seenal] when you hear the tone...

ovelha f [ov**ayl**-ya] sheep

P

pá f spade

pacote m [pakotee] carton; pack

pacote de férias [dee fehr-yas] package holiday

padaria f [padaree-a] bakery

padeiro m [padayroo] baker

padrasto m [padrastoo] stepfather

padre m [padree] priest

pagamento m [pagamayntoo] payment

pagamento em dinheiro [ayng deen-yayroo] cash payment

pagar to pay

pagar em dinheiro to pay cash

página f [paJeena] page

páginas amarelas [amarehlas] yellow pages

pai m [pī] father

painel m [pīnehl] dashboard; panel

País de Gales m [pa-ees dee galees] Wales

país m [pa-ees] country; nation; homeland

pais mpl [pīs] parents

paisagem f [pīzaJayng] scenery

palácio m [palas-yoo] palace

palavra f word

palco m [palkoo] stage

paletó m [paleeto] jacket; coat

pálido [paleedoo] pale

pandeiro m [pandayroo] tambourine

pane f [panee] breakdown

panela f [panehla] pan, saucepan

panfleto m [panflaytoo] leaflet

pano m [panoo] fabric, cloth

pano de prato [dee pratoo] tea towel, dishcloth

papai m [papī] dad

papel m [papehl] paper

papel-alumínio [aloomeen-yoo] aluminium foil

papel de carta [dee] writing paper, notepaper

papel de embrulho [aymbrool-yoo] wrapping paper

papel higiênico [eeJ-yayneekoo] toilet paper

papel usado [oozadoo] waste paper

papelaria f [papaylaree-a] stationer

par m pair

um par de... [oong dee] a couple of...; a pair of...

para [para] into; for; to; towards

para alugar [aloogar] for hire; to rent

para onde? [ohndee] where to?

parabéns! [parabayngs] congratulations!; happy birthday!

pára-brisa m [para-breeza] windscreen

pára-choque m [parashokee] bumper

parada f [parada] stop

parafuso m [parafoozoo] screw

paraibano [para-eebanoo] born or living at Paraíba

paranaense m/f [parana-**ayn**see]
born or living at Paraná

parapente m [parapa**ayn**tee] paragliding

parar to stop

pare! [**paree**] stop!

pare com isso! [kohng **ee**soo]
stop it!

pare, olhe e escute stop, look
and listen

parecer [paray**sayr**] to look like

parede f [para**ay**dee] wall

parente m/f [para**ayn**tee] relative

parentes por afinidade mpl
[poor afeeneed**a**dee] in-laws

parque [**par**kee] park

parque de diversões [dee
deevayr**soy**ngs] amusement
park

parte f [**par**tee] part

em parte nenhuma [nayn-
yooma] nowhere

em toda a parte [**toh**da]
everywhere

parte posterior [pohstayr-y**ohr**]
back (part)

particular [parteekoo**lar**] private

partida f [par**tee**da] departure

partida de futebol [dee footay**bol**]
football match

partido m [par**tee**doo] party
(political)

partilhar [parteel-**yar**] to share

partir [par**teer**] to leave

a partir de [dee] from

Páscoa f [**pask**wa] Easter

passado m [pas**a**doo] past

no ano passado [noo **a**noo]
last year

semana passada [say**ma**na]
last week

passageira f [pasaJ**ay**ra],
passageiro m [pasaJ**ay**roo]
passenger

passagem f [pasaJ**ayng**] ticket
(de excursão) [dee ayskoors**owng**]
excursion ticket

uma passagem de ida [**dee**da]
single ticket, one-way ticket

**uma passagem de ida e
volta** [**dee**da ee] return ticket,
round trip ticket

uma passagem aberta
[a**behr**ta] open ticket

uma passagem simples m
[**seem**plees] single ticket, one-
way ticket

passagem de nível f [pasaJ**ayng**]
level crossing, (US) grade
crossing

passagem de pedestres
[payd**eh**strees] pedestrian
crossing, (US) crosswalk

passagem subterrânea [soo-
btayH**an**-ya] underpass

passaporte m [pasa**por**tee]
passport

passar a ferro [a feh-**Hoo**] to
iron

passar to pass

pássaro m [p**as**aroo] bird

passatempo m [pasat**aym**poo]
hobby

passe go, walk, cross now

passeio m [pas**ay**-oo]: **dar um
passeio** to go for a walk

passeio turístico [toor**ee**steekoo]
sightseeing tour

pasta f [pasta] briefcase

pasta de dentes [dee dayntees] toothpaste

pastilhas para a garganta fpl [pasteel-yas] throat pastilles

patinar [pateenar] to skid; to skate

patins de gelo mpl [pateens dee Jayloo] ice skates

patrão m [patrowng] boss

paulista m/f [powleesta] born or living at the state of São Paulo

paulistano [powleestanoo] born or living at São Paulo city

pavilhão de esportes [paveel-yowng] sports pavilion

pé m [peh] foot
a pé on foot
ficar de pé [feekar dee] to stand
ir a pé to walk

peça de teatro f [pehsa dee tay-atroo] play

peça sobresselente [sohbraysalayntee] spare part

pechincha f [paysheensha] bargain

pedaço m [paydasoo] piece

pedágio m [paydaJ-yoo] toll

pedestre m [paydehstree] pedestrian

pedir [paydeer] to ask; to order

pedir carona [karohna] to hitchhike

pedir emprestado [aympraystadoo] to borrow

pedra f [pehdra] stone, rock

pegar [paygar] to catch; to pick up

peito m [paytoo] breast; bust; chest

peixaria f [paysharee-a] fishmonger's

pela(s) [payla] through the; by the; about the
pelas três horas [trays oras] by three o'clock

pele f [pehlee] skin; leather; suede; fur

peleteiro m [paylaytayroo] furrier

pelo [payloo] through the; by the; about the

pelos [payloos] through the; by the; about the

pena: é uma pena [eh ooma payna] it's a pity
não vale a pena [nowng val-ya] there's no point
que pena! [kee] what a pity!
tenho muita pena [tayn-yoo mweengta] I'm so sorry

pensão f [paynsowng] guesthouse

pensão completa [komplehta] full board

pensar [paynsar] to think

pente m [payntee] comb

pequeno [paykaynoo] little, small

perdão [payrdowng] sorry

perder [payrdayr] to lose; to miss

perdido [payrdeedoo] lost

perfeito [payrfaytoo] perfect

perfumaria f [payrfoomaree-a] perfume shop

pergunta f [payrgoonta] question

perguntar [payrgoontar] to ask

perigo m [payreegoo] danger
 perigo: pare danger: stop
perigo de desmoronamento
 danger of landslides [dee days-mohroh-namayntoo]
perigo de incêndio beware of
 starting fires [insaynd-yoo]
perigo de morte extreme
 danger [mortee]
perigoso [payreegohzoo]
 dangerous
período m [payree-oodoo] period
permanente f [payrmanayntee]
 perm
permitido [payrmeeteedo] allowed
permitir [payrmeeteer] to allow
perna f [pehrna] leg
 de pernas para o ar [dee
 pehrnas proo ar] upside down
pernambucano
 [payrnambookanoo] born or
 living at Pernambuco
persianas fpl [payrs-yanas]
 blinds; shutters
pertencer [payrtaynsayr] to
 belong
perto [pehrtoo] near
 perto daqui [dakee] nearby,
 near here
 perto de [dee] next to
perturbar [payrtoorbar] to disturb
peruca f [payrooka] wig
pesadelo m [payzadayloo]
 nightmare
pesado [payzadoo] heavy
pesca f [pehska] fishing
pesca submarina [soob-mareena] underwater fishing
pescar [payskar] to fish

pescoço m [payskohsoo] neck
peso m [payzoo] weight
peso líquido [leekeedoo] net
 weight
pessoa f [paysoh-a] person
pessoal m [paysoo-al] staff,
 employees
pia f [pee-a] washhand basin
piada f [p-yada] joke
piauiense m/f [p-yow-ee-aynsee]
 born or living at Piauí
picada f [peekada] bite; sting
picada de inseto [dinsehtoo]
 insect bite
picado [peekadoo] stung
picante [peekantee] hot, spicy
picar [peekar] to sting; to chop
 finely
picolé m [peekoleh] ice lolly
píer m [peer] jetty
pijama m [peeJama] pyjamas
pilha f [peel-ya] battery
pílula f [peeloola] pill
pinça f [peensa] tweezers
pincel m [peensehl] paintbrush
pintar [peentar] to paint
pintura f [peentoora] picture
pior [p-yor] worse; worst
 o pior the worst
piquenique m [peekeeneekee]
 picnic
pires m [peerees] saucer
pirulito m [peerooleetoo] lollipop
pisca-alerta m [peeska alehrta]
 sidelights
piscina f [peeseena] swimming
 pool
piscina coberta [kohbehrta]
 indoor pool

piscina infantil [infanteel] children's pool

pista f [peesta] runway

pista escorregadia slippery road surface

pista irregular uneven road surface [eeHaygoolar]

placa indicativa f [plaka indeekateeva] signpost

placa de carro f [dee kaHoo] licence plate

plano m [planoo] plan; flat (adj)

planta f plant

plástico m [plasteekoo] plastic

plataforma f [plataforma] platform, (US) track

platéia f [plateh-ya] audience; ground floor of auditorium

platinados mpl [plateenadoos] points

playground m playground

pneu m [p-nay-oo] tyre

pó m [paw] dust; powder

pobre [pobree] poor

pode [podee] you can/he/she can

pode me dar...? [podee mee dar] can I have a...?, may I have...?

pode-se...? [podeesee] is it OK to...?

você pode...? [vohsay] can you...?

poder [pohdayr] to be able to; power

poderia [pohdayree-a] could

poderia me servir...? could I have...?

você poderia...? could you...?

podre [pohdree] rotten

põe [poyng] he/she/it puts; you put

põem [poh-ayng] you/they put

pões [poyngs] you put

polegada f [pohlaygada] inch

polegar m [pohlaygar] thumb

polícia f [pohlees-ya] police

policial m/f [poolees-yal] policewoman, policeman

poliéster polyester

política f politics

político political

poluído [pohloo-eedoo] polluted

polvo m [pohlvoo] octopus

pomada f [pohmada] ointment

pomos [pohmoos] we put

pônei m [ponay] pony

ponho [pohn-yoo] I put

ponte f [pohntee] bridge; crown

ponto de encontro m [pohntoo dee aynkohntroo] meeting place/point

ponto de ônibus [dee ohneeboos] bus stop

ponto de táxi [dee taxi] taxi rank

população f [pohpoolasowng] population

pôr [pohr] to put

por [poor] through; by

por avião by airmail

por cento [sayntoo] per cent

por favor [favohr] please

por noite [noh-itee] per night

por quê? [poorkay] why?

por que não? [nowng] why not?

188

porca f [porka] nut (for bolt)
porção f [pohrsowng] portion
porção para crianças [para kr-yan-sas] children's portion
porcaria f [pohrkaree-a] dirt; mess
porcelana f [pohrsaylana] china
porco m [pohrkoo] pig
pôr-do-sol m [pohr doo] sunset
porque [poorkay] because
porta f [porta] door
porta-malas m [malas] boot, (US) trunk
porta-moedas m [moh-ehdas] purse
portão m [pohrtowng] gate
portão de embarque [dee aymbarkee] gate (at airport)
portão número... [noomayroo] gate number...
porteiro m [pohrtayroo] doorman, porter
porteiro da noite [noh-itee] night porter
porto m harbour, port
português m [pohrtoogays] Portuguese; Portuguese man
em português in Portuguese
os portugueses the Portuguese
portuguesa f [pohrtoogayza] Portuguese; Portuguese woman
posologia f dose
possível [pohseevil] possible
posso [posoo] I can
posso...? can I...?
postagem f [pohstaJayng] postage

posta-restante f [posta Haystantee] poste restante, (US) general delivery
pôster m poster
posterior: parte posterior [pohstayr-yohr] back (part)
posto de polícia m [pohstoo dee poolees-ya] police station
posto de combustível [dee kohmboosteevil] service station
potiguar m/f [pohteegwar] born or living at Rio Grande do Norte
pouco [pohkoo] a little
pouco comum [kohmoong] unusual
um pouco [oong] a little bit
um pouco caro [karoo] a bit expensive
um pouco disto [deestoo] some of this
poucos [pohkoos] few; a few
pouquinho: um pouquinho [oong pohkeen-yoo] a little bit
pousada f [pohsada] small hotel
pouso m [pohzoo] landing
pouso de emergência [emayrJayns-ya] emergency landing
povo m [pohvoo] people
praça f [prasa] square
praia f [prī-a] seafront; beach
na praia on the beach
prancha de windsurfe f [pransha] sailboard
prata f [prata] silver
prateleira f [prataylayra] shelf
praticar [prateekar] to practise
praticar jogging to go jogging

praticar windsurfe to windsurf

prático [prateekoo] practical

prato m [pratoo] course, dish; plate

prato feito (PF) [pratoo faytoo (pay-**eh**fee)] today's menu, set menu

prazer: (muito) prazer em conhecê-lo/conhecê-la [(mweengtoo) prazayr ayng kohn-yaysayloo] pleased to meet you

precisar [prayseezar] to need

preciso de... [prayseezoo dee] I need...

preço m [praysoo] price; charge

preço de custo [koostoo] cost price

preço por dia [poor dee-a] price per day

preço por pessoa [paysoh-a] price per person

preço por semana [saymana] price per week

preços reduzidos [Haydoozeedoos] reduced prices

prédio de apartamentos m [prehd-yoo dee apartamayntoos] apartment block

preencher [pray-aynshayr] to fill in

prefeitura f [prayfaytoora] town hall

preferência: dar a preferência [prafayrayns-ya] give way, yield

preferencial f right of way [prafayrayns-ya0]

preferir [prayfayreer] to prefer

prefiro... [prayfeeroo] I prefer...

prego m [prehgoo] nail (metal)

preguiçoso [praygeesohzoo] lazy

prendedor de roupa m [prayndaydohr dee Hohpa] clothes peg

prender [prayndayr] to arrest

preocupação f [pray-ohkoopasowng] worry

preocupado [pray-ohkoopadoo] worried

preocupar-se com to worry about

preparar [prayparar] to prepare

presente m [prayzaynt] present, gift

presentes fpl [prayzayntees] gifts

preservativo m [prayzayrvateevoo] condom

presidente m/f [prayzeedayntee] president

pressa: estou com pressa f [eestoh kohng prehsa] I'm in a hurry

não há pressa [nowng a] there's no hurry

pressão f [praysowng] pressure

pressão alta high blood pressure

pressão arterial [artayr-ya0] blood pressure

presta: não presta [nowng prehsta] it's no good

prestativo [prestateevoo] helpful

preto [praytoo] black

preto-e-branco black and white

previsão do tempo f [prayveezowng doo taympoo] weather forecast

prima f [preema] cousin

primavera f [preemavehra]

190

spring

primeira [preem**ay**ra] first

a primeira à esquerda [a
ees**kay**rda] first on the left

a primeira vez f [vays] the
first time

primeira classe [kl**ah**see] first
class

primeiro [preem**ay**roo] first

primeiro andar first floor, (US)
second floor

**primeiro nome/nome de
batismo** [n**oh**mee/bat**ees**moo]
Christian name, first name

primeiro-ministro m
[meen**ees**troo] prime minister

primeiros-socorros mpl
[prim**ay**roos soh**ko**Hoos] first aid

primo m [pr**eem**oo] cousin

princesa f [preens**ay**za] princess

principal [preens**eepa**l] main

principalmente
[preens**eepalmayntee**] mostly

príncipe m [pr**eens**eepee] prince

principiante m/f [preenseep-
yantee] beginner

princípio: a princípio [preens**eep**-
yoo] at first

prioridade f priority [pr-
yohr**eedadee**]

prisão f [preez**owng**] jail

prisão de ventre [dee **vay**ntree]
constipation

problema m [prohbl**ay**ma]
problem

procissão f [prohsees**owng**]
procession held to celebrate
religious days

procissão à luz de velas f

[a loos dee **veh**las] candlelit
procession

procurar [prohkoor**ar**] to look
for; to search

produto m [prohd**oo**too] product

produtos alimentícios
[aleemaynt**ees**-yoos] foodstuffs

produtos de beleza [dee
bayl**ay**za] beauty products

produtos de limpeza
[leemp**ay**za] household
cleaning materials

produtos regionais [rayJ-yohn**ais**]
regional goods, typical goods
from the region

produtos têxteis textiles
[**tay**stays]

professor m [prohfays**ohr**],
professora f [prohfays**oh**ra]
teacher

programa m [prohgr**a**ma]
program(me)

proibida [proo-eeb**ee**da]
forbidden

proibida a entrada de... [proo-
eeb**ee**da] no admittance to...

**proibida a entrada de
cachorros** no dogs

**proibida a entrada de
menores de... anos** no
admittance to those under...
years of age

proibida a passagem no
access

proibido [proh-eeb**ee**doo]
forbidden

proibido... no...

proibido acampar no
camping

proibido a pessoas estranhas ao serviço personnel only

proibido estacionar no parking

proibido fazer fogueira no campfires

proibido fumar no smoking

proibido nadar no swimming

proibido para menores de... anos no admission to those under... years of age

proibido parar no stopping

proibido pescar no fishing

proibido tirar fotografias no photography

proibido tomar banho no bathing

proibido ultrapassar no overtaking

prometer [prohmayayr] to promise

pronto [prohntoo] ready

pronto-socorro m [prohntoo sohkoh-Hoo] first-aid post

pronunciar [prohnoons-yar] to pronounce

propósito: de propósito [dee prohpozeetoo] deliberately

própria: sua própria [soo-a propr-ya], seu próprio [say-oo propr-yoo] his/her/its/your/their own

propriedade particular f [prohpr-yaydadadee parteekoolar] private property

proteger [prohtayJayr] to protect

proteger do calor e da umidade store away from heat and damp

protestante m/f [prohtaystantee] Protestant

protetor labial m [prohtaytohr lab-yal] lip salve

protetor solar sunblock

prova: à prova d'água [dagwa] waterproof

provador m [prohvadohr] fitting room

provar [prohvar] to try; to try on; to taste

provavelmente [prohvavilmayntee] probably

próximo [prosimoo], próxima [prosima] near; next

o/a mais próximo/próxima [mīs] the nearest...

próxima sessão às... horas [saysowng] next showing at... o'clock

próximo de [dee] next to

pua f [poo-a] splinter

público m [poobleekoo] audience; public

pular [poolar] to jump

pulga f [poolga] flea

pulmões mpl [poolmoyngs] lungs

pulseira f [poolsayra] bracelet; watchstrap

pulseira de relógio [dee Hay-loJ-yoo] watch strap

pulso m [poolsoo] wrist

pura lã pure wool

pura lã virgem pure new wool

puxar [pooshar] to pull

puxe pull

puxe (a alavanca) em caso de emergência pull (lever) in case of emergency

Q

Q (em torneiras) hot

quadra de tênis [kwadra dee taynees] tennis court

quadril f [kwadreel] hip

qual [kwal] which

  quais? [kwis] which?; which ones?

  qual? which?

  qual deles? [daylees] which one?

qualidade f [kwaleedadee] quality

qualquer [kwalkehr] any

  qualquer coisa [koh-iza] anything

  qualquer medicamento deve ficar fora do alcance das crianças keep all medicines out of the reach of children

quando? [kwandoo] when?

quantia f [kwantee-a] amount

quanto [kwantoo] how much

  quanto custa? [koosta] how much does it cost?

  quanto é? [kwantweh] how much is it?

  quantos? [kwantoos] how many?

quarenta [kwaraynta] forty

quarentena f [kwarayntayna] quarantine

quarta parte f [partee] quarter

quarta-feira f [kwarta fayra] Wednesday

quarto fourth

  quarto andar fourth floor,

(US) fifth floor

quarto m [kwartoo] bedroom; room

  alugam-se quartos rooms to let (in a private house)

  um quarto com duas camas [kohng doo-as kamas] twin room

  um quarto de casal [oong dee kazal] double room

  um quarto de solteiro [sohltayroo] single room

  um quarto duplo [dooploo] double room

  um quarto para duas pessoas [doo-as paysoh-as] double room

  um quarto para uma pessoa [ooma] single room

quase [kwazee] almost, nearly

  quase nunca [noonka] hardly ever

quatro [kwatroo] four

quatrocentas [kwatroosayntas], **quatrocentos** [kwatroosayntoos] four hundred

que [kay] that; than

  o que é isso? [oo k-yeh eesoo] what's that?

  que...! what a...!

  quê/o quê? what?

  que bom! [kee bohng] that's nice!

quebrado m [parteedoo] broken

quebrar [kaybrar] to damage; to break down

  quebre em caso de emergência break in case of emergency

queda f [**keh**da] fall
queda de pedras falling stones
queda de rochas falling rocks
queimado [kay**ma**do] burnt
queimado de sol [dee]
sunburnt
queimadura f [kayma**doo**ra] burn
queimadura de sol sunburn
queimar [kay**mar**] to burn
queixa f complaint
queixo m [**kay**shoo] chin
quem? [kayng] who?
de quem? [dee] whose?
de quem é isto? [eh **ees**too]
whose is this?
quem é? [kayng**eh**] who is it?
quem fala? who's calling?
quente [**kay**ntee] warm; hot
querer [kay**rayr**] to want
quer...? [kehr] would you
like...?, do you want...?
queria [kay**ree**-a] I want; I'd
like
quermesse f [kayrm**eh**see] local
fair with fireworks, singing
and dancing
quero [**keh**roo] I want
não quero [**now**ng] I don't
want (to)
não quero nada I don't want
anything
quieto [k-**yeh**too] still
quilo m [**kee**loo] kilo
quilometragem ilimitada f
[keeloohmaytra**Jayng** eeleemeet**a**da]
unlimited mileage
quilômetro m [kee**loh**maytroo]
kilometre
quinhentas [keen-**yay**ntas],

quinhentos [keen-**yay**ntoos] five
hundred
quinta-feira f [**kee**nta **fay**ra]
Thursday
quinto [**kee**ntoo] fifth
quinze [**kee**nzee] fifteen
quinzena f [keen**zay**na] fortnight
quiosque m [k-**yos**kee] kiosk
quitanda [keet**a**nda]
greengrocer's; fruits and
vegetables shop

R

radiador m [Had-yad**ohr**] radiator
radiografia f [Had-yohgraf**ee**-a]
X-ray
rainha f [Ha-**een**-ya] queen
raio m [**Hī**-oo] lightning, ray,
beam; spoke
raios X mpl [Ha-yoos shees] X-ray
rapaz m [Ha**pas**] young boy
rápido [Ha**pee**doo] fast, quick
raquete f [Hak**eh**te] racket
raquete de tênis tennis racket
raro [Ha**roo**] rare, uncommon
rato f [Ha**too**] rat
razão f [Haz**ow**ng] reason
você tinha razão [teen-ya
Haz**ow**ng] you were right
razoável [Hazw**a**vil] reasonable
real real m [Hay-**al**] (Brazilian unit
of currency)
realmente [Hay-alm**ay**ntee] really
reaver [Hay-av**ayr**] to get back
reboque m [Hayb**o**kee] trailer (for
carrying tent etc)
recado m [Hayk**a**doo] message

deixar um recado [dayshar oong] to leave a message

receber [Haysaybayr] to receive

receita f [Haysayta] recipe; prescription

recepção f [Haysepsowng] reception

recepcionista m/f [Haysepsyohneesta] receptionist

receptor m [Haysayptohr] receiver

recibo m [Hayseeboo] receipt

reclamação f [Hayklamasowng] complaint

reclamações fpl complaints

reclamar [Hayklamar] to complain

recomendar [Haykohmayndar] to recommend

reconhecer [Haykohn-yaysayr] to recognize

rede f [Haydee] net; hammock

redondo [Haydohndoo] round

reembolsar [Hay-aymbohlsar] to refund

reembolso m [Hay-aymbohlsoo] refund

refeição f [Hayfaysowng] meal

refugo m [Hayfoogoo] rubbish

região f [HayJ-yowng] region; area

da região local

regional [HayJ-yohnal] regional, local

registrado [HayJeestradoo] registered

regulamento m regulation

rei m [Hay] king

Reino Unido m [Haynooneedoo] United Kingdom

relâmpago m [Haylampagoo] lightning

religião f [HayleeJ-yowng] religion

relógio m [HayloJ-yoo] clock; watch, wristwatch

relógio de pulso [dee poolsoo] watch, wristwatch

relojoaria f [raylohJwaree-a] watchmaker's shop

remar to row [Haymar]

remédio m [Haymehd-yoo] medicine

remetente m/f [Haymaytayntee] sender

renda f [Haynda] lace

repelente de insetos m [Haypaylayntee dinsehtoos] insect repellent

repetir [Haypayteer] to repeat

repousar [Haypohzar] to rest

repouso m [Haypohzoo] rest

representante m/f [Hayprayzayntantee] agent

repugnante [Haypoognantee] revolting

reserva f [Hayzehrva] reservation

reserva de lugares [dee loogarees] seat reservation

reservado [Hayzayrvadoo] reserved

reservar [Hayzayrvar] to book, to reserve

resfriado f [Haysfree-adoo] cold

estou resfriado [eestoh] I have a cold

respirar [Hayspeerar] to breathe

responder [Hayspohndayr] to answer

responsável [Hayspohnsavil] responsible

resposta f [Haysposta] answer

ressaca f [Haysaka] hangover

restaurante m [Haystowrantee] restaurant

restaurante de frutos-do-mar [dee frootoos doo] seafood restaurant

resto m [Hehstoo] rest, remainder

retalhos mpl [Haytal-yoos] oddments

retirada de bagagem f [Hayteerada dee bagaJayng] baggage claim

retorno proibido no U-turns

retrato m [Haytratoo] portrait

reumatismo m rheumatism [Hay-oomateesmoo]

reunião f [Hay-oon-yowng] meeting

Réveillon New Year's Eve

revelação de filmes f [Hayvaylasowng dee feelmees] film developing

revelar [Hayvaylar] to develop (film)

revista f [Hayveesta] magazine

riacho m [Hee-ashoo] stream

rico [Heekoo] rich

ridículo [Heedeekooloo] ridiculous

rímel m [Heemil] mascara

rinque de patinação m [Heenkee de pateenasowng] ice rink

rins mpl [Heens] kidneys

rio m [Hee-oo] river

rir [Heer] to laugh

rocha f [Hosha] rock

rochedo m [Hohshaydoo] cliff

rock rock (music)

roda f [Hoda] wheel

rodada f [Hohdada] round

rodovia f [Hohdohvee-a] motorway, highway, freeway

rodovia nacional [nas-yohnal] national highway

rolha f [Hohl-ya] cork

romance m [Hohmansee] novel

roncar [Honkar] to snore

rondoniense [Hohndohn-yaynsee] born or living at Rondônia

roraimense m/f [Horīmaynsee] born or living at Roraima

rosa f [Hoza] rose

rosto f face [Hohstoo]

rotatória f [Hohtator-ya] roundabout

rótulo m [Hotooloo] label

roubado [Hohbadoo] robbed

roubar [Hohbar] to steal

roubo m [Hohboo] burglary; theft; rip-off

roupa f [Hohpa] clothes

roupa de baixo [dee bīshoo] underwear

roupa de banho [dee ban-yoo] swimming costume

roupa de cama [dee kama] bed linen

roupa de ginástica [dee Jeenasteeka] tracksuit

roupa feminina [faymeeneena] ladies' wear

roupa infantil f [infanteel] children's wear

roupa masculina [maskooleena] menswear

roupa para lavar laundry, washing

roupão m [Hohpowng] dressing gown

roxo [Hohshoo] purple

rua f [Hoo-a] road; street

rua interditada [intayrdeetada] road blocked

rua principal [preenseepal] main road

rua secundária [saykoondar-ya] side street

rua sem saída [sayng sa-eeda] cul-de-sac, dead end

rubéola f [Hoobeh-oola] German measles

ruínas fpl [Hweenas] ruins

ruivo [Hoo-ivoo] red-headed

S

S. saint

sábado m [sabadoo] Saturday

saber [sabayr] to know; to be able to

sabia [sabee-a] I knew

não sabia [nowng] I didn't know

sabonete m [sabohnaytee] soap

sabor m [sabohr] taste; flavour

saboroso [sabohrohzoo] tasty, delicious

sacana! bastard!

saca-rolhas m [sakaHohl-yas] corkscrew

sacerdote m [sasayrdotee] priest

saco f [sakoo] bag

saco de lixo m [sakoo] bin liner

saco de dormir [dee dohrmeer] sleeping bag

sacola f [sakola] bag

sacola plástica [plasteeka] plastic bag

sacola de compras [dee kohmpras] shopping bag

saguão m [sagwowng] lobby

saia f [sī-ya] skirt

saída f [sa-eeda] departure; exit

saída de emergência [dee aymayrJayns-ya] emergency exit

sair [sa-eer] to get off, to get out; to go out; to leave

eu saio saio [sī-oo] I get off; I go out; I leave

saia! get out!

saiu [sa-ee-oo] he/she is out; he/she has gone out

sais de banho mpl [sīs dee ban-yoo] bath salts

sala de chá tea room

sala de embarque [dee aymbarkee] departure lounge

sala de espera [eespehra] lounge, departure lounge

sala de estar [aystar] living room

sala de jantar [Jantar] dining room

salão m lounge

salão de beleza [salowng dee belayza] beauty salon

salão de cabeleireiro [dee kabaylayrayroo] hairdressing salon

saldos mpl [saldoos] sale

salgado [salgadoo] savoury; salty

salto m [saltoo] heel (of shoe)

salva-vidas [veedas] lifeguard

samba m [samba] typical Brazilian rhythm

sambista m/f [sambeesta] singer/dancer of traditional samba songs

sandálias fpl [sandal-yas] sandals

sangrar to bleed

sangue m [sangee] blood

são [sowng] they are; you are

sapataria f [sapataree-a] shoe shop

sapataria rápida [Hapeeda] heel bar

sapateiro m [sapatayroo] shoe repairer's

sapatos mpl [sapatoos] shoes

sarampo m [sarampoo] measles

sardinha f [sardeen-ya] sardine

satisfeito [sateesfaytoo] satisfied, full

saudável [sowdavil] healthy

saúde f [sa-oodee] health

  à sua saúde! [soo-a] your health!

  saúde! cheers!; bless you!

se [see] if; yourself; himself; herself; themselves; yourselves; itself; oneself

secador de cabelo m [saykadohr dee kabayloo] hairdryer

secadora de roupa f [saykadohra dee Hohpa] spin-dryer

seção f [saysowng] section; department

seção de achados e perdidos [dee ashadoos ee payrdeedoos] lost property office, lost and found

seção de crianças [dee kry-ansas] children's department

secar [saykar] to dry

secar com secador (de mão) [kohng saykadohr (dee mowng)] to blow-dry

seco [saykoo] dry

secreto [saykrehtoo] secret

século m [sehkooloo] century

seda f [sayda] silk

sede: ter sede [tayr saydee] to be thirsty

Sedex® [saydehks] express mail

seguida: em seguida [ayng saygeeda] straight away

seguinte [saygeentee] following; next

  o dia seguinte m the day after

seguir [saygeer] to follow

  siga pela direita [payla deerayta] keep to your right

  siga pela esquerda [eeskayrda] keep to your left

segunda classe f [saygoonda klasee] second class

segunda mão: de segunda mão [saygoonda mowng] second-hand

segunda-feira f [saygoonda fayra] Monday

segundo m [saygoondoo] second

segundo andar second floor, (US) third floor

segurar [saygoorar] to hold

seguro m [saygooroo] insurance; safe; sure

seguro de viagem [dee v-yaJayng] travel insurance

sei [say] I know

seis [says] six

seiscentas [says-sayntas], seiscentos [says-sayntoos] six hundred

sela f [sehla] saddle

selo m [sayloo] stamp

selvagem [saylvaJayng] wild

sem [sayng] without

sem chumbo [sayng shoomboo] leadfree, unleaded

sem conservantes does not contain preservatives

sem corantes does not contain artificial colouring

sem corantes nem conservantes does not contain artificial colouring or preservatives

sem refeições no meals served

semáforo m [saymafohroo] traffic lights

semana f [saymana] week

na próxima semana [proseema] next week

semelhante [saymayl-yantee] similar

semestre escolar m [saymehstree ayskohlar] term

sempre [saympree] always

sempre em frente [saymprayng frayntee] straight ahead

senão [saynowng] otherwise

senha f [sayn-ya] password

senhor (m) sir; gentleman; you

do senhor [doo] your; yours

dos senhores [doos sayn-yohrees] your; yours

o senhor [oo] you

os senhores [oos sayn-yohrees] you

senhor [sayn-yohr] Mr

senhora madam; lady; you

a senhora you

as senhoras [as sayn-yoras] you

da senhora, das senhoras your; yours

senhora [sayn-yora] Mrs

sensato [saynsatoo] sensible

sensível [saynseevil] sensitive

sentar(se) [sayntarsee] to sit, to sit down

sente-se [saynteesee] sit down

sentimento m [saynteemayntoo] feeling

sentir [saynteer] to feel

como se sente? [kohmoo see sayntee] how are you feeling?

eu me sinto [ay-oo mee seentoo] I feel

eu me sinto bem [bayng] I'm OK, I'm fine

separadamente [sayparadamayntee] separately

separado [sayparadoo] separate; separated

ser [sayr] to be

será [sayra] he/she/it/you will be

serão [sayrowng] you/they will be

serás [sayras] you will be

serei [sayray] I will be

seremos [sayraymoos] we will be

sergipano [sayrJeepanoo] born or living at Sergipe

sério [sehr-yoo] serious

serve-se... das... horas às... horas... served from... o'clock until... o'clock

serviço m [sayrveesoo] service

serviço 24-horas 24-hour service

serviço de emergência [dee aymayrJayns-ya] casualty department

serviço de guincho [geenshoo] breakdown service

serviço de funilaria [fooneelaree-a] bodywork repairs

serviço de quarto [dee kwartoo] room service

serviço expresso [esprehsoo] express service

serviço incluído [inklweedoo] service included

serviço internacional [intayrnas-yohna] international service

servir [sayrveer] to serve; to suit; to be convenient

sessenta [saysaynta] sixty

sete [sehtee] seven

setecentas [sehteesayntas], setecentos [sehteesayntoos] seven hundred

setembro [saytaymbroo] September

setenta [setaynta] seventy

setentrional [setayntr-yohna]

northern

sétimo [sehteemoo] seventh

seu [say-oo], seus [say-oos] his; her; hers; its; your; yours; their; theirs

sexo m [sehksoo] sex

sexta-feira f [saysta fayra] Friday

Sexta-Feira Santa Good Friday

sexto [saystoo] sixth

shopping centre m shopping centre

shorts mpl shorts

siga-me [seegamee] follow me

significar [seegneefeekar] to mean

silêncio m [seelayns-yoo] silence

silencioso [seelayns-yohzoo] quiet

sim [seeng] yes; it is

simpático [seempateekoo] friendly

simples [seemplees] simple, easy

sinagoga f [seenagoga] synagogue

sinal m [seena] sign; signal; roadsign

sinal de alarme [dee alarmee] emergency alarm

sincero [seensehroo] sincere

sino m [seenoo] bell

sintético [seentehteekoo] synthetic

só [saw] alone; just; only
só pode ser vendido com receita médica available only on prescription

sobrancelha f [sohbrans**ayl**-ya] eyebrow

sobrar: sobraram dois [sohbra**rowng** d**oh**-is] there are two left

sobre [**sohbree**] about, concerning; on

sobrenome m [sohbray**nohmee**] surname; family name

sobretudo m [sohbraytoo**doo**] overcoat

sobrinha f [sohbr**een**-ya] niece

sobrinho m [sohbr**een**-yoo] nephew

sóbrio [**sobr**-yoo] sober

sociedade f [sohs-yad**dadee**] society; company

socorro! [sohk**oh**-Hoo] help!

sofá m [soh**fa**] sofa; couch

sofisticado [sohfeesteek**adoo**] sophisticated; upmarket

sogra f mother-in-law

sogro m [**sohg**roo] father-in-law

sol m sun

  ao sol [ow] in the sun

  está (fazendo) sol [ees**ta** (faz**ayndoo**)] it's sunny

solo m [s**oloo**] ground

  no solo [noo] on the ground

solteiro m [sohlt**ayroo**] single; bachelor

solto [**sohl**too] loose

solução de limpeza f [sohloos**owng** dee leemp**ayza**] cleaning solution

solução para lentes de contato [para la**yn**tees dee kohnt**atoo**] soaking solution

soluço m [sohl**oo**soo] hiccup

sombra f [**soh**mbra] shade; shadow

  à sombra in the shade

sombra de olho [dee o**l**-yoo] eye shadow

sombrinha f [sohmbr**een**-ya] guarda-chuva

somente [som**ayn**tee] only; just

somos [**sohm**oos] we are

sonho m [**soh**n-yoo] dream

sonífero m [sohn**ee**fayroo] sleeping pill

sono m [**soh**noo] sleep

  estar com sono [eestar kohng] to be sleepy

sopé: no sopé do... [noo sohp**eh** doo] at the bottom of...

sorrir [soh-H**eer**] to smile

sorriso m [soh-H**ee**zoo] smile

sorte f [**sor**tee] luck

sorvete m [sohr**vay**tee] ice cream

sorvete de casquinha m [dee kask**een**-ya] ice-cream cone

sorveteria f [sohrvaytay**ree**-a] ice-cream parlour

soteropolitano [sohtehroo-pohl**eet**anoo] born or living at Salvador, Bahia

sou [soh] I am

  sou de... [dee] I am from...

sozinha [soz**een**-ya], **sozinho** [soz**een**-yoo] by myself

spa m spa

spray de cabelo m [dee kab**ayloo**] hair spray

Sr. Mr

Sra. Mrs

Srta. Miss

Sta. f saint
Sto. m saint
sua [soo-a] his; her; hers; its; your; yours; their; theirs
suar [soo-ar] to sweat
suas [soo-as] his; her; hers; its; your; yours; their; theirs
suave [swavee] delicate; mild
subir [soobeer] to go up
subitamente [soob-tamaynte] suddenly
sucesso m [soosehsoo] success
sudeste m [soodehstee] southeast
sudoeste m [soodoh-ehstee] southwest
sueca f [swehka], sueco m [swehkoo] Swedish; Swede
Suécia f [swehs-ya] Sweden
suficiente [soofees-yaynte] enough
suficientemente [soofees-yaynteemaynte] enough
suíça f [sweesa], suíço m [sweesoo] Swiss
Suíça f [sweesa] Switzerland
sujeira f [sooJayra] dirt
sujeito m [sooJaytoo] guy
sujo [sooJoo] dirty
sul m [sool] south
no sul [noo] in the south
sul-africana f [soolafreekana], sul-africano m [soolafreekanoo] South African
supermercado m [soopaymayrkadoo] supermarket
suplemento m [sooplaymayntoo] supplement, extra charge

supositório m [soopohzeetor-yoo] suppository
surdo [soordoo] deaf
surfar to surf
surpreendente [soorpr-yayndayntee] surprising
surpresa f [soorprayza] surprise
sutiã m [soot-yang] bra

T

tabacaria f [tabakaree-a] tobacconist; tobacco store; tobacco goods
tabaco m [tabakoo] tobacco
talão de cheques [talowng dee shehkees] cheque book
talco m [talkoo] talcum powder
talheres mpl [tal-yehrees] cutlery
talvez [talvays] maybe, perhaps
talvez não [nowng] perhaps not
tamanho m [taman-yoo] size
também [tambayng] also, too, as well
eu também [ay-oo] so am I; so do I; me too
tampa f cap, lid
tampa do ralo f [doo Haloo] plug (in sink)
tampões mpl [tampoyngs] tampons
tanque m [tankee] tank
tanto [tantoo] so much
tanto faz [fas] it's all the same to me
tão [towng] so

tão... como... as... as...

tão... quanto [kwantoo] as... as

tão... quanto possível [pohseevil] as... as possible

tapete m [tapaytee] carpet

tarde f [tardee] afternoon; late

à tarde in the afternoon

da tarde p.m.

esta tarde [ehsta] this afternoon

três da tarde 3 p.m.

tarifa f [tareefa] charges

taxa de serviço f [tasha dee sayrveesoo] service charge

taxa extra m [ehstra] supplement, extra charge

taxista m [takseesta] taxi-driver

tchau! cheerio!

te [tay] you; to you; yourself

teatro m [t-yatroo] theatre

tecido m [tayseedoo] fabric, cloth

tel. telephone

tela f [tehla] screen

telefone m [taylayfohnee] telephone

teleférico m [taylayfehreekoo] cable car

telefonar [taylayfohnar] to call, to phone

telefone celular m [sayloolar] mobile phone

telefone de cartão [dee kartowng] cardphone

telefone público [poobleekoo] payphone

telefonista m/f [taylayfohneesta] operator

televisão f [taylayveezowng] television

telhado m [tayl-yadoo] roof

tem [tayng] he/she/it has; you have

ele/ela tem de... he/she must...

tem...? have you got any...?, do you have...?

têm [tay-ayng] you/they have

temos [taymoos] we have

temos de... [dee] we've got to..., we must...

temperatura f [taympayratoora] temperature

tempestade f [taympaystadee] storm

tempo m [taympoo] time; weather

a tempo on time

por quanto tempo? [poor kwantoo] for how long?

temporada f [taymporada] station; season

alta temporada high season

baixa temporada [bisha] low season

tenho [tayn-yoo] I have; I am; I have to

não tenho [nowng] I don't have any

tenho de... [dee] I must...

tênis m [di traynoo] trainers, sneakers; tennis

tênis de mesa [di mayza] table tennis

tens [tayns] you have

tensão f [taynsowng] tension

tentar [tayntar] to try

ter [tayr] to have; to hold;

to be; to contain; to have to
ter de to have to
terça-feira f [**tayr**sa **fay**ra] Tuesday
terça-feira de carnaval Mardi gras
terceiro [tayr**say**roo] third
terceiro andar m third floor, (US) fourth floor
terminado [tayrmeen**a**doo] over; finished
terminal m [tayrmee**nal**] terminus
terminal de ônibus [dee **oh**neeboos] bus station
terminar [tayrmee**nar**] to finish
termômetro m [tayrm**oh**maytroo] thermometer
terno m [**tehr**noo] suit
terra f [**teh**-Ha] earth
terraço m [tay**Ha**soo] terrace
térreo m ground floor, (US) first floor
terrível [tay-**Hee**vil] terrible
tesoura f [tay**zoh**ra] scissors
testa f [**teh**sta] forehead
testemunha m/f [taystaym**oo**n-ya] witness
teto m [**teh**too] ceiling
teu [**tay**-oo], **teus** [**tay**-oos] your; yours
teve [**tay**vee] he/she/it/you had
ti [tee] you
tia f [**tee**-a] aunt
tigela f [tee**Jeh**la] bowl
tijolo m [tee**Joh**loo] brick
time f [**tee**mee] team
tímido [**tee**meedoo] shy

tinha [**teen**-ya] I/he/she/it/you used to have
tinham [**teen**-yowng] you/they used to have
tínhamos [**teen**-yamoos] we used to have
tinhas [**teen**-yas] you used to have
tinta f [**teen**ta] paint; tint
tinta fresca [**fray**ska] wet paint
tinto (wine) [**teen**too] red
tinturaria f [teentoorar**ee**-a] dry-cleaner
tio m [**tee**-oo] uncle
típico [**tee**peekoo] typical
tipo m [**tee**poo] sort, type, kind
tiragem f [teera**Jayng**] edition; circulation
tirar to remove
tirar o fone do gancho lift the receiver
tive [**tee**vee] I had
tivemos [teev**ay**moos] we had
tiveram [teev**eh**rowng] you/they had
tiveste [teev**eh**stee] you had
toalete m [twal**eh**tee] toilet, rest room
toalha f [**twal**-ya] towel
toalha de banho [dee ban-yoo] bath towel
toalha de mesa [**may**za] tablecloth
toca-discos m [**to**ka dee**skoos**] record player
tocantinense m/f [tokanteen**ayn**see] born or living at Tocantins
tocar [to**hkar**] to touch

todas [**toh**das] all; all of them

todas as vezes [as **vay**zees] every time

todo [**toh**doo] all; all of it

todo mundo [**moon**doo] everyone

todo o dia [dee-a] all day

todos [**toh**doos] all; all of them

para todos suitable for all age groups

todos os dias [**toh**dooz-oos dee-as] every day, daily

toma lá [**toh**ma] there you are

tomada f [**toh**mada] socket; plug; power point

tomada para barbeador elétrico [para barbay-ad**ohr** el**eh**treekoo] shaving point

tomar [tohm**ar**] to take

o que vai tomar? [oo kee vī] what'll you have?

tomar antes de se deitar to be taken before going to bed

tomar após as refeições to be taken after meals

tomar banho [ban-yoo] to have a bath

tomar conta de [**koh**nta] to look after, to take care of

tomar cuidado take care

tomar em jejum take on an empty stomach

tomar sol to sunbathe

tomar... vezes ao dia to be taken... times a day

tônico m [**toh**neekoo] toner

tonturas: sinto tonturas [**seen**too tont**oo**ras] I feel dizzy

topo: no topo de... [**toh**poo dee]

at the top of...

toque (a campainha) ring (the bell)

torcedor m [tohrsayd**ohr**] fan

torcedora f [tohrsayd**oh**ra]

torcer [tohrs**ayr**] to sprain; to twist

tornar-se [tohrn**ar**see] to become

torneira f [tohrn**ay**ra] tap, faucet

tornozelo m [tohrnohz**ay**loo] ankle

torre f [**toh**-Hee] tower

tosse f [**toh**see] cough

tossir [tohs**eer**] to cough

totalmente [tohtalm**ayn**tee] totally; altogether

touca de banho f [**toh**ka dee ban-yoo] bathing cap

tóxico [**tok**seekoo] toxic, poisonous

trabalhar [trabal-y**ar**] to work

trabalho m [trabal-yoo] work

tradição f [tradees**ow**ng] tradition

tradicional [tradees-yohn**al**] traditional

tradução f [tradoos**ow**ng] translation

tradutor m [tradoot**ohr**], tradutora f [tradoot**oh**ra] translator

traduzir [tradooz**eer**] to translate

tragédia f [traʝ**eh**d-ya] disaster

trailer f caravan, (US) trailer

trajeto m [traʝ**eh**too] route

trampolim [trampohl**eeng**] diving board

trancar [trankar] to lock

tranquilo [trankweeloo] peaceful

transferência f [transfayrayns-ya] transfer

trânsito m [tranzeetoo] traffic

trânsito congestionado [kohnjayst-ohnadoo] traffic congestion

trânsito nos dois sentidos [nohs doh-is saynteedoos] two-way traffic

trânsito proibido no thoroughfare

transmissão f [transmeesowng] transmission

traseiro m [trazayroo] bottom (of person); back

traumatismo m [trowmateesmoo] traumatism

travessa f [travehsa] tray

travesseiro m [almoofada] pillow

travessia f [travaysee-a] crossing

trazer [trazayr] to bring

trazer de volta [dee] to bring back

trem m [trayng] train

de trem [dee] by train

trem expresso express train

três [trays] three

treze [trayzee] thirteen

trezentas [trayzayntas], trezentos [trayzayntoos] three hundred

tribunal m [treeboonal] court

tricotar [treekohtar] to knit

trinta [treenta] thirty

tripulação f [treepoolasowng] crew

triste [treestee] sad

trocar [trohkar] to change (money)

troco m [trohkoo] change (money)

trombose f [trombozee] thrombosis

trovão m [trohvowng] thunder

trovoada f [trohvwada] thunder

tu [too] you

tua [too-a], tuas [too-as] your; yours

tudo [toodoo] everything

é tudo [eh] that's all

tudo bem! [bayng] no problem!

tudo bem? how are you?

tudo incluído [incklweedoo] all-inclusive

túnel m [toonil] tunnel

turismo m [tooreesmoo] tourist information office

turista m/f [tooreesta] tourist

U

UE [oo eh] EU

úlcera f [oolsayra] ulcer

último [oolteemoo] last, latest

ultrapassar [ooltrapasar] to overtake, to pass

um [oong], uma [ooma] a, an; one

uma vez [ooma vays] once

umas [oomas] some

úmido [oomeedoo] damp; humid

unha f [oon-ya] fingernail

União Européia f [oonee-owng

ay-oorohp**eh**-ia] European
Union
universidade f
[ooneevayrseed**a**dee] university
uns [oons] some
urgência f [oor**J**ayns-ya]
casualty, emergencies
urgente [oor**J**ayntee] urgent
usar [oozar] to use
uso m [**oo**zoo] use
utensílios de cozinha mpl
[ootaynse**el**-yoos dee kohz**een**-ya]
cooking utensils
utensílios domésticos
[dohm**eh**steekoos] household
goods
útil [**oo**til] useful

V

vaca f cow
vacina f [vas**een**a] vaccine
vacinação f [vaseenas**ow**ng]
vaccination
vagão m [vag**ow**ng] carriage,
coach
vagão-leito [**l**aytoo] sleeper,
sleeping car
vagão-restaurante
[Haystowr**a**ntee] dining car
vai [vi] he/she/it goes; you go
vais [vīs] you go
vale m [v**a**lee] valley
vale postal internacional
international money order
validação de bilhetes
[valeedas**ow**ng dee beel-y**ay**tees]

punch your ticket here
válido [val**ee**doo] valid
válido até... valid until...
valioso [val-y**oh**zoo] valuable
valor m [val**oh**r] value
válvula f [v**a**lvoola] valve
vamos [v**a**moos] we go
vamos! let's go!
vão [vowng] you/they go
varal m clothes line
varicela f [varees**eh**la]
chickenpox
variedade f [var-yed**a**dee] range
vaso f [v**a**zoo] vase
vassoura f [vas**oh**ra] broom
vaza! go away!
vazio [vaz**ee**-oo] empty
vegetariana f [vay**J**aytar-y**a**na],
vegetariano m [vay**J**aytar-y**a**noo]
vegetarian
veículo m [vay-e**ek**ooloo] vehicle
veículo pesado heavy vehicle
[payz**a**doo]
veio [v**ay**-oo] he/she/it came,
he/she/it has come; you
came, you have come
vela f [v**eh**la] spark plug; sail;
candle
velejar [vaylay**J**ar] to sail; sailing
velho [v**eh**l-yoo] old
velocidade f [vaylohseed**a**dee]
speed
velocidade máxima... km/h
maximum speed... km/h
velocímetro m [vaylohs**ee**maytroo]
speedometer
vem [vayng] he/she/it comes;
you come
vêm you/they come

venda f [**vay**nda] sale
 à venda for sale
vendedor de jornais m
 [vayndayd**ohr** dee Jorn**ī**s]
 newsagent, news vendor
vendem-se [**vay**ndaynsee] for
 sale
vender [vaynd**ayr**] to sell
vende-se [**vay**ndeesee] for sale
 vende-se este ponto premises
 for sale
veneno m [vayn**ay**noo] poison
venenoso [vaynayn**oh**zoo]
 poisonous
venho [**vay**n-yoo] I come
vens [vayns] you come
ventilador m [vaynteelad**ohr**] fan
 (electrical)
vento m [**vay**ntoo] wind
ver [vayr] to look; to have a
 look; to see
verão m [vayr**ow**ng] summer
verdade f [vayrd**a**dee] truth
 é verdade? [dee] really?
verdadeiro [vayrdad**ay**roo] real;
 true
verde [**vay**rdee] green
verificar [vayreef**eekar**] to check
vermelho [vayrm**ay**l-yoo] red
vespa f [**vay**spa] wasp
vestido m [vayst**ee**doo] dress
vestir [vayst**eer**] to dress
vestir-se [vayst**eer**see] to get
 dressed
veterinário m [vaytayreen**a**r-yoo]
 vet
vez f [vays] time
 a próxima vez [**pro**sima] next
 time

às vezes [as v**ay**zees]
 sometimes
 a última vez [**oo**ltima] last time
 em vez [ayng] instead
 em vez de... [dee] instead of...
 esta vez [**eh**sta] this time
via f [v**ee**-a] via
 por via aérea by airmail
via intravenosa intravenously
via oral to be taken orally
via retal [Hay**ta**l] per rectum
viagem f [v-ya**J**ayng] journey
 para viagem to take away, to
 go (food)
viagem de negócios [dee
 nayg**o**s-yoos] business trip
viajar [v-ya**J**ar] to travel
vida f [v**ee**da] life
vidraçaria f [veedrasar**ee**-a]
 glazier's
vidro m [v**ee**droo] glass
viela f [v-y**eh**la] lane
viemos [v-y**ay**moos] we came,
 we have come
vieram [v-y**eh**rowng] you/they
 came, you/they have come
vieste [v-y**eh**stee] you came,
 you have come
vim [veeng] I came, I have
 come
vimos [v**ee**moos] we come;
 we saw
vindima f [vind**ee**ma] grape
 harvest
vindo [v**ee**ndoo] come
vinha f [v**ee**n-ya] vineyard
vinte [v**ee**ntee] twenty
vinte e um [v**ee**ntee-oong]
 twenty-one

viola f [v-y**o**la] traditional 10-string acoustic guitar used in Brazilian folk music

violão m [v-yol**ow**ng] traditional Brazilian acoustic guitar

vir [veer] to come

vir de carro [veer dee k**a**Hoo] to drive

virabrequim m [veerabraykeeng] crankshaft

virar [veer**ar**] to turn; to turn off

vire à esquerda/direita [veer-ya eesk**ay**rda/deer**ay**ta] turn left/right

vírgula f [veerg**oo**la] comma; decimal point

visita f [veez**ee**ta] visit

visita guiada [gee-**a**da] guided tour

visitar [veezeet**ar**] to visit

visor m [veez**oh**r] viewfinder

vista f [v**ee**sta] view

vista panorâmica m scenic view, vantage point

visto m [v**ee**stoo] visa; seen

vitrine f [veetr**ee**nee] shop window

viu [v**ee**-oo] you have seen

viúva f [v-y**oo**va] widow

viúvo m [v-y**oo**voo] widower

viver [veev**ayr**] to live

vivo [v**ee**voo] bright; alive

vizinha f [veez**ee**n-ya], **vizinho m** [veez**ee**n-yoo] neighbour

voar [v-w**ar**] to fly

você [voh**say**] you

você primeiro [preem**ay**roo] after you

vocês [voh**says**] you

de vocês [dee] your; yours

volante m [voh**la**ntee] steering wheel

com volante à direita [kohng] right-hand drive

volta: por volta de... [poor] about...; approximately...

voltagem f [vohltaJ**ay**ng] voltage

voltar to go back, to get back, to come back, to return

voltar a telefonar [voltar a taylayfohn**ar**] to ring back

volto já [v**o**ltoo Ja] back in a minute

vomitar [vohmeet**ar**] to be sick, to vomit

vontade f [vohnt**a**dee] wish

estou com vontade de... I feel like...

vôo m [v**oh**-oo] flight

vôo de conexão [dee kohnayks**ow**ng] connecting flight

vôo direto [deer**eh**too] direct flight

vôo doméstico [dohm**eh**shteekoo] domestic flight

vôo fretado [frayt**a**doo] charter flight

vôo regular [Haygoolar] scheduled flight

vou [voh] I go

voz f [vos] voice

W

windsurfe m windsurf

X

xadrez m [shadrays] chess
xampu m [shampoo] shampoo
xarope m [sharopee] cough
 medicine; cordial
xícara f [sheekara] cup

Z

zangado [zangadoo] angry;
 mad
zero [zehroo] zero
zíper zip, zipper

zona azul f [zohnazool] payable
 parking zone
zona para pedestres
 pedestrian precinct
zona perigosa danger zone

Menu
Reader:
Food

Essential Terms

bread pão [powng]
butter manteiga [mantayga]
cup xícara [sheekara]
dessert sobremesa [sobraymayza]
fish peixe [payshee]
fork garfo [garfoo]
glass copo [kopoo]
knife faca
main course prato principal [pratoo preenseepal]
meat carne [karnee]
menu cardápio [kardap-yoo]
pepper pimenta [peemaynta]
plate prato [pratoo]
salad salada
salt sal
set menu menu de preço fixo [maynoo dee praysoo feeksoo]
soup sopa [sohpa]
spoon colher [kohl-yehr]
starter entrada [ayntrada]
table mesa [mayza]

another..., please outro/outra..., por favor [ohtroo – poor favohr]
excuse me! (to call waiter/waitress) por favor! [poor favohr]
could I have the bill, please? pode me trazer a conta, por favor?
 [podee mee trazayr a kohnta]

à la carte[kartee] à la carte

à moda de... [dee]...-style

abacate [abakatee] avocado

abacaxi [abakashee] pineapple

abóbora [abobohra] osumpkin

abobrinha com creme ao forno
[abobreen-ya kohng kraymee ow
fohrnoo] baked courgettes/
zucchini served with cream

abobrinha frita [freeta] fried
courgettes/zucchini

acarajé [akaraJeh] black eyed
peas dough ball deep- fried
and served with a paste of
shrimp and lots of pepper

açúcar [asookar] sugar

agrião [agr-yowng] watercress

aipo [īpoo] celery

alcachofra [alkashohfra]
artichoke

alecrim [alaykreeng] rosemary

alface [alfasee] lettuce

alho [al-yoo] garlic

alho-poró [al-yoo pohro] leek

almoço [almohsoo] lunch

almôndegas [almohndaygas]
meatballs

almôndegas com molho de
tomate [kohng mohl-yoo dee
tohmatee] meatballs with
tomato sauce

amêijoas [amayJwas] clams

ameixa [amaysha] plum

ameixa seca [sayka] prune

amêndoa [amayndwa] almond

amendoins [amayndweens]
peanut

amora [amora] blackberry

anchova [anshohva] anchovy

anis [anees] aniseed

ao natural [ow natooral] plain

ao ponto [pohntoo] medium-
rare

apimentado [apeemayntadoo]
hot, spicy

arroz [aHohs] rice

arroz árabe [arabee] fried rice
with nuts and dried fruit

arroz branco [brankoo] plain
rice

arroz de cabidela [dee
kabeedehla] rice cooked in
birds' blood

arroz de carreteiro [dee
kaHaytayroo] rice cooked with
dried beef, typical fare of
truck drivers

arroz-doce [dohsee] sweet rice
dessert

arroz e feijão [ee fayJowng] rice
and beans: a staple food in
Brazil

asa [aza] wing

aspargo [aspargoo] asparagu

assado [asadoo] roasted

atum [atoong] tuna

avelã [avaylang] hazelnut

aves [avees] poultry

azeite [azaytee] olive oil

azeitona [azaytohnas] olives

azeitonas recheadas [Hay-shay-
adas] stuffed olives

azeitonas recheadas com
pimenta [kohng peemaynta]
olives stuffed with pimentos

bacalhau à Gomes de Sá
[bakal-yow a gohmees dee] dried

cod fried with onions, boiled eggs, potatoes and black olives

bacalhau assado [asadoo] roast dried cod

bacalhau à Zé do Pipo [zeh doo peepoo] dried cod with egg sauce

bacalhau dourado [dohradoo] dried cod baked in the oven

bacalhau grelhado [grayl-yadoo] grilled dried cod

bacalhau na brasa [braza] barbecued dried cod

bacalhau salgado [salgado] dried salted cod

banana flambada [flambada] flambéed banana

batata [batata] potatoe

batata assada [batatasada] baked potato

batata-baroa [baroh-a] when boiled, this root has about de same uses as potatoes, including side dishes as purrés, dumplings, gnocchi, pastries etc.

batata cozida [kohzeeda] boiled potato

batata frita [freeta] chips, French fries

batata palha [pal-ya] French fries in chips

batata salteada [salt-yada] sautéed potato

baunilha [bowneel-ya] vanilla

bauru [bowroo] popular Brazilian sandwich, whose original recipe calls for

mozzarella cheese melted in bain-marie, slices of roast beef, tomato and pickled cucumber; there is a simplified version with ham, cheese and tomato

bavaroise [bavarwaz] dessert made from egg whites and cream

bem passado [bayng pasadoo] well-done

berbigão [bayrbeegowng] shellfish similar to mussels

berinjela [bayreenJehla] aubergine, eggplant

beterraba [baytay-Haba] beetroot

bife [beefee] steak

bife a cavalo [a kavaloo] steak with a fried egg on top

bife acebolado [a-saybohladoo] thin slices of steak with onions

bife com fritas [beefee kohng freetas] steak and chips/ French fries

bife de alcatra [dee alkatra] rump steak

bife de javali [dee Javalee] wild boar steak

bife grelhado [grayl-yadoo] grilled steak

bife tártaro [tartaroo] steak tartare

bifinhos de porco [beefeen-yoos dee pohrkoo] small slices of pork

bolacha [bohlasha] biscuit, cookie

bolinho de bacalhau [boleenyoo dee bakal-**yow**] fried cod dumplings

bolinho de mandioca [dee mand-**yo**ka] fried manioc dumplings

bolo [**boh**loo] cake

bolo de carne [**boh**loo dee **karne**] meat loaf

bolo de cenoura [say**noh**ra] carrot cake

bolo de chocolate [shoh**koh**la**tee**] chocolate cake

bolo de fubá [**foo**ba] corn meal cake

bolo de nozes [**no**zees] walnut cake

bolo inglês [ing**lays**] sponge cake with dried fruit

bolos e bolachas [**boh**looz ee boh**la**shas] cakes and biscuits/cookies

bomba de café [**boh**mba dee kafeh] coffee éclair

bomba de chantilly [dee shantee**lee**] whipped cream éclair

bomba de chocolate [shoh**koh**la**tee**] chocolate éclair

bomba de creme [**boh**mba dee kraymee] cream puff

brigadeiro [breega**day**roo] Brazilian chocolate candy

brioche [br-**yo**shee] slightly sweet round bun

broa [**broh**-a] maize/corn bread or rye bread

cabrito [ka**bree**too] kid

cabrito assado [a**sa**doo] roast kid

caçarola de perdiz [kasa**ro**la dee payr**dee**s] partridge casserole

caçarola de porco [kasa**ro**la dee **poh**rkoo] pork casserole

cachorro-quente [ka**shoh**-Hoo **kay**ntee] hot dog

café-da-manhã [ka**feh** da man-yang] breakfast

caldeirada [kalday**ra**da] fish stew

caldo [**kal**doo] broth

caldo de carne [dee **karnee**] meat soup

caldo de galinha [dee ga**leen**-ya] poultry soup

caldo verde [**vayr**dee] potato and kale soup, served with slices of fried or boiled pork sausage

camarão na moranga [kama**rown**g na moh**ran**ga] pumpkin stuffed with shrimps

camarões graúdos [kama**roy**ngs gra-**oo**doos] prawns

camarões graúdos grelhados [grayl-**ya**doos] grilled prawns

canela [ka**neh**la] cinnamon

canja de galinha [**kan**Ja dee ga**leen**-ya] chicken soup

carambola starfruit

caranguejo [karang**ay**Joo] crab

caranguejo gratinado [grateen**a**doo] crab with cheese sauce browned under the grill

carapau [kara**pa**-oo] mackerel

carapaus em escabeche [ayng ayska**beh**shee] marinated mackerel carapaus fritos [freetoos] fried mackerel

carne [karnee] meat

carne à jardineira [Jardeenayra] meat and vegetable stew

carne com massa folhada [kohng masa fohl-yada] meat in pastry

carne de cabrito [dee kabreetoo] kid

carne de caça [kasa] game

carne de porco [pohrkoo] pork

carne de porco com batatas [kohng batatas] pork with potatoes

carne de porco dessossada [dayzohsada] thin slices of pork

carne de vaca [vaka] beef

carne seca [sayka] dried salted meat, ingredient of many Brazilian dishes

carneiro [karnayroo] mutton

carneiro assado [asadoo] roast mutton

carnes [karnees] meats

caseiro [kazayroo] home-made

casquinha de siri [kaskeen-ya dee seeree] blue crab carapace filled with the edible parts of the crab, coated with cheese

castanhas [kastan-yas] chestnuts

cebola [saybohla] onion

ceia [saya] supper

cenoura [saynohra] carrot

cereja [sayrayJa] cherry

chantilly [shanteelee] whipped cream

charlotes [sharlotees] biscuits/

cookies with fruit and cream

cherne [shernee] sea bream

chouriço [shohreesoo] spiced sausage

churrasco [shooHaskoo] barbecue

churrasco de frango [dee frangoo] barbecued chicken

churrasquinho no pão [shooHaskeen-yoo noo powng] bread with fried/grilled meat

churro [shooHoo] long thin fritters

codorna [kohdohrna] quail

codorna frita [freeta] fried quail

coelho [kwayl-yoo] rabbit

coelho à caçadora [kasadohra] rabbit casserole with rice

coelho em escabeche [ayng ayskabehshee] marinated rabbit

coelho frito [freetoo] fried rabbit

coentro [koh-ayntroo] coriander

cogumelos [kohgoomehloos] mushrooms

cogumelos com alho [kohng al-yoo] mushrooms with garlic

comida congelada [kohmeeda kohnJaylada] frozen food

compota stewed fruit

conquilhas [kohnkeel-yas] baby clams

consomê [kohnsohmay] consommé, clear meat soup

coquetel de camarão [kohkeetehl dee kamarowng] prawn cocktail

coração [kohrasowng] heart

corações de alcachofra

[kohrasoyngs dee alkashohfra]
artichoke hearts

cordeiro [kohrdayroo] lamb

corvina [kohrveena] large
saltwater fish

costela [kohstehla] rib

costeleta [kohstaylayta] chop

costeletas de carneiro
[kohstaylaytas dee karnayroo]
lamb chops

costeletas de porco [dee
pohrkoo] pork chops

costeletas fritas [freetas] fried
chops

costeletas grelhadas [grayl-
yadas] grilled chops

couve [kohvee] kale

couve-de-bruxelas [kohvee dee
brooshehlas] Brussels sprouts

couve-de-bruxelas com creme
[kohng kraymee dee laytee]
Brussels sprouts with cream

couve-de-bruxelas salteada
[salt-yada] sautéed Brussels
sprouts

couve-flor [kohvee flohr]
cauliflower

couve-flor com creme de leite
[kohng kraymee dee laytee]
cauliflower with cream

couve-flor com molho branco
no forno [mohl-yoo brankoo ow
fohrnoo] cauliflower in white
sauce

couvert cover charge

coxinha [kohsheen-ya] minced
chicken and seasonings,
enclosed in wheat flour
batter and deep fried

cozido [kohzeedoo] boiled;
stewed; poached; cooked
(either in a sauce or with olive oil);
stew

cozido [kohzeedoo] meat stew

cozido à portuguesa
[pohrtoogayza] stew made from
meat, sausage, potatoes and
vegetables

creme de cogumelos [kraymee
dee kohgoomehloos] cream of
mushroom soup

creme de leite [dee laytee]
cream

creme de mariscos [mareeskoos]
cream of shellfish soup

croquete de camarão
[krohkehtee dee kamarowng] fried
shrimp dumplings

croquete de carne [dee karnee]
fried meat dumplings

cru/crua [kroo/kroo-a] raw

curry curry

damasco [damaskoo] apricot

defumado [dayfoomadoo]
smoked

dobradinha [dohbradeen-ya]
tripe

dobradinha com feijão branco
[kohng fayJowng brankoo] tripe
with white beans

dobradinha com grão-de-bico
[growng dee beekoo] tripe with
chickpeas

doce [dohsee] jam; any sweet
dish or dessert

doce de abóbora [dee abobohra]
pumpkin dessert

doce de amêndoas [dee amayndwas] almond dessert

doce de ovos [dee ovoos] type of egg custard

doces regionais [HayJ-yohnīs] regional desserts

dourado [dohrado] dory (saltwater fish); browned, golden brown

empadão de carne [aympadowng dee karnee] large meat pie

empadão de peixe [payshee] large fish pie

empadinha [aympadeen-ya] dough based on flour and butter, filled with chicken, heart of palm, shrimp, a common ready-to-go item at fast-food counters

enguia [ayngee-a] eel

enguia frita [freeta] fried eel

ensopado [aynsopadoo] stewed

ensopado de coelho [dee kwayl-yoo] jugged rabbit

ensopado de cordeiro [kordayroo] lamb stew

ensopado de enguias [ayngee-as] eel stew

entradas [ayntradas] starters, appetizers

entrecosto [ayntraykohstoo] entrecôte

entrecosto frito [freetoo] fried entrecôte

erva-doce [ehrva dohsee] fennel

ervas [ehrvas] herbs

ervilhas [ayrveel-yas] peas

ervilhas com bacon [ayrveel-yas kohng] peas in butter with bacon

ervilhas na manteiga [mantayga] peas in butter

escalope à milanesa [eeskalopee a meelanayza] breaded escalope

escalope ao Madeira [eeskalopee ow madayra] escalope in Madeira wine

escalope de carneiro [dee karnayroo] mutton escalope

escalope de porco [pohrkoo] pork escalope

escargô [ayskargoh] snail

espaguete à bolonhesa [eespagehtee a bohlohn-yayza] spaghetti bolognese

espaguete ao sugo [ow soogoo] spaghetti with light tomato sauce

espaguete com vôngole [kohng vohngohlee] spaghetti with clams

especiaria [eespays-yaree-a] spice

espetinho de coração de frango [eespayteen-yoo dee kohrasowng dee frangoo] chicken heart kebab

espetinho de frango chicken kebab

espetinho de lombo de porco [dee lohmboo dee pohrkoo] pig loin kebab

espetinho misto [meesto] mixed kebab

espinafre [ayspeenafree] spinach

espinafre gratinado [grateenadoo] spinach with

cheese sauce browned under
the grill

espinafre salteado [salt-**ya**doo]
spinach sautéed in butter

estragão [eestrag**ow**ng] tarragon

faisão [fi**zow**ng] pheasant

farinha [fa**reen**-ya] flour

fatia [fa**tee**-a] slice

favas [**fa**vas] broad beans

feijão [fay**Jow**ng] beans

feijoada [fayJ**wa**da] bean and
meat stew

feijões [fay**Joy**ngs] beans

fígado [**fee**gadoo] liver

figo [**fee**goo] fig

figo seco [**say**koo] dried fig

filé [fee**leh**] fillet

filé com foie gras [kohng fwa gra]
beef fillet with foie gras

filé de atum [dee at**oo**ng] tuna
steak

flã [flang] crème caramel

folhado de linguiça [fohl-**ya**do
dee leeng**wee**sa] sausage roll

fondue de carne [fon**dee** dee
karnee] meat fondue

fondue de chocolate
[shohkoh**la**tee] chocolate
fondue

fondue de queijo [**kay**Joo]
cheese fondue

framboesa [frambw**ay**za]
raspberry

frango [**fran**goo] chicken

frango com quiabo [kohng kee-
aboo] chicken stew with okra

frango com vinho do Porto
[kohng **veen**-yoo doo] chicken

casserole with Port and
almonds

frango grelhado [grayl-**ya**doo]
grilled chicken

frango no espeto [noo eespay**too**]
spit-roasted chicken

fricassê [freekas**ay**] small pieces
of chicken, pork, veal etc
boiled in a hearty sauce

fricassê de coelho [freekas**ay** dee
kw**ay**l-yoo] rabbit fricassee

fricassê de galinha [ga**leen**-ya]
chicken fricassée

fricassê de peru [pay**roo**]
turkey fricassée

frios [**free**-oos] selection of cold
meats

fritar [free**tar**] to fry

frito [**free**too] fried

fruta [**froo**ta] fruit

fruta da época [**eh**pohka]
seasonal fruit

fruta-do-conde [doo **kohn**dee]
custard apple

galantina de carne [galan**tee**na
dee **kar**nee] cold meat roll

galantina de coelho [dee kw**ay**l-
yoo] cold rabbit roll

galantina de galinha [ga**leen**-ya]
cold chicken roll

galantina de vegetais [vayJay**tİs**]
cold vegetable roll

galinha [ga**leen**-ya] chicken

galinha-d'angola [d**ang**ola]
guinea fowl

ganso [**gan**soo] goose

garoupa [ga**roh**pa] fish similar
to bream, very tasty

gaspacho [gaspashoo] chilled vegetable soup

geléia de frutas [Jayleh-ia dee frootas] fruit jam

geléia de laranja [dee laranJa] marmalade

gengibre [JaynJeebree] ginger

goiabada [goh-ee-abada] conserve made of guava, sugar and water

gordura [gohrdoora] fat

grão-de-bico [growng dee beekoo] chickpeas

grapefruit grapefruit

grelhado [grayl-yadoo] grilled

groselha [grohzehl-ya] redcurrant

guisado de carne [geezadoo dee karnee] stewed meat

hambúrguer simples [seemplees] hamburger in a roll

hortaliças [ohrtaleesas] green vegetables

hortelã [ohrtaylang] mint

iogurte [yohgoortee] yoghurt

jantar [Jantar] evening meal, dinner

jardineira de legumes [Jardinayra dee laygoomees] mixed vegetables

lagosta [lagohsta] lobster

lagosta à Americana [amayreekana] lobster with tomato and onions

lagosta à thermidor [tayrmeedohr] lobster thermidor, with béchamel sauce, cream and brandy

lagostim [lagohsteeng] saltwater crayfish

lanche [lanshee] afternoon tea

laranja [laranJa] orange

lasanha [lasan-ya] lasagne

legumes [laygoomees] vegetables

leitão assado [laytowng asadoo] roast sucking pig

leite [laytee] milk

limão [leemowng] lemon

língua [leengwa] tongue

língua de boi [boh-i] ox tongue

língua de porco [dee pohrkoo] pig's tongue

linguado [leengwadoo] sole

linguado à meunière [moon-yehr] sole dipped in flour and fried in butter

linguado frito [freetoo] fried sole

linguado grelhado [grayl-yadoo] grilled sole

linguado no forno [noo fohrnoo] baked sole

linguiça de frango [leengweesa dee frangoo] chicken sausage

linguiça de porco [pohrkoo] pork sausage

lista de preços [leesta dee praysoos] price list

lombo [lohmboo] loin

lombo de porco [dee pohrkoo] loin of pork

lombo de vaca [vaka] sirloin

louro [lohroo] bay leaf

lula [loola] squid

lula com creme [kohng kraymee

dee **laytee**] stewed squid with cream

lula empanada [aym**pana**da] seasoned squid dipped in flour and fried in oil

lula frita [**free**ta] fried squid

lula guisada [gee**za**da] stewed squid

lula recheada [Hay**shay**-**a**da] stuffed squid

maçã [ma**sang**] apple

maçã assada [a**sa**da] baked apple

macarrão ao alho e óleo [maka**How**ng ow **al**-yoo ee **ol**-yo] pasta with garlic and olive oil

maionese [mi-ohn**eh**zee] mayonnaise

maionese de alho [dee **al**-yoo] garlic mayonnaise

maionese de ovo [**oh**voo] egg mayonnaise

malpassado [pa**sa**doo] rare

mandioca frita [mand-**yo**ka **free**ta] deep fried cassava/manioc

mandioquinha [mand-yo**keen**-ya] when boiled this root has about de same uses as potatoes, including side dishes as purrés, dumplings, gnocchi, pastries etc.

manga mango

manjar branco [man**Jar bran**koo] coconut milk custard with prune sauce

manjericão [manJayreek**ow**ng] basil

manteiga [mant**ayga**] butter

margarina [margar**ee**na] margarine

marinada [maree**na**da] marinade

mariscada [maree**ska**da] mussels in light tomato sauce, parsley, onion and pepper

mariscos [mare**eskoos**] shellfish

marmelada [marmay**la**da] quince jam

marmelo [marm**eh**loo] quince

marmelo assado [marm**eh**loo a**sa**doo] roast quince

massa pasta

meia porção [**may**-a pohr**sowng**] half portion

melancia [maylan**see**-a] watermelon

melão [may**lowng**] melon

melão com presunto [kohng prayz**oon**too] melon with ham

menu de preço fixo [**may**noo dee **pray**soo **feek**so] set menu

merenda [mayr**aynda**] tea; snack

merengue [mayr**ayngee**] meringue

mexilhões [maysheel-y**oyngs**] mussels

mexilhões ao vinagrete [ow veenagr**eh**tee] mussels in vinaigrette dressing

mil-folhas [meel **fohl**-yas] millefeuille, custard slice, (US) napoleon

miolo [m-**yo**loo] brains

miolos com ovos [kohng **o**voos] brains with eggs

misto quente [**mee**sto **kayn**tee] toasted ham and cheese sandwich molho [**mohl**-yoo] sauce

molho bearnaise [baym**ehz**] béarnaise sauce

molho bechamel [baysham**ehl**] béchamel sauce, white sauce

molho branco [**bran**koo] white sauce

molho de queijo [dee kay**Joo**] cheese sauce

molho holandês [ohland**ays**] hollandaise sauce

molho Madeira [mad**ayra**] Madeira wine sauce

molho tártaro [**tarta**roo] tartare sauce

molho velouté [vaylool**tay**] white sauce made from cream and egg yolks

moqueca [mohk**ehka**] seafood stew made of fish, onions, garlic, tomatoes, coriander and pepper

morango [mohr**ango**o] strawberry

morangos com chantilly [kohng shantee**lee**] strawberries and whipped cream

morcela [mohrs**ehla**] black pudding, blood sausage

mostarda [mohstarda] mustard

musse de chocolate [**moo**see dee shohkoh**la**tee] chocolate mousse

musse de leite condensado [**lay**tee kohndaynsadoo] mousse made from condensed milk

musse de manga [dee manga] mango mousse

na brasa [**braza**] charcoal-grilled

nectarina [naykta**ree**na] nectarine

nêsperas [**nays**payras] loquats

nhoque gnocchi

no espeto [noo eesp**aytoo**] spit-roasted

no forno [**fohr**noo] baked

nozes [**no**zees] walnuts

noz-moscada [nos mohskada] nutmeg

óleo [**ol**-yoo] oil

omelete [omayl**eh**tee] omelette

omelete com ervas [kohng **ehr**vas] vegetable omelette

omelete de cogumelos [dee kohgoom**eh**loos] mushroom omelette

omelete de presunto [prayz**oon**too] ham omelette

omelete de queijo [kay**Joo**] cheese omelette

ostra [**oh**stra] oyster

ovo [**oh**voo] egg

ovo cozido [kohz**ee**doo] hard-boiled egg

ovo frito [**free**too] fried egg

ovo poché [pohsh**ay**] poached egg

ovo quente [**kayn**tee] soft-boiled egg

ovos mexidos [maysh**ee**doos] scrambled eggs

ovos mexidos com tomate [kohng tohm**a**tee] scrambled eggs with tomato

ovos nevados [**o**voos nayvadoos] cream with egg whites, sugar and cinammon ovos recheados [Hayshay-adoos] eggs stuffed with a mixture of egg yolks, mayonnaise and parsley

pamonha [pamohn-ya] paste made from corn and milk, boiled wrapped in corn husk

panqueca [pankehka] pancake

panqueca de camarão [pankehka dee kamarowng] prawn crêpe

panqueca de carne [karnee] meat crêpe

panqueca de cogumelos [kohgoomehloos] mushroom crêpe

panqueca de espinafre [ayspeenafree] spinach crêpe

panqueca de legumes [laygoomees] vegetable crêpe

pão [powng] bread

pão branco [brankoo] white bread

pão de centeio [dee sayntay-oo] rye bread

pão de milho [meel-yoo] bread made from maize flour, corn bread

pão de queijo [kayJoo] small rolls made of cassava flour and eggs, flavored with matured hard white cheese ou fresh white cheese

pão integral [intaygral] wholemeal bread

pão torrado [toh-Hadoo] toasted bread

pão-de-ló [law] sponge cake

pargo [pargoo] sea bream

pargo assado [asadoo] roast bream

pargo cozido [kohzeedoo] bream cooked in a sauce or with olive oil

passas [pasas] raisins

pastel [pastehl] fritter (usually filled with meat, cheese, heart of palm or other flavour)

pastel de bacalhau [dee bakal-yow] fritter filled with cod

pastel de carne [karnee] fritter filled with beef

patê de fígado [patay dee feegadoo] liver pâté

patê de galinha [galeen-ya] chicken pâté

pato [patoo] duck

pato assado [asadoo] roast duck

pato com laranja [kohng laranJa] duck à l'orange

peixe [payshee] fish

peixe grelhado [grayl-yadoo] grilled fish

peixe-espada [ayspada] swordfish

peixe-espada em escabeche [ayng ayskabehshee] marinated swordfish

pepino [paypeenoo] cucumber

pêra [payra] pear

pêra com calda de chocolate [kohng kalda dee shohkohlatee] pear in chocolate sauce

perdiz [payrdees] partridge

perdiz em escabeche [ayng ayskabehshee] marinated partridge

223

perdiz frita [freeta] fried
partridge

perna de rã [perrna dee rang]
frogs' legs

pernil [payrneel] leg

pernil de carneiro assado [dee
karnayroo asadoo] roast leg of
lamb

pernil de carneiro recheado
[Hayshay- adoo] stuffed leg of
lamb

peru assado [asadoo] roast
turkey

peru recheado [Hayshay-adoo]
stuffed turkey

pescada [payskada] hake

pescada cozida [kohzeeda]
hake cooked in a sauce or
with olive oil

pêssego [paysaygoo] peach

petiscos [payteeskoos] savouries

picadinho [peekadeen-yoo]
minced meat

picante [peekantee] hot, spicy

pimenta [peemaynta] pepper

pimenta-preta [prayta] black
pepper

pimentão [peemayntowng]
peppers, capsicums

pirão de peixe [peerowng
dee payshee] fish broth
thickened with manioc flour

polvo [pohlvoo] octopus

porção [pohrsowng] portion

porção para crianças [kr-yansas]
children's portion

porco [pohrkoo] pork

prato [pratoo] dish; course

prato do dia [doo dee-a]
today's special

prato especial da casa [eespays-
yal da kaza] speciality of the
house

prato principal [preenseepal]
main course

presunto [prayzoontoo] ham

presunto caramelizado
[karamayleezadoo] glazed ham

presunto cozido [prayzoontoo
kohzeedoo] ham

pudim de laranja [poodeeng dee
laranJa] orange custard

pudim de leite [laytee] milk and
eggs custard with caramel

pudim de ovos [ovoos] egg
pudding

pudim de pão [powng] bread
custard with raisins

purê de batata [pooray dee
batata] mashed potatoes

purê de castanhas [kastan-yas]
chestnut purée

purê de ervilha [ayrveel-ya] peas
purée

queijadinha [kayJadeen-ya] small
tarts with a filling made from
milk, eggs, sugar and vanilla

queijo curado [kooradoo] matured
cheese ready for consumption
when the juice has evaporated
and the cheese has solidified
and turned into a yellowish
tint; it has a stronger taste

queijo de cabra [dee] goat's
cheese

queijo de coalho [kwah-lyoo]
firm but very light cheese

with a "squeaky" texture, commonly eaten off a stick, much like a lollipop

queijo de leite de cabra [kayjoo dee laytee dee kabra] goat's cheese

queijo de ovelha [dee ovayl-ya] sheep's cheese

queijo frescal [frayskal] served quite fresh, about 4-10 days after preparation, still white and tender, with a mild taste

queijo fresco [frayskoo] medium-firm mild cheese, like queijo-de-minas

queijo meia-cura [maya koora] slightly matured frescal cheese, very soft

queijo-de-minas [dee meenas] cheese traditionally produced in the state of Minas Gerais; it comes in three varieties: frescal, meia-cura and curado

quibebe [keebehee] salted pumpkin purée

quiche de cogumelos [keesh dee kohgoomehloos] mushroom quiche

quindim [keendeeng] popular Brazilian baked dessert, a type of custard made from sugar, egg yolks and ground coconut

rabanadas [Habanadas] French toast

raia [Hī-a] skate

rapadura [Hapadoora] pure dried sugacane juice in the form of a brick, extremely sweet

refeição leve [Hafaysowng lehvee] snack, light meal

refeições [Hafaysoyngs] meals

refogado [Hayfohgadoo] stewed

repolho [Haypohl-yoo] cabbage

repolho ao vinagrete [ow veenagrehtee] white cabbage with vinegar

repolho refogado com salsichas [Hayfohgadoo kohng salseeshas] stewed cabbage with sausage

repolho roxo [Hohsoo] red cabbage

requeijão [HaykayJowng] cream cheese with a mild taste; its consistency varies from solid to creamy

rim [reeng] kidney

rim ao Madeira [ow madayra] kidneys cooked in Madeira wine

riosoto de mariscos [mareeskoos] a soupy dish of rice with mixed seafood

risoto de erva-doce [Heezohtoo dee ehrva dohsee] rice with fennel

risoto de frango [Heezohtoo dee frangoo] rice with chicken

risoto de lula [loola] rice with squid

rissole [Heesolee] deep-fried meat patties

rissole de camarão [dee kamarowng] prawn rissole

robalo [Hohbaloo] rock bass

rodízio [Hohdeez-yoo] restaurant

serving as much meat as you can eat; the waiters move around with skewers, slicing meat onto the client's plate
rosbife roast beef

sal salt
salada salad
salada de agrião [dee agr-**yow**ng] watercress salad
salada de alface [al**fa**see] green salad
salada de atum [a**too**ng] tuna salad
salada de batata [ba**ta**ta] boiled potato salad
salada de chicória [sheek**o**r-ya] chicory salad
salada de frutas [sa**la**da dee **froo**tas] fruit salad
salada de lagosta [la**goh**sta] lobster salad
salada de palmito [pal**mee**too] heart of palm salad
salada de tomate [toh**ma**tee] tomato salad
salada mista [**mee**sta] mixed salad
salada russa [**Hoo**sa] diced vegetables in mayonnaise
salgado [salg**a**doo] savoury, salty
salmão [sal**mow**ng] salmon
salmão defumado [dayfoo**ma**doo] smoked salmon
salmonete [salmohn**ay**tee] red mullet
salmonete grelhado [grayl-**ya**doo] grilled red mullet

salsa parsley
salsicha [sal**see**sha] sausage
salsicha de coquetel [sal**see**sha dee kohkeet**eh**l] cocktail sausages
salteado [salt-**ya**doo] sautéed
sanduíche de linguiça [leeng**wee**sa] sausage sandwich
sanduíche de lombo [**loh**mboo] pork sandwich
sanduíche de mortadela [mohrtad**eh**la] mortadella sandwich (Italian cold cut made of finely ground heat-cured pork sausage)
sanduíche de presunto [dee pray**zoo**ntoo] ham sandwich
sanduíche de queijo [**kay**Joo] cheese sandwich
sanduíche misto [**mee**sto] mixed sandwich, usually ham and cheese (hot or cold)
sanduíche quente [**kay**ntee] toasted sandwich
sanduíche sandwich
sardinha [sar**deen**-ya] sardine
sardinha assada [a**sa**da] roast sardine
sashimi de atum tuna sashimi
seleção de queijos [saylay**sow**ng dee **kay**Joos] selection of cheeses
siri [**seeree**] blue crab
sobremesas [sohbray**may**zas] desserts
solha [**soh**l-ya] flounder
solha ao forno [ow **foh**rnoo] baked flounder

solha frita [free ta] fried flounder

solha recheada [Hayshay-a da] stuffed flounder

sonho [sohn-yoo] type of doughnut

sopa de abóbora [sohpa dee abobohra] pumpkin soup

sopa de alho-poró [al-yoo pohro] leek soup

sopa de aspargos [aspargoos] asparagus soup

sopa de camarão [kamarowng] prawn soup

sopa de caranguejo [karangayJoo] crab soup

sopa de cebola gratinada [saybohla grateenada] French onion soup with melted cheese on top

sopa de cogumelos [kohgoomehloos] mushroom soup

sopa de ervilha [ayrveel-ya] pea soup

sopa de feijão [fayJowng] beans soup

sopa de fubá com agrião [fooba kohng agr-yowng] corn meal soup with watercress

sopa de grão-de-bico [growng dee beekoo] chickpea soup

sopa de lagosta [lagohsta] lobster soup

sopa de legumes [laygoomees] vegetable soup

sopa de lentilha [laynteel-ya] lentil soup

sopa de mandioquinha [mand-yokeen-ya] arracacha soup

sopa de mariscos [mareeskoos] shellfish soup

sopa de milho [meel-yoo] corn soup

sopa de ostras [ohstras] oyster soup

sopa do dia [doo dee-a] soup of the day

sopa juliana [Jool-yana] vegetable soup

sorvete [sorvaytee] ice cream

sorvete de baunilha [dee bowneel-ya] vanilla ice cream

sorvete de chocolate [shohkohlatee] chocolate ice cream

sorvete de coco coconut ice cream

sorvete de frutas [frootas] fruit ice cream

suflê de camarão [sooflay dee kamarowng] prawn soufflé

suflê de chocolate [shohkohlatee] chocolate soufflé

suflê de cogumelo [kohgoomehloos] mushroom soufflé

suflê de espinafre [ayspeenafree] spinach soufflé

suflê de peixe [payshee] fish soufflé

suflê de queijo [kayJoo] cheese soufflé

taxa de serviço [tasha dee sayrveesoo] service charge

tempero de salada [taympayroo dee salada] salad dressing

tira-gosto [teera gohstoo] hors d'œuvres

tomate [tohmatee] tomato

tomates recheados [tohmatees Hayshay-adoos] stuffed tomatoes

tomilho [tohmeel-yoo] thyme

torrada [toh-Hada] toast

torresmo [toh-Haysmoo] small fried rasher of bacon

torta de amêndoas [torta dee amayndwas] almond tart

torta de limão [leemowng] lemon tart

torta de maçã [masang] apple pie

torta de nozes [dee nozees] walnut tart

torta tart

tortilha [toorteel-ya] Spanish-style omelette with potato

trufas de chocolate [troofas dee shohkohlatee] chocolate truffles

truta [troota] trout

truta ao forno [ow fohrnoo] baked trout

truta cozida [kohzeeda] trout cooked in a sauce or with olive oil

truta frita [freeta] fried trout

uva [oova] grape

uva branca [oova branka] green grape

uva moscatel [mohskatehl] musscatel grape

uva preta [oova prayta] black grape

vagem [vajayng] French beans

vinagre [veenagree] vinegar

vitela [veetehla] veal

zabaione [zaba-yohnee] dessert made from egg yolks and white wine

Menu
Reader:
Drink

Essential Terms

beer cerveja [sayrvayJa]
bottle garrafa [gaHafa]
brandy conhaque [kohn-yakee]
coffee café [kafeh]
 a cup of... uma xícara de... [ooma sheekara dee]
gin o gim [Jeeng]
 gin and tonic gim-tônica [Jeeng tohneeka]
glass copo [kopoo]
 a glass of... um copo de... [oong kopoo dee]
milk leite [laytee]
mineral water água mineral [agwa]
orange juice suco de laranja [sookoo dee laranJa]
port vinho do Porto [veen-yoo doo pohrtoo]
red wine o vinho tinto [teentoo]
rosé rosé [Hohzay]
soda (water) club soda
soft drink bebida não alcoólica [baybeeda nowng alko-oleeka]
sugar açúcar [asookar]
tea chá [sha]
tonic (water) água tônica [agwa]
vodka vodca
water água [agwa]
whisky uísque [weeskee]
white wine vinho branco [veen-yoo brankoo]
wine vinho
wine list carta de vinhos [karta dee veen-yoos]

another..., please outro/outra..., por favor [ohtroo – poor favohr]

açúcar [asookar] sugar

água de coco [agwa dee]
coconut water

água mineral [agwa meenayral]
mineral water

aguardente [agwardayntee]
clear spirit/brandy (literally:
'firewater'), distilled from
wine or grape skins

aguardente de pêra [dee payra]
brandy with a pear or pears
in the bottle

aguardentes bagaceiras
[agwardayntees bagasayras] clear
spirit/brandy distilled from
grape skins

aguardentes velhas [vehl-yas]
matured brandies

aguardentes velhas ou
preparadas [vehl-yaz oh
preparadas] brandies matured
in oak

álcool [alkohl] alcohol

aperitivo [apayreeteevoo] aperitif

bagaço [bagasoo] clear spirit/
brandy, distilled from grape
skins

bebida [baybeeda] drink

cacau [kakow] cocoa

cachaça [kashasa] clear spirit
distilled from sugarcane

café [kafeh] coffee

café com conhaque [kohn-
yakee] espresso with brandy

café com leite [kohng laytee]
white coffee, coffee with
milk (large cup)

café duplo [dooploo] two
espressos in the same cup

café solúvel [soh-loovil] instant
coffee

cafezinho [kafehzeen-yoo] small
black espresso-type coffee

caipirinha [kīpeeree-nya]
cocktail mixing lime
muddled with sugar,
"cachaça" and ice cubes

caipirosca [kīpeeroska]
cocktail mixing lime
muddled with sugar, vodka
and ice cubes

carioca [kar-yoka] small weak
black coffee

carta de vinhos [karta dee veen-
yoos] wine list

cerveja [sayrvayJa] beer

cerveja preta [prayta] bitter,
dark beer

chá [sha] tea

chá com leite [kohng laytee] tea
with milk

chá com limão [leemowng]
lemon tea

chá com mel [mehl] tea with
honey

chá de erva-doce [ehrva dohsee]
fennel tea

chá de hortelã [ohrtaylang] mint
tea

chá de limão [dee leemowng]
infusion of hot water with a
lemon rind

chá de tília [teel-ya] linden
blossom tea

champanhe [shampan-yi]
champagne

chimarrão [sheemaHownng] hot and bitter tea made with hot water and mate herb

chocolate gelado [shohkohlatee Jayladoo] hot chocolate

chocolate quente [shohkohlatee kayntee] hot chocolate

chope [shohpee] draught beer

cidra [seedra] cider

com gás [kohng gas] carbonated

com gelo [Jayloo] with ice, on the rocks

conhaque [kohn-yakee] cognac, brandy

cubo de gelo [kooboo dee Jayloo] ice cube

descafeinado [deeskafaynadoo] decaffeinated

doce [dohsee] sweet (usually very sweet)

espumante [eespoomantee] sparkling

espumante natural [natooral] sparkling wine made by the champagne method

expresso [aysprehsoo] espresso

extra seco [saykoo] extra-dry

fanta® [fanta] orange soft drink

garrafa [gaHafa] bottle

gelo [Jayloo] ice

jarra [JaHa] jug

leite [laytee] milk

licor [leekohr] liqueur; sweet flavoured spirit

licor de abacaxi [dee abakashee] pineapple home made liqueur

licor de amêndoa amarga [amayndwa amarga] bitter almond liqueur

licor de jenipapo [Jayneepapoo] home made liqueur made from the fruits of the species *Genipa americana*

licor de pêra [payra] pear liqueur

licor de uísque [weeskee] whisky liqueur

limonada [leemohnada] fresh lemon juice with water and sugar

lista de preços [leesta dee praysoos] price list

maduro [madooroo] mature

meia de seda [may-a dee sayda] cream, cocoa cream, gin and cinnamon cocktail

meia garrafa [may-a gaHafa] half-bottle

meio seco [may-oo saykoo] medium-dry (usually fairly sweet)

milkshake milkshake

moscatel [mohskatehl] muscatel wine

não alcoólico [nowng alko-oleekoo] non-alcoholic

pingado [peengadoo] coffee with drops of milk

ponche [**poh**nshee] punch

pré-pagamento pay in advance

rabo-de-galo [**H**aboo dee galoo] "cachaça" with a little bit of red vermouth

raspadinha de café [**H**aspadeen-ya dee kaf**eh**] coffee drink with crushed ice

raspadinha de chocolate [shohkohl**a**tee] chocolate drink with crushed ice

raspadinha de groselha [grohz**eh**l-ya] redcurrant drink with crushed ice

raspadinha de morango [moh**ra**ngoo] strawberry drink with crushed ice

região demarcada wine-producing region subject to official controls

reserva especial aged wine set aside by the producer in years of exceptional quality

saquinhos de chá [sak**ee**n-yoos dee sha] teabags

seco [**say**koo] dry

selo de garantia seal of guarantee

sem gás [sayng gas] still

sem gelo [**Jay**loo] without ice

servir à temperatura ambiente serve at room temperature

servir fresco serve cool

servir gelado serve chilled

suco de laranja [**soo**koo dee lara**nJa**] orange juice

suco de limão [leem**owng**] lemon juice

suco de maçã [mas**a**ng] apple juice

suco de tomate [toh**ma**tee] tomato juice

tulipa [too**lee**pa] tall and narrow glass for drinking beer

uísque de malte [**wee**skee dee **ma**ltee] malt whisky

velhíssimo [vehl-y**ee**seemo] very old (spirits)

velho [**veh**l-yoo] old, mature

vermute branco [vayrm**oo**tee **bra**nkoo] white vermouth

vermute tinto [**teen**too] red vermouth

vinho branco [**vee**n-yoo **bra**nkoo] white wine

vinho clarete [klar**ay**tee] claret wine

vinho da casa [da **Ka**za] house wine

vinho de aperitivo [dee apayreet**ee**voo] aperitif

vinho de mesa [dee **may**za] table wine

vinho do Porto [doo **poh**rtoo] port

vinho espumante [eespoom**a**ntee] sparkling wine

vinho moscatel [mohskat**eh**l] muscatel wine

vinho rosé [**H**ohz**ay**] rosé wine

vinho tinto [**teen**too] red wine

vinho verde [**vay**rdee] young,

233

slightly sparkling white, red,
or rosé wine

xarope de groselha [sharopee
dee grohzehl-ya] redcurrant
syrup mixed with water
xerez [shayrays] sherry

How the Language Works

Pronunciation

In this phrasebook, the Brazilian Portuguese has been written in a system of imitated pronunciation so that it can be read as though it were English, bearing in mind the notes on pronunciation given below:

a	as in c**a**r (in Brazil sometimes 'a' is pronounced as in r**u**n, but you will have no difficulty to make yourself understood)
ay	as in m**ay** (but in Portuguese this sound is much shorter)
eh	as in g**e**t
g	as in **g**oat
H	as in **h**ome (initial 'r' and 'rr' are pronounced this way)
i	as in **i**t
ī	as the 'i' sound in m**i**ght
J	as in plea**s**ure
o	as in n**o**t
oh	like the exclamation **oh**
oo	as in b**oo**t
ow	as in n**ow**

In words such as **não** [nowng] and **bem** [bayng], the final 'g' in the pronunciation signifies a nasal sound and should barely be sounded. As you talk and listen, the sounds will become more and more familiar. The same word can be transcribed in different ways due to different needs of expression, and in our system letters given in bold type indicate the part of the word to be stressed.

Abbreviations

adj	adjective	pl	plural
f	feminine	pol	polite
fam	familiar	sing	singular
m	masculine		

Nouns

All nouns in Portuguese have one of two genders: masculine or feminine. Generally speaking, those ending in -o are masculine:

> **o sapato**
> oo sap**a**too
> the shoe

Nouns ending in **-or** are masculine. To make the corresponding feminine, add **-a**:

> **o professor**   **a professora**
> oo prohfays**oh**r   a prohfays**oh**ra
> the (male) teacher   the (female) teacher

Nouns ending in **-a**, **-ade** or **-ão** are usually feminine (although there are exceptions):

> **a cama**   **a cidade**   **a pensão**
> a k**a**ma   a seed**a**dee   a payns**ow**ng
> the bed   the city   the boarding house

A small number of nouns ending in **-a** and **-e** (usually professions) can be either masculine or feminine:

> **o/a guia**   **o/a intérprete**
> oo/a g**ee**-a   oo/a int**eh**rpraytee
> the tourist guide   the interpreter

Plural Nouns

The plurals of nouns are formed according to the rules below.

For nouns ending in a vowel, add **-s**:

> **a garçonete**   **as garçonetes**
> a garsohn**eh**tee   as garsohn**eh**tees
> the waitress   the waitresses

The plural of most nouns ending in **-ão** is formed by removing the **-ão** and adding **-ões**:

a pensão	**as pensões**
a payns**ow**ng	as paynsoyngs
the guesthouse	the guesthouses

But in some nouns you have to add **-s** or **-ães**:

o cidadão	**os cidadãos**
oo seedad**ow**ng	oos seedad**ow**ngs
the citizen	the citizens

o escrivão	**os escrivães**
oo ayskreev**ow**ng	oos ayskreev**ay**ngs
the notary public	the notaries public

To obtain the plural of nouns ending in **-l**, remove the **-l** and add **-is**:

o hotel	**os hotéis**
oo oht**ehl**	ooz oht**eh**-is
the hotel	the hotels

To obtain the plural of nouns ending in **-m**, remove the **-m** and add **-ns**:

o homem	**os homens**
oo **o**mayng	ooz **o**mayngs
the man	the men

For nouns ending in other consonants, the plural is formed by adding **-es**:

o promotor	**os promotores**
oo prohmoht**ohr**	oos prohmoht**oh**ris
the prosecutor	the prosecutors

uma mulher	**umas mulheres**
ooma mool-y**ehr**	**oo**mas mool-y**eh**rees
a woman	some women

Articles

The words for articles in Portuguese depend on the number (singular or plural) and gender of the noun.

The Definite Article

The definite article (the) is as follows:

	singular	plural
masculine	o [oh]	os [oos]
feminine	a [a]	as [as]

o livro	**os livros**
oo **lee**vroo	oos **lee**vroos
the book	the books
a piscina	**as piscinas**
a pee**see**na	as pee**see**nas
the swimming pool	the swimming pools

When the definite article is used in combination with **a** (to), **de** (of), **em** (in, on) or **por** (by), it changes as follows:

	o	a	os	as
a +	ao	à	aos	às
	ow	a	ows	as
de +	do	da	dos	das
	doh	da	doos	das
em +	no	na	nos	nas
	noh	na	noos	nas
por +	pelo	pela	pelos	pelas
	payloo	**pay**la	**pay**loos	**pay**las

vamos ao museu	**perto do hotel**
vamooz ow moo**say**-oo	**peh**rtoo doo ohte**hl**
let's go to the museum	near the hotel

The Indefinite Article

The indefinite article (a, an, some) also changes according to the gender and number of the accompanying noun:

	singular	plural
masculine	**um** [oong]	**uns** [oons]
feminine	**uma** [**oo**ma]	**umas** [**oo**mas]

um selo	**uns selos**
oong **say**loo	oons **say**loos
a stamp	some stamps
uma menina	**umas/algumas meninas**
ooma mayn**ee**na	**oo**mas mayn**ee**nas
a girl	some girls

When the indefinite article is used in combination with **em** (in, on) it changes as follows:

masculine	**em** + **um** = **num** [noong]
feminine	**em** + **uma** = **numa** [**noo**ma]

gostaria de ir numa viagem ao Brasil
gohstar**ee**-a deer n**oo**ma v-y**a**Jayng ow braz**eel**
I'd like to go on a trip to Brazil

Adjectives and Adverbs

Adjectives must agree in gender and number with the noun they refer to. In the English-Portuguese section of this book, all adjectives are given in the masculine singular. Unlike English, Portuguese adjectives usually follow the noun.

The feminine singular of the adjective is formed by changing the masculine endings as follows:

masculine	feminine
-o	-a
-or	-ora
-ês	-esa

um cozinheiro ótimo
oong kohzeen-**yay**roo **o**timoo
a wonderful cook

uma cozinheira ótima
ooma koozeen-**yay**ra **o**tima
a wonderful cook

um senhor encantador
oong sayn-**yohr** aynkantad**ohr**
a nice man

uma senhora encantadora
ooma sayn-**yo**ra aynkantad**o**ra
a nice woman

um rapaz inglês
oong H**a**paz ingl**ays**
an English boy

uma moça inglesa
ooma m**oh**sa ingl**ay**za
an English girl

For other types of adjective, the feminine form is the same as the masculine:

um homem agradável
oong **o**mayng agrad**a**vil
a nice man

uma mulher agradável
ooma mool-**yeh**r agrad**a**vil
a nice woman

Note that the adjective **mau** (bad) is irregular: the feminine is **má**.

The plurals of adjectives are formed in the same way as the plurals of nouns, by adding an **-s**, an **-es** or changing **-l** to **-is**:

o preço alto
oo pr**ay**soo **a**ltoo
the high price

os preços altos
oos pr**ay**sooz **a**ltoos
the high prices

uma taxa alta
ooma t**a**sha **a**lta
a high rate

as taxas altas
as t**a**shaz **a**ltas
the high rates

um homem agradável
oong **o**mayng agrad**a**vil
a nice man

uns homens agradáveis
oonz **o**mayngz agrad**a**vay-is
some nice men

When the adjective ends in **-ês**, the **ê** is replaced by **e** in the plural:

um rapaz inglês	uns rapazes ingleses
oong rap**az** ingl**ays**	oons rap**az**eez ingl**ay**zees
an English boy	some English boys

Comparatives

The comparative is formed by placing **mais** (more) or **menos** (less) in front of the adjective or adverb and **que** (than) after it:

bonito	mais bonito
bohn**ee**too	mīs bohn**ee**too
beautiful	more beautiful

quente	menos quente
kayntee	ma**y**noos **kay**ntee
hot	less hot

este hotel é mais/menos caro que o outro
aystee oht**eh**l eh mīs/**may**noos ka**ro**o kee oo **oh**troo
this hotel is more/less expensive than the other one

tem um quarto mais barato?
ta**y**ng oong kw**ar**too mīs bar**at**oo?
do you have a cheaper room?

pode falar mais devagar, por favor?
p**o**dee falar mīs deevag**ar**, poor fav**ohr**?
could you speak more slowly please?

Superlatives

Superlatives are formed by placing one of the following before the adjective: **o/a mais** or **os/as mais** (depending on the noun's gender and number):

qual é o mais divertido?
kwal**eh** oo mīs deevayrt**ee**doo
which is the most entertaining?

o dia mais quente	o carro mais rápido
oo d**ee**-a mīs **kay**ntee	oo ka**H**oo mīs **H**apeedoo
the hottest day	the fastest car

The following adjectives have irregular comparatives and superlatives:

bom	good	**melhor**	better	**o melhor**	the best
bohng		mayl-**yor**		oo mayl-**yor**	
grande	big	**maior**	bigger	**o maior**	the biggest
gr**a**ndee		mī-**or**		oo mī-**or**	
mau	bad	**pior**	worse	**o pior**	the worst
mow		p-**yor**		oo p-yor	
pequeno	small	**menor**	smaller	**o menor**	the smallest
peek**ay**noo		may**nor**		oo may**nor**	

Note that **mais pequeno** (smaller) is also used.

'As... as...' is translated as follows:

> **O Rio de Janeiro está tão bonito como sempre!**
>
> oo H**ee**-o dee Jan**ay**roo ayst**a** towng bohn**ee**too k**oh**moo s**ay**mpree
>
> Rio de Janeiro is as beautiful as ever!

The superlative form ending in -**íssimo** indicates that something is 'very/extremely...' without actually comparing it to something else:

lindo	**lindíssimo**
l**ee**ndoo	leend**ee**seemoo
beautiful	very beautiful

Adverbs

There are two ways to form an adverb. If the adjective ends in -o, take the feminine and add -**mente** to form the corresponding adverb:

exato	**exatamente**
ayz**a**too	ayzatam**ay**ntee
accurate	accurately

If the adjective ends in any other letter, add -**mente** to the basic masculine form:

feliz	felizmente
fay**lees**	fayleesm**ay**ntee
happy	happily

Possessive Adjectives

Possessive adjectives, like other Portuguese adjectives, agree with the noun in gender and number:

	singular		plural	
	masculine	feminine	masculine	feminine
my	**o meu**	**a minha**	**os meus**	**as minhas**
	oo **may**-oo	a **meen**-ya	oos**may**-oos	as **meen**-yas
your	**o teu**	**a tua**	**os teus**	**as tuas**
(sing)	oo **tay**-oo	a **too**-a	oos **tay**-oos	as **too**-as
his/her/its,	**o seu**	**a sua**	**os seus**	**as suas**
your, their	oo **say**-oo	a **soo**-a	oos **say**-oos	as **soo**-as
our	**o nosso**	**a nossa**	**os nossos**	**as nossas**
	oo **no**soo	a **no**sa	oos **no**soos	as **no**sas

A more formal way of translating 'your' is:

	singular	plural
masculine	**do senhor**	**dos senhores**
	doo sayn-**yohr**	doos sayn-**yoh**rees
feminine	**da senhora**	**das senhoras**
	da sayn-**yo**ra	das sayn-**yo**ras

See page 248 for when to use this.

a **tua** casa	os **seus** comprimidos
a **too**-a **ka**za	oos **say**-oos kohmpreem**ee**doos
your house	his/her/your/their tablets
a **sua** mala	os **nossos** amigos
a **soo**-a **ma**la	os **no**sooz am**ee**goos
his/her/your/their suitcase	our friends

If when using **o seu**, **a sua** etc, it is unclear whether you mean 'his', 'her', 'your' or 'their', you can use the following after the noun instead:

dele	[**day**lee]	his
dela	[**deh**la]	her
deles	[**day**lees]	their (m)
delas	[**deh**las]	their (f)
de vocês	[dee voh**says**]	your (pl)

o dinheiro dela	o dinheiro dele	o dinheiro de vocês
oo deen-**yay**roo **deh**la	oo deen-**yay**roo **day**lee	oo deen-**yay**roo dee voh**says**
her money	his money	your money

Possessive Pronouns

To translate 'mine', 'yours', 'theirs' etc, use one of the following forms. Like possessive adjectives, possessive pronouns must agree in gender and number with the object or objects referred to:

	singular		plural	
	masculine	feminine	masculine	feminine
mine	**meu**	**minha**	**meus**	**minhas**
	may-oo	**meen**-ya	**may**-oos	**meen**-yas
yours (sing)	**teu**	**tua**	**teus**	**tuas**
	tay-oo	**too**-a	**tay**-oos	**too**-as
his/hers, yours, theirs	**seu**	**sua**	**seus**	**suas**
	say-oo	**soo**-a	**say**-oos	**soo**-as
ours	**nosso**	**nossa**	**nossos**	**nossas**
	n**o**soo	n**o**sa	n**o**soos	n**o**sas

246

A more formal way of translating 'yours' is:

	singular	plural
masculine	**do senhor**	**dos senhores**
	doo sayn-**yohr**	doos sayn-**yoh**rees
feminine	**da senhora**	**das senhoras**
	da sayn-**yo**ra	das sayn-**yo**ras

See the section on subject pronouns for when to use this.

Generally, possessive pronouns are used with the definite article.

> **esta é a sua chave e esta é a minha**
> **eh**steh a **soo**-a sha**vee eh**steh a **meen**-ya
> this is your key and this is mine

> **este carro não é o seu**
> **ay**stee ka**H**oo nowng eh oo **say**-oo
> this car is not yours

If when using **seu**, **sua** etc, it is unclear whether you mean 'his', 'hers', 'yours' or 'theirs', you can use the following after the noun instead:

dele	[**day**lee]	his
dela	[**deh**la]	hers
deles	[**day**lees]	theirs (m)
delas	[**deh**la]	theirs (f)
de vocês	[dee voh**says**]	yours (pl)

> **não é dele, é dos amigos dele**
> nowng eh **day**lee, eh dooz am**ee**goos **day**lee
> it's not his, it's his friends'

Personal Pronouns

Subject Pronouns

eu	[**ay**-oo]	I
tu	[too]	you (sing)
ele	[**ay**lee]	he, it
ela	[**eh**la]	she, it
você	[voh**say**]	you (sing)
nós	[nos]	we
eles	[**ay**lees]	they (m)
elas	[**eh**las]	they (f)
vocês	[voh**says**]	you (pl)

Vós, the second person form of verbs in plural, is not used in current speaking due to its formality.

Tu is used when speaking to one person and is the familiar form generally used when speaking to family, close friends and children, but it is rarely used in Brazil.

Você and **vocês** are the familiar words to address people in Brazilian Portuguese. They take the third person forms of verbs: **você** takes the same form as 'he/she/it'; **vocês** takes the same form as 'they'.

There is another way of saying 'you', which is used to address complete strangers or in formal situations. These forms all take the third person of the verb, i.e. the same as 'he/she/it' for the singular and 'they' for the plural:

	singular	plural
masculine	**o senhor**	**os senhores**
	oo sayn-y**oh**r	oos sayn-y**oh**rees
feminine	**a senhora**	**as senhoras**
	a sayn-y**o**ra	as sayn-y**o**ras

(Note that **senhor** also means 'Mr' and **senhora** means 'Mrs'.)

a senhora é a mãe da Rita?
a sayn-**yo**ra eh a mayng da H**ee**ta
are you Rita's mother?

In Portuguese the subject pronoun is usually omitted:

não sabem   **está cansado**
nowng s**a**bayng   ays**ta** kans**a**doo
they don't know   he is tired

But it may be retained for emphasis or to avoid confusion:

sou eu!   **somos nós!**
soh **ay**-oo   **soh**moos nos
it's me!   it's us!

eu pago os sanduíches e você paga as cervejas
ay-oo p**a**goos sandwee**shee**s ee vohs**ay** p**a**gas sayrv**vay**Jas
I'll pay for the sandwiches and you pay for the beers

ele é inglês e ela é americana
aylee **eh** ingl**ayz** ee ehl**eh** amayreek**a**na
he's English and she's American

Object Pronouns

object pronoun added to verb

me	[may]	me
te	[tay]	you (sing)
o	[oh]	him, it, you (sing)
a	[a]	her, it, you (sing)
você	[vohsay]	you (sing)
nos	[nohs]	us
os	[oos]	them (m), you (mpl)
as	[as]	them (f), you (fpl)
vocês	[vohsays]	you (pl)

object pronoun used with prepositions

mim	[meeng]	me
ti	[tee]	you (sing)

ele	[aylee]	he, it
ela	[ehla]	she, it
você	[vohsay]	you (sing)
nós	[nos]	we
eles	[aylees]	them (m)
elas	[ehlas]	them (f)
vocês	[vohsays]	you (pl)

The object pronouns (as listed in the previous first table) can follow the verb or come first:

pode ajudar-me?
podee aJoodarmee
can you help me?

comprei-as
kompray-as
I bought them

pode me ajudar?
podee mee aJoodar
can you help me?

eu as comprei
ay-oo as kompray
I bought them

But note the word order in the following:

não o vi
nowng oo vee
I didn't see him

The object pronouns listed in the second table of the previous page are used after prepositions:

para você
para vohsay
for you

com ele
kohng aylee
with him

sem ela
sayng ehla
without her

depois de você
daypoh-is dee vohsay
after you

isso é para mim	**isso é para ti**
eesoo eh **pa**ra meeng	**ee**soo eh **pa**ra tee
that's for me	that's for you

After the preposition **com** (with), **mim** and **ti** change as follows:

comigo	**contigo**
koh**mee**goo	kohn**tee**goo
with me	with you

If you are using an indirect object pronoun to mean 'to me', 'to you' etc (although 'to' might not always be said in English), you generally use the following:

me	[mee]	to me
te	[tee]	to you (sing, fam)
lhe	[l-yi]	to him, to her, to you (sing, pol)
o/a	[oh/a]	to it
nos	[noos]	to us
lhes	[l-yis]	to them, to you (pl)

comprei-lhe flores	**pedi-lhe um favor**
kohm**prayl**-yi **floh**rees	pay**deel**-yi oong fa**vohr**
I bought flowers for him/her	I asked him/her a favour

importa-se de lhe pedir que...?
im**por**tasee dee l-yi pay**deer** kee
could you ask him/her to...?

Reflexive Pronouns

These are used with reflexive verbs like **lavar-se** 'to wash (oneself)', i.e. where the subject and the object of the verb are one and the same person:

me	[mee]	myself
te	[tee]	yourself (fam)
se	[see]	himself, herself, itself, yourself (pol), themselves, yourselves, oneself
nos	[noos]	ourselves

apresentar-se to introduce oneself

posso me apresentar? meu nome é Richard
posoo mee aprayzayntar? m**ay**-oo n**oh**mee eh Richard
may I introduce myself? my name's Richard

divertir-se to enjoy oneself

nós nos divertimos muito na festa
nos noos deevayrt**ee**moos m**wee**ngtoo na f**eh**sta
we enjoyed ourselves a lot at the party

Demonstratives

The English demonstrative adjective 'this' is translated by **este**. 'That' is translated either by **esse** or **aquele**. **Esse** refers to something nearby. **Aquele** refers to something further away.

Like other adjectives, demonstrative adjectives agree with the noun they qualify in gender and number but they are positioned in front of the noun. Their forms are:

masculine singular			feminine singular		
este	esse	aquele	esta	essa	aquela
aystee	**ay**see	ak**ay**lee	**eh**sta	**eh**sa	ak**eh**la

masculine plural			feminine plural		
estes	esses	aqueles	estas	essas	aquelas
aystees	**ay**sees	ak**ay**lees	**eh**stas	**eh**sas	ak**eh**las

este restaurante	esse garçom	aquela praia
aystee Haystowr**a**ntee	**ay**see gars**oh**ng	ak**eh**la pr**ī**-a
this restaurant	that waiter	that beach (in the distance)

The demonstrative pronouns 'this one', 'that one', 'those', 'these' etc are the same as demonstrative adjectives in Portuguese:

queria estes/esses/aqueles
kayr**ee**-a **ay**stees/**ay**sees/ak**ay**lees
I'd like these/those/those (over there)

However, a neuter form also exists which is used when no specific noun is being referred to:

isto	**isso**	**aquilo**
eestoo	**ee**soo	akeeloo
this	that	that (over there)

isso não é justo	**o que é isto?**
eeso nowng eh J**oo**stoo	oo kee eh **ee**stoo
that's not fair	what is this?

Verbs

The basic form of the verb given in the **English-Portuguese** and **Portuguese-English** sections is the infinitive (e.g. to drive, to go etc). There are three verb types in Portuguese which can be recognized by their infinitive endings: -ar, -er, -ir. For example:

amar	[amar]	to love
comer	[kohm**ay**r]	to eat
partir	[part**ee**r]	to leave

Present Tense

The present tense corresponds to 'I leave' in English. To form the present tense for the three main types of verb in Portuguese, remove the -ar, -er or -ir and add the following endings:

amar to love

am-o	[**a**moo]	I love
am-as	[**a**mas]	you love (sing)
am-a	[**a**ma]	he loves, she loves, you love (sing)
am-amos	[ama**moo**s]	we love
am-am	[**a**mowng]	they love, you love (pl)

comer to eat

com-o	[**koh**moo]	I eat
com-es	[**ko**mees]	you eat (**sing**)
com-e	[**ko**mee]	he eats, she eats, you eat (**sing**)
com-emos	[kohm**ay**moos]	we eat
com-em	[**ko**mayng]	they eat, you eat (**pl**)

partir to leave

part-o	[**par**too]	I leave
part-es	[**par**tees]	you leave (**sing**)
part-e	[**par**tee]	he leaves, she leaves, it leaves, you leave (**sing**)
part-imos	[par**tee**moos]	we leave
part-em	[**par**tayng]	they leave, you leave (**pl**)

Some common verbs are irregular:

dar to give

dou	[doh]	I give
dás	[das]	you give (**sing**)
dá	[da]	he gives, she gives, it gives, you give (**sing**)
damos	[**da**moos]	we give
dão	[downg]	they give, you give (**pl**)

ir to go

vou	[voh]	I go
vais	[vīs]	you go (**sing**)
vai	[vī]	he/she/it goes, you go (**sing**)
vamos	[**va**moos]	we go
vão	[vowng]	they go, you go (**pl**)

pôr to put

ponho	[**poh**n-yoo]	I put
pões	[poyngs]	you put (**sing**)
põe	[poyng]	he/she/it puts, you put (**sing**)
pomos	[**poh**moos]	we put
põem	[**poh**-ayng]	they put, you put (**pl**)

ter to have

tenho	[**tayn**-yoo]	I have
tens	[**tayngs**]	you have (**sing**)
tem	[**taynɡ**]	he/she/it has, you have (**sing**)
temos	[**taymoos**]	we have
têm	[**tay**-aynɡ]	they have, you have (**pl**)

vir to come

venho	[**vayn**-yoo]	I come
vens	[**vayngs**]	you come (**sing**)
vem	[**vaynɡ**]	he/she/it comes, you come (**sing**)
vimos	[**veemoos**]	we come
vêm	[**vay**-aynɡ]	they come, you come (**pl**)

The first person singular (the 'I' form) of the following verbs is irregular:

dizer	to say	digo	[**dee**goo]
fazer	to do, to make	faço	[**fa**soo]
saber	to know	sei	[say]
sair	to go out	saio	[**sī**-oo]
poder	to be able	posso	[**po**soo]

See page 262 for the present tense of the verbs **ser** and **estar**.

Past Tense:

Preterite Tense

The preterite is the tense most commonly used to express a completed action that has taken place in the past. To form the preterite tense for the three main types of verb in Portuguese, remove the -**ar**, -**er** or -**ir** and add the following endings:

am-ei	[am**ay**]	I loved
am-aste	[am**astee**]	you loved (**sing**)
am-ou	[am**oh**]	he loved, she loved, you loved (**sing**)

255

am-amos	[ama**moos**]	we loved
am-aram	[ama**rowng**]	they loved, you loved (pl)
com-i	[koh**mee**]	I ate
com-este	[koh**may**stee]	you ate (sing)
com-eu	[koh**may**-oo]	he ate, she ate, it ate, you ate (sing)
com-emos	[koh**may**moos]	we ate
com-eram	[koma**yrowng**]	they ate, you ate (pl)
part-i	[par**tee**]	I left
part-iste	[par**tee**stee]	you left (sing)
part-iu	[par**tee**-oo]	he left, she left, it left, you left (sing)
part-imos	[par**tee**moos]	we left
part-iram	[par**tee**rowng]	they left, you left (pl)

The following verbs are irregular in the preterite:

dizer to say

disse	[dee**see**]	I said
disseste	[dee**seh**stee]	you said (sing)
disse	[dee**see**]	he said, she said, you said (sing)
dissemos	[dee**say**moos]	we said
disseram	[dee**seh**rowng]	they said, you said (pl)

fazer to do

fiz	[fees]	I did
fizeste	[fee**zeh**stee]	you did (sing)
fez	[fays]	he did, she did, it did, you did (sing)
fizemos	[fee**zay**moos]	we did
fizeram	[fee**zeh**rowng]	they did, you did (pl)

ter to have

tive	[tee**vee**]	I had
tiveste	[tee**veh**stee]	you had (sing)
teve	[**tay**vee]	he had, she had, it had, you had (sing)

tivemos	[teevay̱moos]	we had
tiveram	[teeve̱hrowng]	they had, you had (pl)

vir to come

vim	[veeng]	I came
vieste	[v-ye̱hstee]	you came (sing)
veio	[va̱y-oo]	he came, she came, it came, you came (sing)
viemos	[v-ya̱ymoos]	we came
vieram	[v-ye̱hrowng]	they came, you came (pl)

The verbs **ser** (to be) and **ir** (to go) are irregular and have the same form in the preterite:

fui	[fwee]	I was; I went
foste	[fo̱hstee]	you were (sing); you went (sing)
foi	[foh-i]	he/she/it was, you were (sing); he/she/it went, you went (sing)
fomos	[fo̱hmoos]	we were; we went
foram	[fo̱hrowng]	they were, you were (pl); they went, you went (pl)

quem disse isso?	**conhecemos seu pai ontem**
kayng de̱esee e̱esoo	kohn-yaysa̱ymoos sa̱y-oo pī o̱hntayng
who told you that?	we met your father yesterday

compramos um carro no ano passado
kohmpra̱mooz oong kaHoo noo a̱noo pasa̱doo
we bought a car last year

See page 262 for the preterite tense of the verbs **ser** and **estar**.

Imperfect Tense

This tense is used to express what was going on regularly over an indefinite period of time and is often translated by 'used to + verb'. It is formed as follows:

amar to love

am-ava	[am**av**a]	I used to love
am-avas	[am**av**as]	you used to love (**sing**)
am-ava	[am**av**a]	he/she used to love, you used to love (**sing**)
am-ávamos	[am**av**amoos]	we used to love
am-avam	[am**av**owng]	they used to love, you used to love (**pl**)

comer to eat

com-ia	[koh**mee**-a]	I used to eat, I was eating etc
com-ias	[koh**mee**-as]	you used to eat (**sing**)
com-ia	[koh**mee**-a]	he/she/it used to eat, used to eat (**sing**)
com-íamos	[koh**mee**-amoos]	we used to eat
com-iam	[koh**mee**-owng]	they used to eat, you used to eat (**pl**)

partir to leave

part-ia	[par**tee**-a]	I used to leave, I was leaving etc
part-ias	[par**tee**-as]	you used to leave (**sing**)
part-ia	[par**tee**-a]	he/she/it used to leave, you used to leave (**sing**)
part-íamos	[par**tee**-amoos]	we used to leave
part-iam	[par**tee**-owng]	they used to leave, you used to leave (**pl**)

todas as quartas-feiras saíamos para dar um passeio

tohdazas kw**ar**tas f**ay**ras sa-**ee**-amoos p**a**ra dar oong pass**ay**-oo

every Wednesday we used to go for a walk, every Wednesday we went for a walk

sempre chegávamos cedo ao trabalho

s**ay**mpree shayg**a**vamoos s**ay**dwow trab**al**-yoo

we always arrived early at work

One useful irregular verb in the imperfect tense is:

ter to have

tinha	[**teen**-ya]	I used to have
tinhas	[**teen**-yas]	you used to have (sing, fam)
tinha	[**teen**-ya]	he/she/it used to have, you used to have (sing, pol)
tínhamos	[**teen**-yamoos]	we used to have
tinham	[**teen**-yowng]	they used to have, you used to have (pl)

See page 262 for the imperfect tense of the verbs **ser** and **estar**.

Future Tense

To form the future tense in Portuguese (I will do, you will do etc), add the following endings to the infinitive. The same endings are used whether verbs end in **-ar**, **-er** or **-ir**:

amar to love

amar-ei	[amar**ay**]	I will love
amar-ás	[amar**as**]	you will love (sing)
amar-á	[amar**a**]	he will love, she will love, you will love (sing)
amar-emos	[amar**ay**moos]	we will love
amar-ão	[amar**owng**]	they will love, you will love (pl)

voltarei mais tarde
vohltar**ay** mīs tardee
I'll come back later

The immediate future can also be translated by **ir** + infinitive:

vamos comprar uma garrafa de vinho tinto
v**a**moos kohmprar **oo**ma gaHafa dee **vee**n-yoo **tee**ntoo
we're going to buy a bottle of red wine

irei buscá-lo
ir**ay** boosk**a**loo
I'll fetch him, I'll go and fetch him

In Portuguese, as in English, the future can sometimes be expressed by the present tense:

o seu avião parte à uma hora
oo **say**-oo av-**yow**ng par**tee** a **oo**ma **o**ra
your plane takes off at one o'clock

However, Portuguese often uses the present tense where the future would be used in English:

eu lhe dou oitocentos reais
ay-oo l-yi doh oh-itoo**say**ntoos Hay-**ī**s
I'll give you eight hundred reais

The following verbs are irregular in the future tense:

dizer to say

dir-ei	[deer**ay**]	I will say
dir-ás	[deer**as**]	you will say (sing)
dir-á	[deer**a**]	he will say, she will say, you will say (sing)
dir-emos	[deer**ay**moos]	we will say
dir-ão	[deer**ow**ng]	they will say, you will say (pl)

fazer to do

far-ei	[far**ay**]	I will do
far-ás	[far**as**]	you will do (sing)
far-á	[far**a**]	he will do, she will do, it will do, you will do (sing)
far-emos	[far**ay**moos]	we will do
far-ão	[far**ow**ng]	they will do, you will do (pl)

See page 262 for the future tense of the verbs **ser** and **estar**.

Use of the Past Participle

There are two auxiliary verbs in Portuguese: **ter** (more commonly used) and **haver**. These two combine with the past

participle to make a compound form of the past tense.
To form the past participle, remove the infinitive endings and
add the endings **-ado** or **-ido** as indicated below:

infinitive	past participle	
amar	am-ado	[ama**doo**]
comer	com-ido	[koh**mee**doo]
partir	part-ido	[par**tee**doo]

ela já tinha comprado o bilhete

ehla Ja **tee**n-ya kohmpra**doo** oo beel-**yay**tee

she had already bought the ticket

Some further examples using the past participle:

este livro foi comprado em São Paulo

aystee **lee**vroo **foh**-i kohmpra**doo** ayng Sowng **Pow**loo

this book was bought in São Paulo

temos comido bem	**ela deve ter partido ontem**
taymoos koh**mee**doo bayng	**eh**la **deh**vee tayr par**tee**doo **oh**ntayng
we've been eating well	she should have left yesterday

Some verbs have irregular past participles:

fazer to do, to make	feito	[**fay**too]
abrir to open	aberto	[a**beh**rtoo]
dizer to say	dito	[**dee**too]
pôr to put	posto	[**poh**stoo]
ver to see	visto	[**vees**too]
vir to come	vindo	[**veen**doo]
satisfazer to satisfy	satisfeito	[satees**fay**too]

The Verb 'To Be'

There are two verbs 'to be' in Portuguese: **ser** and **estar**. They
are conjugated as follows:

Present Tense

ser

sou	[soh]	I am
es	[ehs]	you are (sing)
é	[eh]	he is, she is, it is, you are (sing)
somos	[**soh**moos]	we are
são	[sowng]	they are, you are (pl)

estar

estou	[eest**oh**]	I am
estás	[eest**as**]	you are (sing)
está	[eest**a**]	he is, she is, it is, you are (sing)
estamos	[eest**a**moos]	we are
estão	[eest**owng**]	they are, you are (pl)

Preterite Tense (I was etc)

ser		estar	
fui	[fwee]	estive	[eest**ee**vee]
foste	[**foh**stee]	estiveste	[eesteev**eh**stee]
foi	[foh-i]	esteve	[eest**ay**vee]
fomos	[**foh**moos]	estivemos	[eesteev**ay**moos]
foram	[**foh**rowng]	estiveram	[eesteev**eh**rowng]

Imperfect Tense (I used to be etc)

ser		estar	
era	[**eh**ra]	estava	[eest**a**va]
eras	[**eh**ras]	estavas	[eest**a**vas]
era	[**eh**ra]	estava	[eest**a**va]
éramos	[**eh**ramoos]	estávamos	[eest**a**vamoos]
eram	[**eh**rowng]	estavam	[eest**a**vowng]

Future Tense (I will be etc)

ser		estar	
serei	[say**ray**]	estarei	[eesta**ray**]
serás	[say**ras**]	estarás	[eesta**ras**]

será	[sayra]	estará	[eestara]	
seremos	[sayraymoos]	estaremos	[eestaraymoos]	
serão	[sayrowng]	estarão	[eestarowng]	

Ser

Ser indicates an inherent quality, a permanent state or characteristic, i.e. something which is unlikely to change:

> a neve é branca
> a nehvee eh branka
> snow is white

Ser is also used with occupations, nationalities, the time and to indicate possession:

> somos escoceses
> sohmoos eeskohsayzees
> we are Scottish

> minha mãe é professora
> meen-ya mayng eh prohfesohra
> my mum is a teacher

> este é o nosso carro
> aystee eh oo nosoo kaHoo
> this is our car

> são cinco da tarde
> sowng seenkoo da tardee
> it's five o'clock in the afternoon

Estar

Estar, on the other hand, is used to describe the temporary or passing qualities of something or someone:

> estou zangado com você
> eestoh zangadoo kohng vohsay
> I'm angry with you

> estou cansado
> eestoh kansadoo
> I'm tired

> este café está frio
> aystee kafeh aysta free-oo
> this coffee is cold

Notice the difference between the following two phrases:

> Isabel é bonita
> eezabehl eh bohneeta
> Isabel is very pretty

> Isabel está bonita (hoje)
> eezabehl eesta boneeta (ohJee)
> Isabel looks pretty (today)

Negatives

To express a negative in Portuguese, to say 'I don't want', 'it's not here' etc, place the word **não** in front of the verb:

entendo	**não entendo**
ayn**tayn**doo	nowng ayn**tayn**doo
I understand	I don't understand
gosto deste sorvete	**não gosto deste sorvete**
gostoo **day**stee sohrv**vay**tee	nowng **go**stoo **day**stee sohrv**vay**tee
I like this ice cream	I don't like this ice cream
aluguei-o aqui	**não o aluguei aqui**
aloog**ay**-oo ak**ee**	nowng oo aloog**ay** ak**ee**
I rented it here	I didn't rent it here
vão cantar	**não vão cantar**
vowng kantar	nowng vowng kantar
they're going to sing	they're not going to sing

Unlike English, Portuguese makes use of double negatives with words like 'nothing/anything' or 'nobody/anybody':

não há ninguém aqui	**não compramos nada**
nowng a ning**ayng** ak**ee**	nowng kohmpra**moos** n**a**da
there's nobody here	we didn't buy anything

não sabemos nada sobre ela
nowng sab**ay**moos n**a**da s**oh**bree **eh**la
we don't know anything about her

To say 'there's no...', 'I've no...' etc, make the accompanying verb negative:

não há vinho	**não tenho fósforos**
nowng a v**een**-yoo	nowng **tayn**-yoo **fo**sfooroos
there's no wine	I've no matches

To say 'not him', 'not her' etc, just use the personal pronoun followed by **não**:

nós, não	**ela, não**	**eu, não**
nos nowng	**eh**la nowng	**ay**-oo nowng
not us	not her	not me

Imperative

The imperative form of the verb is used to give commands. To form the imperative, remove the **-ar**, **-er** or **-ir** from the infinitive and add these endings:

	tu	você	vocês
amar to love	**ama**	**am-e**	**am-em**
	ama	a**mee**	**a**mayng
comer to eat	**come**	**com-a**	**com-am**
	komee	**koh**ma	**koh**mowng
partir to leave	**parte**	**part-a**	**part-am**
	partee	**par**ta	**par**towng

coma devagar
kohma deeva**gar**
eat slowly

When you are telling someone not to do something, use the forms above and place **não** in front of the verb:

não me interrompa, por favor
nowng mintay**Hoh**mpa poor favo**hr**
don't interrupt me, please

não beba álcool!
nowng **bay**ba **al**kohl!
don't drink alcohol!

não venha esta noite
nowng **vay**n-ya **eh**sta **noh**-itee
don't come tonight

por favor, não fale tão rápido (to one person)
poor favo**hr**, nowng **fa**lee towng **Ha**peedoo
please, don't speak so fast

265

por favor, não falem tão rápido (to several people)
poor favohr nowng falayng towng Hapeedoo
please, don't speak so fast

Pronouns are added to the end of the imperative form:

acorde-me às oito, por favor
akordeemee azoh-itoo, poor favohr
wake me up at eight o'clock, please

ajude-me, por favor
aJoodeemee poor favohr
help me please

However, when the imperative is negative, pronouns are placed in front of it:

não as deixe aqui
nowng as dayshee akee
don't leave them her

Questions

Often the word order remains the same in a question, but the intonation changes, the voice rising at the end of the question:

você quer dançar?
vohsay kehr dansar?
do you want to dance?

fica longe?
feeka lohnJee?
is it far?

Dates

Use the numbers on page 269 to express the date.

um de setembro [oong dee saytaymbroo] the first of September
dois de dezembro [doh-is dee dayzaymbroo] the second of December
vinte e um de janeiro [veentee-oong dee Janayroo] the twenty first of January

Days

Monday segunda-feira [saygoonda fayra]
Tuesday terça-feira [tayrsa fayra]
Wednesday quarta-feira [kwarta fayra]
Thursday quinta-feira [keenta fayra]
Friday sexta-feira [saysta fayra]
Saturday sábado [sabadoo]
Sunday domingo [dohmeengoo]

Months

January janeiro [Janayroo]
February fevereiro [fayvayrayroo]
March março [marsoo]
April abril [abreel]
May maio [mī-oo]
June junho [Joon-yoo]
July julho [Jool-yoo]
August agosto [agohstoo]
September setembro [saytaymbroo]
October outubro [ohtoobroo]
November novembro [nohvaymbroo]
December dezembro [dayzaymbroo]

Time

what time is it? que horas são? [k-**yo**ras sowng]

one o'clock uma hora [**oo**ma **o**ra]

two o'clock duas horas [**doo**-az**o**ras]

it's one o'clock é uma hora [eh **oo**ma **o**ra]

it's two o'clock são duas horas [sowng doo-az**o**ras]

it's three o'clock são três horas [trayz**o**ras]

five past one uma e cinco [**oo**mi **seen**koo]

ten past two duas e dez [**doo**-az**i**dehs]

quarter past one uma e quinze [**oo**mi-**keen**zee]

quarter past two duas e quinze [**doo**-azi-**keen**zee]

half past ten dez e meia [dehzi **may**-a]

twenty to ten vinte para as dez [**veen**tee **pa**ras dehz]

quarter to ten quinze para as dez [**keen**zee **pa**ras dehz]

at eight o'clock às oito horas [az**oh**-itoo **o**ras]

at half past four às quatro e meia [as kw**a**troo ee **may**-a]

2 a.m. duas da manhã [**doo**-as da man-y**a**ng]

2 p.m. duas da tarde [**tar**dee]

6 a.m. seis da manhã [says]

6 p.m. seis da tarde [says da **tar**dee]

noon meio-dia [**may**-oo **dee**-a]

midnight meia-noite [**may**-a n**oh**-itee]

an hour uma hora [**oo**ma **o**ra]

a minute um minuto [oong meen**oo**too]

two minutes dois minutos [**doh**-is meen**oo**toos]

a second um segundo [oong sayg**oo**ndoo]

a quarter of an hour quinze minutos [**kee**nzee]

half an hour meia hora [**may**-a **o**ra]

three quarters of an hour quarenta e cinco minutos [kwar**ay**nta ee **seen**koo]

Numbers

0	zero [**zeh**roo]	90	noventa [nohv**ay**nta]
1	um [oong]	100	cem [sayng]
2	dois [**doh**-is]	101	cento e um
3	três [trays]		[**say**ntwi oong]
4	quatro [**kwa**troo]	120	cento e vinte [**veen**tee]
5	cinco [**seen**koo]	200	duzentos [dooz**ay**ntoos],
6	seis [says]		duzentas [dooz**ay**ntas]
7	sete [**seh**tee]	300	trezentos [trayz**ay**ntoos],
8	oito [**oh**-itoo]		trezentas [trayz**ay**ntas]
9	nove [**no**vee]	400	quatrocentos
10	dez [dehs]		[kwatros**ay**ntoos],
11	onze [**ohn**zee]		quatrocentas
12	doze [**doh**zee]		[kwatros**ay**ntas]
13	treze [**tray**zee]	500	quinhentos [keen-
14	catorze [kat**ohr**zee]		**yay**ntoos], quinhentas
15	quinze [**keen**zee]		[keen-y**ay**ntas]
16	dezesseis [deezays**ays**]	600	seiscentos [saysay**ay**ntoos],
17	dezessete [deezay**eh**tee]		seiscentas [saysay**ay**ntas]
18	dezoito [deez**oh**-itoo]	700	setecentos [sehtees**ay**ntoos],
19	dezenove [deezay**no**vee]		setecentas [sehtees**ay**ntas]
20	vinte [**veen**tee]	800	oitocentos
21	vinte e um [**veen**ti-oong]		[oh-itoos**ay**ntoos],
22	vinte e dois [**veen**ti **doh**-is]		oitocentas
23	vinte e três [**veen**ti trays]		[oh-itoos**ay**ntas]
30	trinta [**treen**ta]	900	novecentos [novees**ay**ntoos],
31	trinta e um [**treen**tĩ-oong]		novecentas [novees**ay**ntas]
32	trinta e dois [**treen**tĩ **doh**-is]	1,000	mil [meel]
40	quarenta [kwar**ay**nta]	2,000	dois mil [**doh**-is]
50	cinquenta [seenkw**ay**nta]	5,000	cinco mil [**seen**koo]
60	sessenta [says**ay**nta]	10,000	dez mil [dehs]
70	setenta [sayt**ay**nta]	1,000,000	um milhão
80	oitenta [oh-it**ay**nta]		[meel-**yow**ng]

um is used with masculine nouns:

> **um carro**
> oong kaHoo
> one car

uma is used with feminine nouns:

> **uma bicicleta**
> **oo**ma beeseekle**eh**ta
> one bike

With multiples of a hundred, the **-as** ending is used with feminine nouns:

> **trezentos homens**
> trayz**ay**ntooz **o**mayngs
> 300 men

> **quinhentas mulheres**
> keen-**yay**ntas mool-**yeh**rees
> 500 women

Ordinals

1st	primeiro	[preem**ay**roo]
2nd	segundo	[sayg**oo**ndoo]
3rd	terceiro	[tayrs**ay**roo]
4th	quarto	[k**wa**rtoo]
5th	quinto	[**kee**ntoo]
6th	sexto	[**say**stoo]
7th	sétimo	[**seh**teemoo]
8th	oitavo	[oh-it**a**voo]
9th	nono	[**noh**noo]
10th	décimo	[**deh**seemoo]

Conversion Tables

1 centimetre = 0.39 inches   1 inch = 2.54 cm

1 metre = 39.37 inches = 1.09 yards   1 foot = 30.48 cm

1 kilometre = 0.62 miles = 5/8 mile   1 yard = 0.91 m

     1 mile = 1.61 km

km	1	2	3	4	5	10	20	30	40	50	100
miles	0.6	1.2	1.9	2.5	3.1	6.2	12.4	18.6	24.8	31.0	62.1

miles	1	2	3	4	5	10	20	30	40	50	100
km	1.6	3.2	4.8	6.4	8.0	16.1	32.2	48.3	64.4	80.5	161

1 gram = 0.035 ounces   1 kilo = 1000 g = 2.2 pounds

g	100	250	500
oz	3.5	8.75	17.5

1 oz = 28.35 g

1 lb = 0.45 kg

kg	0.5	1	2	3	4	5	6	7	8	9	10
lb	1.1	2.2	4.4	6.6	8.8	11.0	13.2	15.4	17.6	19.8	22.0

kg	20	30	40	50	60	70	80	90	100
lb	44	66	88	110	132	154	176	198	220

lb	0.5	1	2	3	4	5	6	7	8	9	10	20
kg	0.2	0.5	0.9	1.4	1.8	2.3	2.7	3.2	3.6	4.1	4.5	9.0

1 litre = 1.75 UK pints / 2.13 US pints

1 UK pint = 0.57 litre   1 UK gallon = 4.55 litre

1 US pint = 0.47 litre   1 US gallon = 3.79 litre

centigrade / Celsius $°C = (°F - 32) \times 5/9$

°C	-5	0	5	10	15	18	20	25	30	36.8	38
°F	23	32	41	50	59	64	68	77	86	98.4	100.4

Fahrenheit $°F = (°C \times 9/5) + 32$

°F	23	32	40	50	60	65	70	80	85	98.4	101
°C	-5	0	4	10	16	18	21	27	29	36.8	38.3

Este livro foi impresso em agosto de 2008 pela Cromosete
sobre papel offset 90 g/m^2.